Interdisciplinary Knowledge Organization

Rick Szostak • Claudio Gnoli
María López-Huertas

Interdisciplinary Knowledge Organization

 Springer

Rick Szostak
University of Alberta
Edmonton, Alberta, Canada

Claudio Gnoli
Università di Pavia
Pavia, Italy

María López-Huertas
University of Granada
Granada, Granada, Spain

ISBN 978-3-319-80732-4   ISBN 978-3-319-30148-8   (eBook)
DOI 10.1007/978-3-319-30148-8

Printed on acid-free paper

This Springer imprint is published by Springer Nature
The registered company is Springer International Publishing AG Switzerland

Preface

This book is motivated by the increased importance of interdisciplinary scholarship within the academy and the widely perceived shortcomings of existing knowledge organization schemes (KOSs) in serving interdisciplinary scholarship. The book reaches a set of very strong conclusions:

- Existing bibliographic classification systems [that is, classifications of works, as in libraries] are organized on a disciplinary basis; as a consequence they serve interdisciplinary research and teaching poorly.
- A novel approach to classification, grounded in the phenomena studied rather than disciplines, would serve interdisciplinary scholarship much better. It would also prove advantageous for disciplinary scholarship. If we can aid all scholars in their search for information, the productivity of scholarship would thus be increased.
- This novel approach is entirely feasible. Various concerns that might be raised can each be addressed. The broad outlines of what a new classification would look like are developed.
- This new approach might serve as a complement to or a substitute for existing classification systems.
- Though the impetus for this novel approach comes from interdisciplinarity, it is also better suited to the needs of the Semantic Web, and a digital environment more generally.

This book thus proposes a novel approach to classification, discusses its myriad advantages, and outlines how such an approach to classification can best be pursued. It should thus be of great interest to scholars of classification research, knowledge organization, digitization, and interdisciplinarity itself. Indeed we hope to encourage a collaborative effort toward the detailed development of such a classification.

Key Features

This is, quite simply, the first book to take interdisciplinary knowledge organization as its central theme. This might seem surprising, given the importance of interdisciplinarity in the contemporary academy. It is even more surprising given that the literature on interdisciplinarity appreciates that finding relevant information is one of the key barriers to interdisciplinarity. The paucity of previous research on interdisciplinary knowledge organization reflects in part the inertia surrounding existing classification systems: those in use in most of the world's libraries were developed many decades ago when neither interdisciplinarity nor digitization was foreseen. It also reflects in part a fear that conceptual ambiguity limits the scope for a truly interdisciplinary approach to classification. In this book, we will discuss how the approach to be recommended might either substitute for or complement existing classification schemes. And we will discuss at length how we can best combat conceptual ambiguity.

The approach that we recommend blends a comprehensive classification with domain-specific classification practices. The book should thus be of interest to advocates of both of these types of research (domain analysis will be explained in Chap. 3, and discussed in detail in Chap. 6).

The logical structure of the book deserves emphasis. Each chapter addresses a coherent set of questions. Later chapters build directly on the preceding analysis. Most importantly:

- Chapter 2 argues that interdisciplinary researchers will want to search by the phenomena and causal relationships studied in a work, the theories and methods applied, and the perspective of the author.
- Chapter 3 then examines what type of classification would facilitate these types of search.
- Chapter 4 reviews some attempts in this direction, and addresses why this type of classification has not already been adopted.
- Chapter 5 describes the feasibility of developing such a classification.
- Chapters 6, 7, and 8 develop strategies for doing so.

The book is thus able to provide a strong justification for a carefully described and novel approach to knowledge organization.

Though the primary focus of the book is on classification systems, the analysis is in places extended to other knowledge organization systems (KOSs) such as thesauri and ontologies (these will also be explained in Chap. 3). The possibility of a comprehensive thesaurus is explored. The classification proposed has many of the advantages sought in ontologies for the Semantic Web. The book will thus be of interest to scholars working in these areas as well.

The authors each bring something unique to this project. Rick Szostak is a scholar of interdisciplinarity (and former president of the Association for Interdisciplinary Studies). He has published several articles in leading journals in information science in recent years regarding the desirability and feasibility of the sort of classification outlined in this book. Claudio Gnoli and María López-Huertas are scholars of information Science (and recently served respectively as vice president and president of the International Society for Knowledge Organization [ISKO]). Claudio Gnoli has also published many articles arguing for the new approach to classification urged in this book. María López-Huertas has published domain analyses of the interdisciplinary field of gender studies, and thus brings a critical perspective on both domain analysis and the needs of interdisciplinary scholars. Many works of each author are drawn upon in this book.

Audience

The primary audience for the book will be information science professionals. The book should be readily accessible to students in the field but at the same time will offer novel insights to experienced practitioners. It is entirely original in its approach but yet makes use of and synthesizes a diverse literature. It holds out the promise of a collaborative effort to develop novel KOSs. As stressed above it should be of interest to both those who perform domain analysis and those who wish to work toward a comprehensive classification.

The second audience will be interdisciplinary scholars, and especially scholars of interdisciplinarity itself. As noted above, such scholars are keenly aware of the information challenges they face, but unaware that there is a possible solution. They should be interested in the broad contours of that solution, and more generally in how KOSs do and could operate. They will then be able to advocate for the development of appropriate KOSs (see Chap. 10). Moreover we shall argue that the detailed development of such a KOS is best performed in concert by scholars of knowledge organization and scholars of interdisciplinarity: the latter can advise on how best to serve their needs (Chaps. 4 and 9). This book will also develop strategies for interdisciplinary communication that are of direct use to interdisciplinary scholars. And there are lessons along the way regarding clarity in expressing causal arguments, theories, and methods; arguments in favor of a coherent scholarly enterprise linked by interdisciplinarity; and descriptions of the nature of the world we live in such as the theory of integrative levels. We will discuss how interdisciplinarity can benefit from the Semantic Web and how the KOSs proposed in this book may be well suited to this enterprise. Last but not least, interdisciplinary scholars may see parallels between the discourse on domain analysis within information science and the broader debates regarding specialized versus interdisciplinary research in the academy. In sum, interdisciplinary knowledge organization is, as the name suggests, a field in which interdisciplinary scholars and knowledge organization scholars should interact; this book introduces each to the other field in order to facilitate that interaction.

Though ontologies are a KOS they have most often been developed by computer scientists and others from outside the field of information science. The formal structure—precise definitions of terms and stipulation of relationships among these—is hoped to facilitate computer navigation of diverse databases. There are, perhaps unsurprisingly, important parallels between the challenges of communicating across disciplines and across databases developed for different purposes by different agents. And it will turn out that the sort of KOS we recommend in this book serves many of the purposes of ontologies. It is particularly well suited to a digital world, and its structure seems well suited to the needs of the Semantic Web. A third audience for this book, then, is scholars of digitization, ontologies, and the Semantic Web.

Governments, granting agencies, and university presidents routinely both laud interdisciplinary scholarship and seek to facilitate it. And it is widely appreciated that scholars have trouble finding relevant knowledge in other fields, understanding it when they do, and communicating back to all relevant audiences. Our book proposes solutions to each of these challenges. This book shows how we can enhance interdisciplinary scholarship through the improved classification of works and the ideas that these contain. Arguably the development of KOSs suited to interdisciplinarity is the single most important policy innovation for facilitating interdisciplinarity. We will revisit in the concluding chapter how the sort of KOSs advocated in the book should be a goal of public policy. This goal cannot be pursued without detailed knowledge of the shape of the desired KOSs. A fourth audience for this book, then, comprises policy-makers interested in facilitating interdisciplinarity.

Timeliness of This Book

The timeliness of the book should be stressed. It comes at a point in time when:

- There is widespread discussion of how best to facilitate interdisciplinarity.
- Digitization allows works to be classified along multiple dimensions, and thus respond to the information needs of interdisciplinarians (while also better facilitating disciplinary research).
- Importantly, digital publication increases the value of a classification that can guide researchers to related works in other fields (rather than stressing shelf placement of like works).
- Online databases abound but each tends to employ a unique classification. The approach outlined in our book addresses potential solutions to this problem as well.

- More generally there is a widespread concern that the world faces information overload. And the best answer to overload is organization: people need not know everything as long as they know how to find what they need. The sort of classification we advocate should simplify search for the general user as well as the scholarly user.

Edmonton, AB, Canada   Rick Szostak
Pavia, Italy   Claudio Gnoli
Granada, Spain   María López-Huertas

Acknowledgments

The authors thank each other for the interdisciplinary and international collaboration that made this book possible. They thank Thomas R. Dousa and four anonymous referees for very detailed advice on the manuscript. We wish also to recognize the immense value of the International Society for Knowledge Organization, its regional chapters, and kindred organizations, for providing the scholarly environment in which the idea for this book emerged and was developed.

Contents

Chapter 1
The Importance of Interdisciplinary Research and Teaching

This book will investigate the possibility that a new approach to knowledge organization is better suited to a contemporary academy characterized by an increased emphasis on interdisciplinarity. The knowledge organization systems (KOSs) that are most widely used in the world were developed when a discipline-based view of the universe of knowledge was common within both information science and the wider academy (see Miksa 1992). To set the stage for our analysis, it is first necessary that we define interdisciplinarity (and disciplines) and discuss the increased importance of interdisciplinarity within both the academy and the world at large. The first several sections of this chapter address definitional matters. The next several sections detail the increased importance of interdisciplinary scholarship, its value for scholarly discovery, and the place of interdisciplinarity within the academy and society. The chapter closes by outlining how we can explore in the rest of the book the ways in which knowledge organization should best facilitate interdisciplinarity.

Defining Interdisciplinarity

We can define interdisciplinarity as involving the following characteristics:

- Interdisciplinarity tackles questions (problems, themes) that are (or at least might be) addressed by multiple disciplines (or 'knowledge communities' more generally).
- Interdisciplinarity seeks to integrate the insights from multiple disciplines in order to generate a superior understanding of a particular question.
- Interdisciplinarity is thus open to theories, methods, philosophical perspectives, and types of data utilized in different disciplines (see AIS 2013).

The definition here borrows heavily from that proposed two decades ago by Klein and Newell (1996): 'A process of answering a question, solving a problem, or

© Springer International Publishing Switzerland 2016
R. Szostak et al., *Interdisciplinary Knowledge Organization*,
DOI 10.1007/978-3-319-30148-8_1

addressing a topic that is too broad or complex to be dealt with adequately by a single discipline or profession ... Interdisciplinary studies draws on disciplinary perspectives and integrates their insights through construction of a more comprehensive perspective.' This definition has since been echoed by many authors and organizations (see Repko 2012).[1] In particular, The U.S. National Academy of Science, the National Academy of Engineering, and the Institute of Medicine (2005, 26) (hereafter referred to as the National Academies) formulated the following definition:

> Interdisciplinary [studies] integrates information, data, techniques, tools, perspectives, concepts and/or theories from two or more disciplines or bodies of specialized knowledge to advance fundamental understanding or to solve problems whose solutions are beyond the scope of a single discipline or area of research practice.

Interdisciplinary scholars and students thus study problems or topics that draw on the phenomena studied, theories applied, or methods applied in more than one discipline. While it is possible that an interdisciplinary project may focus on phenomena studied in only one discipline (but applying theories or methods from others), interdisciplinarians most often study relationships between phenomena studied in different disciplines. They thus also often need to confront different theoretical and methodological approaches as well as philosophical perspectives. Interdisciplinary research, then, is usually organized around interdisciplinary causal linkages, where the word 'causal' should be interpreted in the broadest sense to mean any sort of influence that one phenomenon might exert on another. The interdisciplinarian may want to know, for example, how inner-city poverty is generated by a variety of economic, social, cultural, and psychological factors, or how acoustic communication between whales is affected by noisy military operations in oceanic environments.

Interdisciplinary researchers will thus be curious regarding previous research that might have been performed in several different fields. Existing bibliographic [library] classification systems will not leap to the aid of the interdisciplinarian. Works on inner-city poverty will be scattered across many discipline-based main classes within a given discipline-based bibliographical classification system. Even works on the relationship between culture and poverty will be classed in different places depending on whether written by an anthropologist, sociologist, economist, or some other scholar. And since different disciplines tend to be organized differently in every classification (or why bother organizing classifications by discipline?), interdisciplinarians will find that they need to use different search terms and strategies as they explore different disciplines.

We should stress at the outset that many attempts have been made to address these problems. For example, verbal subject heading systems and alphabetical indexes of classifications can aid the researcher in identifying subject terms to search for across disciplines. We will discuss in later chapters the degree to which it

---

[1] We draw on Repko (2012) extensively in this chapter. As the first textbook on how to perform interdisciplinary research it summarizes an extensive and diverse literature.

is possible through such strategies to facilitate interdisciplinary inquiry within discipline-based KOSs. We should also note that keyword searching (where the user can input any search term and will retrieve any items where the term appears in the title or perhaps keywords, abstract, or full text depending on the database) is a popular alternative to subject searching (where the user must first identify the terms or classes utilized within a particular KOS). This also will be discussed later; it can be noted here that even advocates of keyword searching have come to recognize the limitations of searching by isolated words. While we will have cause to address strategies for interdisciplinary search within existing discipline-based KOSs, we stress that this book is focused on the development of a new approach to KOSs that would better meet the information needs of interdisciplinary scholars and students.

There are of course other definitions of interdisciplinarity that can be found in the literature. There are a handful of key issues that underlie these differences in definition. These are summarized in Table 1.1. The key point to take away from Table 1.1 is that these differences in definition do not suggest differences in information needs (though these may be more keenly felt the greater the distance between disciplines being engaged). We can thus speak in this book of the typical information needs of interdisciplinary scholars. Interdisciplinary scholars and students will want access to relevant causal arguments, theories, and methods from multiple disciplines. They will inevitably face difficulty in accessing these in KOSs organized on a disciplinary basis.

These implications become even clearer if we move from an examination of how interdisciplinarity is defined to a discussion of how it is practiced. Repko (2012), the first textbook on interdisciplinary practice, stresses the identification, evaluation, and integration of disciplinary 'insights.' These insights are in turn causal arguments made within disciplines which are often but not always explicitly grounded in theories. Repko also discusses the strengths and weaknesses of different methods but says less about integrating these due to his primary audience being undergraduate students. Other works, such as Bergmann et al (2012) or McDonald et al. (2009), speak more to the need to draw upon multiple methods in interdisciplinary research. These latter works also discuss the challenges of team research (see also Stokols et al. 2010). For present purposes it is worth noting that research teams often face severe communication difficulties for two reasons: team members employ terminology differently, and team members make different assumptions rooted in disciplinary perspective regarding both subject matter and research methodologies (see O'Rourke et al. 2014). We discuss elsewhere in this chapter and book the fact that classification can reduce terminological ambiguity. We can also hope to provide interdisciplinary researchers with ready access to understandings of disciplinary perspective. It has been found that familiarity with the perspectives of others improves communication within research teams (Eigenbrode et al. 2007). In sum, key works on how interdisciplinary research is and should be performed confirm that interdisciplinary researchers need access to the phenomena, causal arguments, theories, methods, and perspectives associated with diverse disciplines.

Table 1.1 Issues in defining interdisciplinarity

What is the attitude toward disciplines? Most interdisciplinarians accept that interdisciplinary research is grounded in the specialized research performed by disciplines (though a minority wish to see disciplines replaced by a more flexible academic structure). Yet while some interdisciplinarians are happy with the present organization of disciplines, others wish that disciplines themselves would become more flexible.[a] While most interdisciplinarians take a problem-oriented focus, and draw on disciplines in order to address a particular problem, others see their goal as generating new interdisciplines. For almost all types of interdisciplinarian, the implications for information science are the same: both interdisciplinary and specialized research need to be respected and facilitated.

Which disciplines are engaged? Interdisciplinarity becomes a greater challenge the greater the differences between the disciplinary approaches embraced in a particular study. *Narrow interdisciplinarity* occurs between (a small number of) disciplines with compatible methods, paradigms, and epistemologies. *Broad interdisciplinarity* takes place between disciplines whose paradigms and methods are incompatible with one another (Klein 2010). That this distinction is made means that knowledge organization systems (KOSs) need often to guide researchers to works in quite different disciplines. Natural scientists engaged in interdisciplinary research will often want to consult information generated in the social sciences and humanities, and vice versa. It may be that natural scientists will find it easier to navigate other natural sciences than to explore the social sciences or humanities (and vice versa).

Is integration essential? Klein and Newell (1996) argue that simply 'adding together' disciplinary insights is just 'multidisciplinarity,' while integrating these is necessary for interdisciplinarity. Repko (2012) and Bergmann et al. (2012) also stress the importance of integration. Lattuca (2001) is sceptical that integration is essential to interdisciplinarity. Note that the multidisciplinarian will be interested in searches similar to those conducted by the interdisciplinarian, and thus the information scientist need not be too troubled by this distinction.

What is integration? The closest synonym is synthesis. Integration involves first an important element of critical reflection on the strengths and weaknesses of different disciplinary insights, and how they might reflect biases inherent either in disciplinary practice or more general academic practice (or indeed limitations on human perception and reasoning). Integration then involves finding common ground among different disciplinary insights. From the point of view of information science, the important point here is that the interdisciplinary scholar wishes to identify relevant insights—that is, scholarly contributions to the understanding of a problem or question, based on research (Repko 2012, 466)—from the widest range of disciplines, but also to understand the overall perspectives of the disciplines in question.

What is the most important focus of integration: is it primarily 'perspectives' or 'insights' or should 'phenomena,' 'theories,' and 'methods' receive equal attention? While insights are central, an emphasis on phenomena, theories, and methods adds a valuable concreteness to interdisciplinary analysis. One can identify, for example, the main strengths and weaknesses of different methods and theories (Szostak 2004), and these understandings are invaluable in identifying strengths and weaknesses in disciplinary insights. Moreover, a discipline's preferences with respect to phenomena, theories, and methods are important components of 'disciplinary perspective,' the general way of looking at the world that characterizes each discipline.[b] Attempting to draw on 'disciplinary perspectives' in interdisciplinary analysis will be unnecessarily challenging if perspectives are not defined carefully in terms of such elements. We will explore in Chap. 2 how knowledge organization can account for and reflect these varied foci of integration.

Are there degrees or levels of integration? Klein (2010) identifies four levels of integration: The lower level is given when interaction is reduced to sharing background or contextual information with other disciplines. The next level takes place when elaboration or explanation of findings is shared, although in a limited way. In the next level, a greater interaction takes place and

(continued)

Table 1.1 (continued)

definitions of variables are shared. In the higher level, fundamental questions are redefined by integrating the approaches of all participants in the research design. Some would see the earlier levels as multidisciplinary. For our purposes we can see successive levels as requiring ever greater familiarity with other disciplines.

Is interdisciplinarity primarily problem-oriented or conceptual? Most interdisciplinary research and teaching is indeed focused upon particular questions or themes, and thus fits the definition provided above very well. But an important minority of interdisciplinarians focus on conceptual questions: some stress how interdisciplinarity can add to disciplines and others how it can replace them (See Salter and Hearn 1997, 30). Note that conceptual interdisciplinarians tend to define interdisciplinarity in terms of its role as critique rather than with respect to its nature. Some see interdisciplinarity as a revolutionary process whose goal should be the subversion of disciplines (Carp 2001). Those who wish to supplant disciplines may object to the tendency of problem-oriented interdisciplinarity to build on disciplinary insights (Salter and Hearn 159). Conceptual interdisciplinarity might be considered as a branch of philosophy of science (though its practitioners are often not philosophers). As such its information needs are distinct from (and likely more straightforward to address than) those of the problem-oriented interdisciplinarity that will be the focus of this book.

Can individuals perform interdisciplinary research? While much of the research on interdisciplinarity examines interdisciplinary teams, and some have argued that interdisciplinarity requires a team approach (Apostel 1972), it is nevertheless true that many individual researchers undertake interdisciplinary research. Indeed Repko (2012) directs much of his advice to the individual researcher. Research teams can rely on the expertise of team members in reviewing the literature (though teams will often look beyond the disciplines of team members). Individual researchers will want to be able to identify relevant literature on their own. They will thus be particularly dependant on KOSs.

[a]Ørom (2003) performed a domain analysis in the field of art studies, and concluded that the field had become increasingly interdisciplinary. If all fields were to follow suit, would disciplinary boundaries become blurred?

[b]We discuss this in more detail below and will engage the importance of disciplinary perspective for interdisciplinary analysis in Chap. 2

Integration

Porter and Rafols (2009) worry that while the number of collaborative research projects has increased substantially in the last 30 years the actual degree of interdisciplinary integration has increased far less. Happily, there has been much success in identifying strategies for successful integration in recent years (Repko 2012; Bergmann et al 2012; AIS 2013).[2] These must be tailored to particular interdisciplinary contexts.

---

[2] The 'About Interdisciplinarity' website of the Association for Interdisciplinary Studies (AIS 2013) surveys the literature on best practices for interdisciplinary research and public policy. It also provides best practices for interdisciplinary teaching and administration. Notably, those who teach and administer the growing number of interdisciplinary courses and programs also need enhanced access to both the literature on interdisciplinarity itself (dispersed across many fields) and literatures from diverse fields.

There are both social and cognitive challenges to integration. Socially, we must appreciate that different scholars bring different sets of assumptions with them from their home disciplines. These assumptions reflect the overall 'disciplinary perspective' of their discipline. Stakeholders from beyond the academy bring their own assumptions and perspectives. The research team will be a mosaic of different models of doing science, and different models of seeing the world that have to be integrated. Team members need to appreciate each other's perspectives if they are to understand each other and work together toward shared goals. The idea is not 'to uproot researchers from their paradigmatic framework. Rather it is to promote understanding and respect for what these ... can offer within and across both the research and policy communities' (Phoenix et al. 2013, 226). If shared goals and understanding can be achieved, then each team member's efforts can be harnessed to achieve collective understanding.

It is critical that efforts toward integration occur early in the team research process. It is of particular importance that the team agree on a guiding research question or questions that are not biased in favour of any one discipline (Repko 2012). Ignaciuk et al. (2012, 153) recommend 'a question which would attract the necessary disciplines but without disciplinary spin.' Participants then need to agree on the theories and methods to be employed in the research project. Another useful strategy is to have team members answer a set of philosophical and methodological questions, and then collectively discuss their answers. Looney et al (2014) have found that such a process not only encourages understanding, but that team members often move toward more moderate positions after conversing. And of course it is crucial that team members be chosen that are experts in their field but that are also willing to cooperate, learn about other fields, and challenge their own assumptions.[3] One critical danger is that some team members think their contribution is the most important, and thus do not fully engage with others.

A second social barrier is that different team members will apply different meanings to shared terminology. If unaware of these different meanings misunderstanding is inevitable. Research teams can seek to develop a shared understanding of the concepts they employ. This task would be much easier if they had recourse to a classification that translated the complex concepts which generate misunderstanding into basic concepts for which broadly shared understanding is feasible (Szostak 2014d).

We can draw four implications from this section for this book: interdisciplinary integration is possible but difficult; interdisciplinary researchers can benefit from access to advice on how to perform interdisciplinary research; researchers need ready access to the literatures of related fields; and researchers also need clarification of terminology.

---

[3] Interviewing participants is an oft-used method to find out their positions regarding their specialties and their contributions to the research project, and to harmonize positions. For instance, in a project on ecosystems-based management (EBM) the interviewees were asked about 'what kind of information is needed to support the EBM here? Is that information being collected? How are you using the social and ecological data that you are collecting? And what is the definition of EBM that you are using here?' (Sievanen et al. 2011, 317). Similar questions can be applied to other topics.

Defining Transdisciplinarity

We will usually employ the word 'interdisciplinary' in this book. But many interdisciplinary scholars instead self-identify themselves as 'transdisciplinary.' The word 'transdisciplinary' has taken on many meanings over the years. It was long associated with the search for grand unified theories (an approach advocated by Nicolescu 1996).[4] Most practicing interdisciplinarians (especially those inspired by postmodernism; see below) are sceptical of the likelihood of a grand theory of everything. Yet in practice the research of the two may look quite similar for it involves integrating across disciplines. And thus for the information scientist the challenges are broadly similar: to allow researchers to identify and integrate insights from diverse disciplines.

More recently, the word 'transdisciplinarity' has become associated with the idea of integrating not just across the academy but with insights generated by agents beyond the academy as well (see the TD-Net website at www.transdisciplinarity. ch). Gibbons et al. (1994) and Nowotny et al. (2001) advocate this approach, and stress that the purpose of transdisciplinarity is to provide contextualized answers to complex questions, rather than seek a unified theory of everything (see below). Nowotny et al. (2001) argues that the critical interaction is that which occurs between science and society. She claims that knowledge is strong, medium or weakly contextualized in relation with its higher or lower degree of interaction with the social context. Self-styled interdisciplinarians are also open to the practice of integrating also across non-academic insights, but place less emphasis on this than transdisciplinarians. This sort of transdisciplinarity may thus be characterized as 'interdisciplinarity plus.' It is noteworthy that many of the strategies employed in integrating across disciplines are equally useful when integrating beyond the academy. For information scientists, the key implication is that both academic and non-academic users may each wish to seek works on a particular topic written by both academics (from multiple disciplines) and non-academics.

Non-academic stakeholders can bring a variety of useful inputs to a research project: the skilled understandings of artisans or farmers, traditional practices embedded in local cultures or religions, understandings of how social and environmental systems work and the incentives provided to particular agents, and much more. The value and use of these and any other forms of non-scientific knowledge will depend upon the research at hand. But the implication for information science is clear: transdisciplinary research requires that researchers be able to identify relevant non-academic literatures. Yet a particular economic activity when reported by a traditional artisan or an anthropologist is likely to be classified with anthropological works on culture rather than with analyses of the exact same process by an economist or engineer. Science is produced not only in universities: any pertinent

---

[4] Nicolescu sees complex plurality and open unity as two facets of the same reality. Reality is multidimensional and it is articulated in levels, levels of reality that have no limitation; the set of levels constitute the transdisciplinary object.

person could and should take part in a research project (López-Huertas 2010). And thus the same strategies that will be recommended for classifying scholarly works should likewise be applied to non-scholarly works. We want to allow both academic and non-academic researchers to readily find works about a particular thing or process both across disciplines and beyond disciplines.

This last point deserves emphasis. While this book emphasizes the needs of interdisciplinary scholarship, its conclusions apply to non-scholarly works and non-scholarly users equally well. The general user often seeks works addressing interdisciplinary causal linkages (why do dogs sometimes bite mail carriers?). They will often have little or no appreciation of the academic disciplines that might inform their research. They will want to follow their curiosity where it leads, regardless of disciplinary boundaries.

While this book will stress transcending disciplinary boundaries, a similar argument can be made with respect to social boundaries. Information scientists should seek to facilitate both within-group communication and across-group understanding. Interdisciplinary scholars have often stressed that the challenges of communicating across social boundaries are similar to the challenges of communicating across disciplinary boundaries. Approaches to classification which facilitate interdisciplinary communication should also serve to encourage communication across other barriers (Szostak 2014a).

It is worth noting here that much interdisciplinary and transdisciplinary research is guided by a desire to affect public policy. If complex social problems require interdisciplinary or transdisciplinary approaches, then citizens wishing to be well informed will need to perform the same sort of searches that interdisciplinary scholars pursue. This provides a further rationale for an interdisciplinary approach to the classification of both scholarly and non-scholarly works.

Defining Multidisciplinarity

Multidisciplinarity (also called pluridisciplinarity [Kockelmanns 1979] and polydisciplinarity [Morin 1995]) is often taken as synonymous with interdisciplinarity, but there is for most authors a quite clear distinction between them. Interdisciplinarity as we have defined it stresses integration. Multidisciplinarity is an approach that instead simply juxtaposes disciplines. Juxtaposition seeks wider knowledge, information, and methods. Nevertheless, disciplines remain separate, the elements of disciplines keep their original identity and the disciplinary structure of knowledge is not criticized. According to Klein (2010), this is the case with conferences, publications, and research projects that present different views of the same topic in serial order. As a result, the studied topic is enriched but the research is still a disciplinary product, limited to the disciplinary framework. In the multidisciplinary approach, interaction does not take place, and this fact differentiates it from interdisciplinarity. In multidisciplinarity there is no interest in blending the different perspectives to generate a more comprehensive understanding.

Though we will not often refer to multidisciplinarity in this book, it should be noted that even the multidisciplinarian will have difficulty with existing discipline-based KOSs. Indeed the multidisciplinarian, seeking particular bits of information from another discipline but lacking the desire to fully engage with the perspective of that discipline or learn its disciplinary language, may find discipline-based KOSs to be particularly frustrating.

Defining Disciplines

Interdisciplinarity as defined above is not a replacement for disciplines but exists in a symbiotic relationship with them. Most practicing interdisciplinarians are very conscious of the advantages of specialized research within disciplines: scholars who study the same phenomena using the same theories and methods can converse readily with each other (and in particular do not have to waste time outlining the assumptions of their theories and methods when publishing their results). Against this important advantage must be counted a variety of disadvantages: if only specialized research is performed the scholarly enterprise as a whole will be incoherent; each community of scholars will be myopic and ignore relevant theories and methods; and each community will have limited inclination or ability to talk to others.

For example, biological nomenclature has adopted increasingly specialized terminology since the times of Linnaeus. This nomenclature includes rules for derivation of higher order group names from that of a reference genus, to be modified with various suffixes according to hierarchical rank. The rigorous methodology known as cladistics taxonomy has encouraged even more specialized nomenclature. As a result, what would usually be called 'Flowering Plants'—a concept familiar to most people—have been labelled as *Angiospermae*, then *Magnoliophyta* by application to the reference genus *Magnolia* of the rules mentioned above. Discipline-based bibliographic classifications are gradually updating their schedules with these new terms (Civallero 2010). While this nomenclature has technical advantages within the discipline of botany, when a layman or a researcher in a very different discipline reads titles involving 'Magnoliophyta' it will be difficult for him/her to understand that simple notion and integrate it with other relevant knowledge from other disciplines.

Specialized researchers often criticize interdisciplinary research for being methodologically and/or theoretically impure. Once the value of multiple theories and methods is appreciated, this objection can be turned on its head. Interdisciplinarians thus try to integrate the insights generated by different specializations. Many interdisciplinarians hope that specialized researchers will become more flexible in their approach in response to an appreciation of the increased insight available through interdisciplinarity. [Some, indeed, hope to change the way that disciplines operate.] Disciplines often evolve precisely because they have learned to borrow some key theoretical or methodological element from other disciplines.

Table 1.2 Key characteristics of disciplines

The disciplinary 'worldview' or 'disciplinary perspective' that shapes analysis in the field. [This embraces the five elements below but also elements of ethics, epistemology, aesthetics, and perhaps ideology.]
A set of phenomena that are the focus of analysis.
One or a few key theories.
One or a few key methods.
A set of concepts, which may be loosely or tightly defined depending on discipline.
The 'rules of the game' governing hiring, promotion, and publication decisions.

It is noteworthy that specialized researchers need knowledge organization much less than the interdisciplinarian. Specialized researchers will know what journals to read in their specialization and who the important authors in their field are. The interdisciplinarian will always be wondering whom to contact and where to look for relevant insights. Nevertheless we should strive in what follows to ensure that the KOSs advocated for interdisciplinarity also serve the specialized researcher. The interdisciplinary researcher will suffer also if specialized researchers are limited in their own access to information.

For this reason, and also because we need to understand the nature of the disciplines that the interdisciplinarian hopes to both navigate and comprehend, it is useful to define disciplines here as well. Both Klein (1990) and Salter and Hearn (1997) have investigated the key characteristics of disciplines. Their analyses can be summarized in Table 1.2 in terms of six main characteristics that define a particular discipline at a point in time (see Szostak 2003; AIS 2013).[5]

Pahre (1996) explores the epistemological status of disciplines. A purely epistemological (or, more precisely, ontological) view of disciplines would suggest that these reflect divisions in nature, but it seems clear that disciplinary boundaries are not natural. The rise of interdisciplinarity would be hard to understand within such a view. A constructivist view—that disciplines are entirely socially constructed— would suggest instead that different cultures might design different disciplines. While disciplinary power structures lend support to a constructivist view, boundary-crossing and hybridization into interdisciplinary fields seems often to be driven by real-world concerns. A constructivist view also implies a very cynical view of information science for if science is not constrained by reality it will not matter how information is organized. Pahre thus recommends a middle ground view in which disciplines are partly natural and partly constructed. Such a view accords with the empirical observation that disciplines evolve through time. Pahre suggests that scholars in crossing disciplinary boundaries may become more influenced by reality because they are free from the disciplining of one discipline and different disciplinary cultures may countervail.

---

[5] They focus on the cognitive aspects of disciplines. Sugimoto and Weingart (2015) survey also the social, historical, communicative, and narrative nature of disciplines.

There are three important implications for information science in Pahre's analysis. First, we are guided not to reify disciplines, but also not to ignore them or the structures of phenomena in which they are in part grounded. Second, we are encouraged in a belief that interdisciplinarity may be supported by appealing to the nature of reality. Third, the constructivist approach provides a further justification for the project pursued in this book. Since information scientists generally strive to reduce the cultural bias inherent in KOSs, the recognition that disciplines are to some degree culturally determined should encourage the pursuit of a general classification not organized around disciplines.

Information scientists should appreciate that disciplines evolve through time, and also that there is diversity within each discipline. The interdependence among the six characteristics enumerated in Table 1.2 should nevertheless be appreciated: disciplines collectively choose methods that are well suited to the investigation of their favored theories, phenomena that can readily be studied with these theories and methods, and rules of the game that reward the application of accepted theories and methods to accepted phenomena. Disciplinary perspectives gain their influence because of the fact that each element reinforces the others. Interdisciplinary scholars should appreciate each element of the disciplinary perspective of the disciplines that they draw upon. Gnoli (2014) discusses knowledge organization in the discipline of history as theorized by historian Marc Bloch, finding that, while history is only loosely defined by its object ('the past,' but usually limited to what concerns humans), methodological approach is also important.

It should also be recognized that some disciplines are much 'looser' than others: they are more flexible with respect to theory and method, and/or with respect to enforcing particular rules of the game. In some disciplines certain sub-disciplines exhibit considerable autonomy (though if hiring decisions are made by the disciplines then any autonomy will be limited in degree). This diversity in disciplinary practices encourages differences in interdisciplinary practice (Apostel 1972). Researchers may in particular need to understand both a broad disciplinary perspective and deviations from this within disciplinary subfields.

Interdisciplinary research, it might be noted, is too diffuse to be characterized by its own 'rules of the game.' One of the challenges for the interdisciplinarian, indeed, is to succeed professionally while often being evaluated in terms of disciplinary standards. Ideally interdisciplinarians should not be evaluated in terms of their mastery of any particular theory or method. Arguably, interdisciplinary research should be evaluated solely in terms of whether it contributes to our collective understanding (Szostak 2003). Interdisciplinary scholars will benefit if administrators, journal editors, and referees are acquainted with advice contained in works such as Lyall et al. (2011) on how interdisciplinary scholarship should be evaluated.

The Increased Importance of Interdisciplinary Scholarship

Disciplines as we have defined them have only existed for a couple of centuries (Klein 1990, 21–2; Lattuca 2001, 23; Burke 2012, chap. 6). While different 'subjects' were long taught in academies and universities, disciplinary specialization only emerged in the eighteenth and nineteenth centuries with specialized degrees and journals, and then disciplinary departments and disciplinary scholarly organizations. Necessarily, interdisciplinarity as we have defined it must be newer than disciplines. Inevitably concerns with the narrowness of disciplines arose as disciplines emerged. Interdisciplinarity has ebbed and flowed in popularity over the last century or so (Weingart 2010). This ebb and flow might lead pessimists to predict that the present interest in interdisciplinarity will inevitably dissipate. The symbiotic perspective outlined above leads us to understand these ebbs and flows in terms of a conflict between the desirability of interdisciplinarity and the difficulty of pursuing interdisciplinary analysis successfully. Previous incarnations of interdisciplinarity, including the interwar blossoming of the 'unity of science' movement, often tended to stress a search for unifying grand theories. Today's interdisciplinarity, on the other hand, stresses instead integration across different theories: the goal is no longer one single, overarching theory but a large number of theories each casting light on different (and overlapping) facets of the world in which we live. This arguably is a much more achievable goal, and thus the future of interdisciplinarity should be brighter than was its past. This approach also accords with an appreciation that no one theory is perfect.

It would be hard to deny that scholarly research is increasingly interdisciplinary. Granting agencies and university presidents around the world applaud this transformation, and dedicate their institutions to its support. And they note the primary cause of this transformation: that complex problems—not least complex problems in public policy—require an interdisciplinary approach. Pressing social and environmental problems in particular call for interdisciplinary analysis. Specialized experts inevitably give advice that is only partially useful. 'The directive force of reason is weakened [because] the leading intellects lack balance. They see this set of circumstances, or that set, but not both together. The task of coordination is left to those who lack either the force or the character to succeed in some definite career' (Alfred N. Whitehead, cited in Brome 1963, 208). Specialized researchers give advice from a limited perspective, but pretend otherwise. Politicians then choose the advice that suits their purposes.

The U.S. National Science Foundation (NSF) report 'Rebuilding the Mosaic' (National Science Foundation 2011) is one of many examples of reports and scholarly works that highlight the growing importance of interdisciplinarity. It is intended to guide the NSF's approach to the social, behavioral, and economic sciences over the next decade or two. The vision expressed in the report is of research that is increasingly 'interdisciplinary, data-intensive, and collaborative.' And the NSF sets itself the task of better supporting this type of research. The report is grounded in 252 'white papers' submitted to the NSF by scholars from across the social and behavioral sciences. The report celebrates the coherence of the advice received. Everyone, it seems, predicts an interdisciplinary and collaborative future. A significant minority of white papers warned the NSF not to go so far in its support of interdisciplinarity that it neglects disciplinary research. The report appreciates that interdisciplinary research is usually stimulated by interest in real-world problems.

This last point deserves emphasis. The increased importance of interdisciplinarity reflects an appreciation—across the natural and social sciences and humanities—that complex problems or questions require an interdisciplinary approach. This recognition in turn reflects both the increased complexity of human society and technology itself (see Nowotny et al. 2001), as well as an appreciation that the specialized disciplinary research that had come to dominate the academy during the last two centuries had contributed much to human understanding but failed to adequately address some of humanity's most pressing concerns (see Morin 1995).

The National Academy of Science, the National Academy of Engineering, and the Institute of Medicine (2005) identified four key drivers of interdisciplinary research. The first of these is the inherent complexity of nature and society. Challenges such as climate change or space exploration simply require an interdisciplinary approach. The second driver is the fact that interesting scientific problems have emerged at the boundaries of disciplines. Biochemistry explores the chemical behavior or organic substances, while cognitive science seeks to understand how the brain performs its various functions. The third is the need to solve societal problems. It is increasingly appreciated that a variety of challenges require insight from multiple disciplines. The fourth involves the stimulus of generative technologies. The Internet in particular has greatly facilitated large research collaborations. Klein (1996b) mentions also the influence of general education programs, liberal studies, and professional programs on interdisciplinary teaching; social and epistemological critiques of disciplines; and in some cases downsizing of faculty numbers. It could well be that interdisciplinarity becomes a self-reinforcing process. As these four drivers and other forces operate, and interdisciplinary scholarship becomes increasingly accepted, more scholars may be attracted to the freedom, flexibility, and opportunities for creativity that interdisciplinarity provides (see Nissani 1997, 201).

It is hard to quantify the scope of the transformation toward interdisciplinarity. Bibliometric analysis (that is, analysis of citation data) can measure the degree of interdisciplinarity and how this varies across the academy, but most studies focus on particular domains (Palmer 2010, 177–9). For example, Chakraborty et al (2013) use citation analysis to trace and analyze increased interdisciplinary interaction in computer science, but such studies are rare.[6] Many scholars may claim to be interdisciplinary—because the term is now in vogue, and because research grants

---

[6] Already in 1992, Hurd found that virtually half of the journals cited by chemists at her research university were from outside chemistry. She thus urged against discipline-based libraries and for better search tools to aid interdisciplinary science.

are available—without really doing interdisciplinary research. On the other hand, interdisciplinary research is often published in disciplinary journals. One imperfect quantitative indicator is the growing importance of interdisciplinary fields and journals: gender studies, biotechnologies, and more recently nanotechnology. There are now dozens if not hundreds of these. Already in 1995 Katz and Hicks found that about one tenth of scientific journals could be considered to be either interdisciplinary or multidisciplinary.

Such interdisciplines often solidify into disciplines over time (Fuchsman 2012). That is to say, they come to pursue a limited set of theories, methods, and phenomena. They are thus not truly interdisciplinary as we have defined the term. Still, information science needs to address the needs of both interdiscipline and interdisciplinarity. Scholars of both types need to access literatures classified across multiple disciplines within existing classification systems. The information needs of scholars within 'solidified' interdisciplines will be similar in type to those of interdisciplinary scholars but more limited in degree. In the early days of founding a new interdiscipline, though, information challenges may be particularly severe as an emerging community of scholars must identify a coherent literature that may be distributed across multiple disciplines.

The majority of scholarly papers is still written by scholars from one discipline and cites only scholars from that discipline (Porter and Rafols 2009). This should not be a surprise: interdisciplinary research must build on a broad base of specialized research. Yet the lesson should be clear: an ideal KOS must facilitate the efforts of both the interdisciplinary and disciplinary scholar. Note in this respect that the same scholar may sometimes perform specialized research and other times perform very integrative research.

Increased interest in interdisciplinary research reflects and reinforces increased interest in interdisciplinary teaching (see Augsburg and Henry 2009 for an overview of the American experience with respect to teaching). Students and employers recognize that life's challenges do not come in neat disciplinary bundles but require the ability to draw connections across different areas of expertise. Librarians in both university and public settings must thus grapple regularly with interdisciplinary search inquiries (see Szostak 2015b).

Undiscovered Public Knowledge

As noted above, the main (but not exclusive) reason for the rising importance of interdisciplinarity is a belief that interdisciplinary analysis can lead to superior understandings of complex problems or questions. One might wonder, then, if in fact there is reason to believe that this is the case.

Insights from History of Science

We can turn first to the field of history of science. Historians of science appreciate that major breakthroughs generally result from some sort of interdisciplinarity.[7] Root-Bernstein (1989) has analyzed the sources of major (mostly natural) scientific breakthroughs. He stresses that those who are familiar with multiple scientific fields tend to make the greatest discoveries (and cites several Nobel laureates to this effect). Since one cannot predict which combinations will yield discoveries, he encourages scientists to familiarize themselves with a variety of fields. Notably, they need not master these. Indeed, newcomers to a field often make the greatest discoveries, for they understand its basic concerns but have not yet absorbed the theoretical and methodological biases of specialists. Root-Bernstein notes that there are a variety of institutional impediments to this sort of interdisciplinary training: graduate schools provide a narrow education; young scholars are not given time to reflect widely before publishing; and granting agencies and journals look for scholarly expertise in a particular area. We might add that bibliographic classifications do not make it easy to identify works that might have some relevance—whether obvious or seemingly tangential—to a scholar's interests.

The basic message that can be taken from the history of science is that important new insights generally represent a novel combination of existing but quite distinct insights. A classification that increases the ability of researchers to make connections across diverse literatures or databases will thus significantly enhance the rate of both scholarly and technological progress. [A similar argument can be made with respect to artistic innovation (Szostak 2014b).] This idea has been captured over the past decades in a literature on 'undiscovered public knowledge' (Swanson 1986; Davies 1989; Swanson et al. 2001). This literature argues that within the voluminous expanse of scholarly literature as a whole, there exist pieces of knowledge that, if combined, would yield new and unexpected knowledge. Efforts by information scientists to facilitate the process of uncovering these potentially generative pieces of knowledge will greatly advance scholarly understanding.

That is, advances in human understanding come from juxtaposing previous bits of understanding that are not obviously related. Any advance in information science that facilitates the ability of researchers (or general users) to make new connections will thus enhance the rate of scholarly (and technical and other sorts of) advance. Yet we tend to evaluate information retrieval only in terms of whether users find what they look for. We should instead/also appreciate the value of alerting them to a range of related paths of exploration (Miksa 1992; Warner 2000). We 'must develop methods to allow online users to serendipitously discover relevant

---

[7] Glassick et al (1997, 9) worried that the 'scholarship of integration' was under-appreciated in the academy. They argued that this was needed to overcome the fragmentation and isolation of disciplines, and to make connections within and across disciplines. In their view, scholars of integration would make bits of disciplinary knowledge more meaningful to non-specialists, and would bring new insights to disciplinary research.

materials' (Knapp 2012). Though scholars cannot search for the unknown, they 'value novelty above all else in their quests for information' (Palmer 2001, 136).

Undiscovered Public Knowledge and Literature Based Discovery

The idea of 'undiscovered public knowledge' (now more commonly called 'literature-based discovery') was formally articulated in the 1960s, though the idea that there were important but unappreciated connections across distinct bodies of knowledge has been voiced since at least Aristotle. Don Swanson and others have produced many articles over the last quarter century showing how advancement in human understanding can come from drawing unappreciated connections within the existing body of knowledge (see Swanson et al. 2001; Beghtol 1995).

Swanson (2008) emphasizes what is often termed the ABC type of literature-based discovery. Sources in one field discuss how A influences B. Sources in another field discuss how B influences C. If these sources are juxtaposed an important discovery involving the impact of A on C may result. Swanson is skeptical that computers can replace humans in recognizing the importance of particular juxtapositions—only a human researcher focused on affecting C is likely to appreciate the possible importance of the role of A—but sees an important task for information science in aiding researchers in discovering possible connections within the literature. 'The goal of Literature Based Discovery in my opinion should be to support and enhance human ability by focusing on the key problems of finding promising pairs of scientific articles that can serve as a stimulus, and on identifying associated literature structures' (Swanson 2008, 5). While it may be difficult to summarize the logical argument of a paper or book it should be easy to identify the key phenomena and relationships investigated (Swanson 2008, 6). Smalheiser and Torvik (2008) concur that juxtapositions are best uncovered by researchers seeking answers to a particular problem (that is, seeking to affect C); their own efforts to alert medical researchers to juxtapositions they have found have elicited little interest. The goal, then, is to facilitate the identification of useful combinations by active researchers, not by experts in information retrieval. We shall argue in this book that this will be facilitated by a classification grounded in phenomena and relationships (A affects B; B affects C) rather than disciplines.

Though the ABC type of discovery is the most obvious, Davies (1989) identified other types of undiscovered knowledge: there may be evidence in one field relevant to a hypothesis in another; there may be weak evidence for a hypothesis in multiple fields that becomes stronger when combined; there may be similar problems in different fields that have yielded different analyses; and there may be novel classifications developed in one field of the phenomena of interest to another. [Pahre (1996) also stresses the value of exchanging hypotheses across fields.] In such cases also a classification grounded in phenomena and relationships should facilitate identification of related hypotheses, evidence, or problems across fields. Notably, Davies (1989) suggested that the amount of undiscovered public knowledge increases geometrically, as every new insight can potentially be combined with all preceding insights.

Most importantly for our purposes, Davies (1989) appreciated that uncovering undiscovered public knowledge would be most difficult when connections needed to be made across disciplines. Differences in terminology across disciplines, and the fact that disciplines are organized differently within general classifications, would in such cases make it particularly difficult to establish connections. And Swanson (2008) urges us to look for situations where one group of scholars studies A and B, and a different group studies B and C; this is when literature based discovery is most likely. Yet the history of science literature tells us that these are likely the most important cases of literature-based discovery.

Much of the research on undiscovered public knowledge has occurred in the medical field: identifying therapies that might alleviate certain illnesses. But there is no theoretical reason that such discoveries need be limited to medicine. Any complex challenge or question might potentially benefit from novel connections across fields. Cory (1997) applied literature-based discovery to hidden analogies in literature. Gordon and Awad (2008) argue that literature-based discovery can be useful for poor countries in both identifying (often old) technologies from developed countries and uses for poor country techniques in rich countries. Importantly their argument again suggests the value of classifying non-scholarly as well as scholarly works in a manner that facilitates literature-based discovery.

Serendipity and Epistemology

The related but distinct literature on 'serendipity' should also be mentioned. Darbellay et al (2014) celebrate the potential importance of serendipitous discoveries to interdisciplinary research. Serendipity requires breaking free from disciplinary constraints, recognizing novel connections, and placing information in a novel context. Foster and Ellis (2014) survey the literature on serendipity in philosophy, sociology, and information science, with special attention to models of interdisciplinary research that stress serendipitous discovery (See also McCay-Peet and Toms 2015). Workman et al. (2014) see causal chains as the key to serendipitous discovery. One either joins A to B and B to C; or starts with a belief that A and C are related and look for intermediate connections. Their analysis parallels that of Swanson above. They hope to develop a user interface that will facilitate such discoveries. We would argue that novel classificatory practices are called for.

There are interesting parallels between both of these literatures (serendipity and literature based discovery) and the pioneering efforts of Wilson (1968) in the epistemology of information science. Wilson identified two key activities (he called them 'powers;' Smiraglia 2012a, suggests 'dimensions'): the 'descriptive' activity by which we attempt to organize our accumulated understandings not just in classification schemes but in encyclopedias and textbooks; and the 'exploitative' activity by which we attempt to develop new understandings. Wilson appreciated that any novel understanding must be a novel combination of existing understandings. For Wilson the key concept is 'efficacy,' the degree to which our descriptive activities facilitate exploitative activities. We will in what follows urge a classification that is more 'efficacious' than existing classifications, particularly with respect to interdisciplinary 'exploitation.' As we have seen this requires us to facilitate connections among phenomena studied across different disciplines.

Interdisciplinarity and Information Science

As Palmer (2001, xii) has noted, if it is useful to enhance the productivity of scholarship, then it is valuable to enhance access to scholarly information, for this lies at the heart of the scholarly project. It was argued above that interdisciplinarians are inherently more reliant on knowledge organization because it is in the nature of interdisciplinarity to seek relevant insights from multiple bodies of knowledge (whereas the truly specialized disciplinary researcher need master only one). The increased importance of interdisciplinarity within the academy is thus a challenge to the information science community: how can this scholarship best be supported?

Many information scientists have recognized the increased importance of interdisciplinarity and the challenges this poses for knowledge organization. 'As research and knowledge become more interdisciplinary, the academic subjects represented in our research libraries become increasingly ill-suited to the conduct of research': a more interdisciplinary scientific enterprise requires radical change in classificatory practice (Palmer 1996, 66). 'Not surprisingly some of the [Information Science] field's most formidable problems stem from the need to develop information systems and services for interdisciplinary researchers' (Palmer 2010, 174). James Duff Brown, Barbara Kyle, Douglas Foskett, Derek Austin, Clare Beghtol, and Nancy Williamson are among the information scientists who have over the years noted that 'disciplines are an arbitrary constraint on classification schemes, and produce obstacles to cross-disciplinary indexing and searching' (Gnoli 2006b, 11). Satija et al. (2014) discuss how the knowledge that needs to be organized grows through several processes associated with academic specialization and several processes associated with interdisciplinary or multidisciplinary interaction. Dahlberg (1994) identified five types of interdisciplinary research, each of which is poorly served by existing classifications.[8] When one discipline is

---

[8] The five were: when a field draws on many others; when a field influences many others, when a subject is studied by many fields, when a certain property is investigated in many fields, and when a subject is studied collaboratively by many disciplines.

informed by many others, or one topic studied by many, related documents are inevitably classified in a dispersed fashion. Bulick (1982) has noted that some subjects thus receive multiple classifications, interdisciplinary subjects receive arbitrary classifications, and confusion occurs when disciplinary boundaries shift.

Knapp (2012) argues not only that interdisciplinarity is important and worthy of much greater consideration by information scientists, but that the existence of interdisciplinarity enhances the importance of the field of information science:

> Regardless of whether printed books cease to exist, or whether every scrap of human knowledge is posted for free on the Internet, librarians can still provide a necessary service: promoting the 'whole;' the broad view. Whether researchers want to call it 'interdisciplinary' or not, it is important to help researchers see how different forms of knowledge interact, how they are related, and understand when it might be appropriate to broaden their searches. . . . It is an important new area, and a new 'academic need' that librarians are uniquely qualified to address.

Knapp touches here on a point that was made above. Specialized disciplinary researchers may be able to master the literature in a well-defined domain without much help from a librarian or a KOS. The interdisciplinary researcher is not so fortunate, but will often need help in identifying relevant literatures. In the words of Bates (1996, 159), 'It certainly seems to be a reasonable preliminary hypothesis that scholars in interdisciplinary fields may have to engage in both substantially more information seeking—and of a different kind—than scholars in a conventional discipline.'

Though university administrators and granting agencies puzzle over how best to facilitate interdisciplinary research, the response of the information science community to this transformation has been much more muted. Some have developed bibliometric and other approaches to test the intensity and the levels of interaction in interdisciplinary research (Song 2003; Qin et al. 1997; Roa-Atkinson and Velho 2005; Palmer 1999; Wenzel 2001). Others have investigated the communication and information-seeking practices of interdisciplinarians (Beers and Boots 2009; Palmer 1999). Shiri (2009) found that interdisciplinary search behavior was different from disciplinary search behavior, and suggested that interdisciplinary queries should be handled differently [though this may be an artifact of the disciplinary structure of KOSs]. Some tools have been created to minimize the problem of communication among persons implicated in interdisciplinary projects. Heterogeneous data bases have been created to make it possible to familiarize scientists with fields different from their own (Bartolo and Trimble 2000). Kimmel (1999) reviewed strategies and tools that could be used by interdisciplinary researchers in navigating discipline-based classifications.

These diverse attempts to measure and/or facilitate interdisciplinary scholarship within an environment of discipline-based KOSs are all valuable. Yet the literatures in both interdisciplinary studies and information science remain clear in their judgment that interdisciplinary scholars and students still face major challenges in information access and dissemination. Our purpose in this book is not to review the strategies that allow interdisciplinary researchers to alleviate somewhat the challenges inherent in the disciplinary organization of knowledge—though these are of course addressed from time to time—but rather to investigate the possibility of an approach to knowledge organization that is intended from the outset to facilitate interdisciplinarity.

A recent survey of the information-seeking practices of scholars found that the greatest problem is 'having enough time,' followed by 'knowing what's available,' followed in turn by 'having access to all information from one place' (see Sparks 2005). A more focused study of interdisciplinary researchers in environmental science found that 85 % did not feel they were keeping up with all relevant research despite the fact that over a third of them were spending 10 hours or more a week on information seeking activities (Murphy 2003). The main contention of this book is that knowledge organization can greatly enhance the ability of interdisciplinary scholars both to find what they want and to discover related information that they would not have known to look for. It can thus significantly enhance the productivity of the entire scholarly enterprise.

If interdisciplinary researchers will have trouble finding what they need, students in interdisciplinary courses will also face grave difficulties. Repko (2012) devotes an entire chapter to the literature search (and discusses problems in searching in other chapters as well). He notes the challenges inherent in the disciplinary organization of both libraries and library catalogues. In particular he notes that interdisciplinary students are often interested in connections between two or more subjects. Lyall et al. (2011) discuss a variety of challenges faced by interdisciplinary graduate students, including their information search needs. Interdisciplinary teaching programs are increasingly common, especially in North America, and university libraries have long struggled to meet the needs of interdisciplinary students (e.g. Searing 1992). Interdisciplinarity is slowly creeping into high school curricula as well (Lenoir and Klein 2010), and thus school and public libraries also need to address interdisciplinary student needs. Undergraduate students, as we have seen, may have less need to address diverse methods than do interdisciplinary scholars; they will, though, wish to identify phenomena, causal arguments, theories, and perspectives. Graduate students will face the full set of interdisciplinary information needs.

The bibliographic classification systems utilized today were all developed at a time when disciplinary specialization was unquestioned, and are thus organized around disciplines (Miksa 1992). It should hardly be surprising that an increasingly interdisciplinary academy requires important changes in the way that the field of information science approaches the classification of scholarly (and other) works.

Relationship of Interdisciplinarity to Other Discourses

The increased importance of interdisciplinarity has been reflected in—and is consonant with—many important academic discourses. The most important of these is almost certainly postmodernism (Szostak 2007). Since interdisciplinarity, especially in the humanities, is often compared with or even confused with postmodernism, this comparison is especially salient. Postmodernism comprises a set of critiques of the contemporary academy, and that academy is still largely organized around disciplines. Thus it is hardly surprising that many postmodern critiques resonate with interdisciplinarians; particularly concerns about scholarly biases, suspicion of overarching 'meta-narratives' (that is, grand theories or ideologies that purport to have an answer for everything) and the celebration of diverse points of view. But interdisciplinarity must in the end hinge on a belief that, through integration, we can achieve understandings that are in important ways more comprehensive and less biased than disciplinary insights, and some versions of postmodernism would doubt such a possibility. Some postmodern thinkers are for this reason hostile to the sort of interdisciplinarity championed in this book. Szostak (2007) discusses some 14 different postmodern critiques of the contemporary academy and how each of these might each be best treated by interdisciplinarians. Similarly, Phoenix et al. (2013) explored in detail the integration of positivist, postpositivist, and interpretivist paradigms in the exploration of environment and human health. Each approach has something to contribute both to scholarly understanding and practical policy advice. The general point that should be made here is that interdisciplinarity can and should embrace most/all postmodern critiques of scholarly process, but must avoid extreme versions of these that deny the very possibility of adding to the body of human understanding.

Other important intellectual currents, such as feminism, complexity analysis,[9] and the unity of science movement share many of the postmodern concerns noted above (Szostak 2007). Some versions of these, though, step away from the postmodern suspicion of meta-narrative in order to pursue some grand theory that will explain much or all of human existence.[10] Most interdisciplinarians no longer seek to formulate all-encompassing grand theory but rather seek to address particular complex problems by integrating various disciplinary insights. Fox and Olson (2012) discuss the implications of feminist theory for knowledge organization; we will discuss in Chap. 9 how the sort of KOS to be recommended in this book addresses the core concern of many feminists with reflecting and respecting social diversity.

Special note might be made of systems theory. Disciplinary boundaries have often been justified in terms of an idea of largely independent systems: economy, polity, culture, human psychology, biology, and so on. If the key phenomena investigated by particular disciplines are judged to interact a lot with each other but very little with the phenomena studied by other disciplines, then disciplinary

---

[9] In the 2001 issue of *Issues in Integrative Studies*, William H. Newell argued that the essence of interdisciplinarity is coping with complexity; while respondents generally appreciated that complex problems (defined by Newell as containing non-linear relationships between variables) were especially suited to interdisciplinary analysis, they doubted that complexity so defined was *necessary* for interdisciplinary analysis.

[10] This was indeed the purpose of the interwar 'unity of science' movement. See Neurath et al. 1937–8). Szostak (2014c) notes that the interdisciplinary coherence sought by that movement can instead be achieved organizationally through KOS.

silos will seem a useful strategy for academic organization. If, however, it is thought that important systems span disciplinary boundaries—and environmental systems leap to mind here, but cognitive science, public health, and many other research programs also link phenomena studied by diverse disciplines—then inter-disciplinary collaboration is called for. General systems theory (Bertalanffy 1968) itself is a cross-disciplinary theory, as it identifies general principles of how parts can interact in any structure, thus helping us to look at phenomena studied by different disciplines in a more abstract, unified way.

The study of systems requires both an appreciation of the phenomena and relationships that comprise the system, and of any emergent properties that can only be understood at the level of the system as a whole. The idea of emergent properties has its home in biology: the idea that certain characteristics of complex organisms such as consciousness could not be understood in terms of any of the component parts of the organism (the elements of its system) but only at the level of the organism as a whole. The idea of emergent properties is now common in systems theories. It is also a key aspect in the theory of integrative levels, itself a guiding principle for the organization of a general phenomenon-based classification (see Chap. 7). Interdisciplinary researchers need to be guided then to discussions of phenomena, relationships, and emergent properties across all disciplines relevant to each particular system.

Philosophical Grounding of Interdisciplinarity

As we have seen above, interdisciplinarity has grown in importance due in large part to the recognition that there are many complex problems or issues that require inputs from multiple disciplines. There is both a practical and a philosophical side to this recognition. The practical recognition that certain problems span disciplinary boundaries was emphasized above, and will be revisited below. Philosophically, there has been an appreciation of the limitations of specialized research. This is an important development, for science has been characterized for centuries by increased specialization, and it was long felt that this increased specialization was the key to increased understanding.

Specialization, to be sure, has its advantages. Scholars can develop expertise in particular theories or methods, and the study of particular phenomena. Communi-ties of scholars can easily communicate regarding these shared theories, methods, and phenomena. But of necessity they then miss possible insights that could be gleaned from alternative theories, methods, and phenomena.

The practical recognition that specialization has limits was associated with a philosophical appreciation of the limits of both reason and empiricism (Wenzel 2001). Specialization fit a philosophical view (see Popper 2005), often termed 'positivism,' that argued that we could prove or at least disprove scientific state-ments. As philosophers came to appreciate that absolute proof was impossible, they encouraged instead a respect for different perspectives. While some postmodern philosophers then doubted the very possibility of enhanced understanding, most philosophers urged the careful compilation and evaluation of different types of argument and evidence (Szostak 2007). Interdisciplinarity fits comfortably within such a philosophical approach (see Alrøe and Noe 2014).

Scholars are thus encouraged to follow questions across disciplinary boundaries. They are also encouraged to engage with stakeholders beyond the academy (a point stressed in the literature on transdisciplinarity), for these might also have useful insights. Science is not considered to proceed only within the limits of a particular field but it is now free to explore any of these as required by the research at hand. Likewise science is not confined to the academic environment either.

This change is captured in the influential literature on Mode 2 science (Nowotny et al. 2001, 29; Gibbons et al. 1994)—which is implicitly contrasted with a 'mode 1' of specialized science pursuing rigorous proof and thus having little need for collaboration with non-scientists. These authors argue that these changes in science mirror changes in society. There too the boundaries between different realms— economy, polity, culture, and so on—have blurred. In Mode 2 society, the boundary between science and society also becomes more porous. In fact, society and science have been brought together in the postmodern era, and science cannot be thought of apart from society. The knowledge being produced in the Mode 2 society is characterized by inter/transdisciplinarity, heterogeneity, organizational diversity, social accountability, reflexivity and integration. Scientists are urged to interact beyond the academy, both gaining insights and communicating these.

This last point deserves emphasis, for it has important implications for knowledge organization. This book focuses primarily on the needs of (especially interdisciplinary) scholars. But if we wish to encourage interaction between scholars and the public, then it is critical that our classification systems be understood by both. Happily, the approach to classification encouraged in this book will also aid the general reader in accessing both the scholarly and general literature.

Social Context for Interdisciplinarity

In Mode 2 society, science is expected to enhance social and individual welfare. 'Mode 2 is characterized by closer interaction among scientific, technological, and industrial modes of knowledge production' (Klein 1996b, 144). Science is expected to interact with society, and thus to respond (much of the time) to societal demands and produce contextualized knowledge which addresses these demands. There is thus a two-way interaction in contrast to the traditional model that it is one way, usually from science to society (López-Huertas 2010).

Romero Lankao et al. (2013) draw a clear distinction between academic-driven and issue-driven interdisciplinarity; they follow others in referring to the latter as contextualized interdisciplinarity (Gibbons et al. 1994; Nowotny et al. 2001). The former is driven by questions within a discipline, or on the boundaries of disciplines, for which insights from multiple disciplines are relevant. The latter is concerned with 'issues that emerge from fundamental societal dilemmas' (Romero-Lankao et al. 2013, 30) that cannot be answered by any one discipline. They characterize this issue-driven research in terms of the following elements: sensitivity to the context, integration, interactivity, reflexivity, and two-way collaboration. From here, the authors point to the main challenges that contextualized interdisciplinary research faces:

- Scholars with different backgrounds, methods, models, and perspectives should be brought together in order to do 'new science.' To fulfil this goal, research should be highly participatory and interactive. Participants need to understand each other and agree on goals and means.
- These new research areas should be interesting to academics by providing the opportunity to arrive at new scholarly insights, and to society by producing practical insights. But it is not always easy to generate both scholarly and practical insights in the same work.
- The interests, values, and insights of all participants need to be appreciated.
- There are a variety of political and sociological issues that may arise at the intersection of science and society.[11]

The last report of the ERA (European Research Area of the European Commission) includes the societal dimension as one of its five components: 'The ERA is firmly rooted in society and responsive to its needs and ambitions' (European Commission 2009, 13). This component leads to the following policy actions: 'societal platforms, involvements of stakeholders, technology assessment, ethical foresight and principles, cohesion and equity.' The ERA expects to support the knowledge society with the following characteristics: 'Trust and dialogue between society and S&T [science and technology]; [Positive] Public attitude to S&T; equity: geographic, social and gender' (European Commission 2009, 14). There are many other examples of interdisciplinary research focused on 'issues that emerge from fundamental societal dilemmas' (Romero-Lankao et al. 2013, 29). The Earth Systems Science Partnership (ESSP) project was created in 2001 by several Global Environmental Change research groups. Ignaciuk et al. (2012) claim that, by the end of the 1990s, there was much greater interest in societal involvement and in interdisciplinary research on this topic. The creation of ESSP was a response to these new needs.

Issue-driven research projects are often initiated by governments, non-governmental agencies, or businesses. These will often have different goals from academic researchers: seeking solutions to particular problems rather than theoretical generalizations. For our purposes they will also face a challenge in that government, business, and academic documents tend to be classified in quite different ways. We will in later chapters explore the possibility that a non-

---

[11] There are also questions of funding. Craig et al. (2005, 372) discuss the issue of 'interdisciplinary overhead.' An interdisciplinary project may require significant funding. If this is not achieved, individual scholars may work independently with little attempt at integration.

discipline-based classification might be useful in archives (and indeed galleries and museums) as well as libraries.

Transdisciplinary research projects differ in the degree to which non-academic stakeholders are integrated into the research team. It is often thought, though, that if external stakeholders are to be involved in a research project, they should be involved from the beginning. They should help choose research questions, and then the theories and methods to be employed (Craig et al. 2005). In addition to this, there must be an active communication of research results with social representatives, media, and the wider public to achieve the desired interaction. If it is hoped that the research will influence public policy then active interaction with policy-makers throughout is recommended.

An example may be useful here. The project surveyed by Ignaciuk et al. (2012) established formal relations with international institutions such as the Food and Agriculture Organization (FAO) and had many discussions with a wide range of stakeholders. As a consequence of integrating the food-chain and food-security communities, a new food system concept was formalized that integrates all related to 'what we do and what we get... The concept is now adopted by main agencies including the FAO...' (Ignaciuk et al. 2012, 152). This example, notably, indicates how terminology can usefully be clarified in interdisciplinary communication.

Many more examples could be provided. The main implication for this book is that we will want KOSs to facilitate a two-way conversation between scholarship (science) and society. Disciplinary boundaries will limit scholarly inquiry, and complicate public access to scientific understanding. We need a KOS that is easy to understand and that does not place arbitrary barriers either between disciplines, or between the academy and societal actors.

Evaluation of Interdisciplinary Research

In an academy structured around disciplines, it often happens that interdisciplinary research is evaluated by disciplinary scholars. Such scholars will often evaluate the research through the lens of their disciplinary perspective. They will employ the standards with which they are familiar for evaluating research in their own discipline. They will thus tend to view interdisciplinary research too harshly. In particular they will be suspicious of methods and theories and subject matter uncommon in their discipline, and object (often subconsciously) to unfamiliar and often implicit philosophical assumptions. The inevitable result is difficulty in communicating interdisciplinary insights. Interdisciplinary journals provide a possible solution, but themselves face the challenge of 'perceived inferiority' (Phoenix et al. 2013, 219).

Nevertheless, it is important that interdisciplinary research be evaluated. The freedom inherent in interdisciplinarity—for scholars are freed to embrace theories, methods, and subject matter ignored by their home discipline—cannot become a license for superficial analysis. Those who will evaluate interdisciplinary research should accept certain principles:

- Foremost, that there is value in integrating the insights generated by diverse disciplines, theories, and methods.
- That there are strategies for doing so, but there is scope both for developing new strategies and for tailoring strategies to particular situations.
- That quality interdisciplinary research requires a serious engagement with the disciplines that are drawn upon.
- That any theories or methods employed in interdisciplinary research must be employed in the correct manner. When these are adapted for interdisciplinary research, the adaptations must be justified (Szostak 2015a).

They should seek to evaluate research in terms first of the importance of results generated (both for the academy and for society), and second an open-minded appreciation of the strength of the arguments and evidence provided. Jacob (2008) identifies five criteria here: validity, utility, learning, satisfying needs, and the benefits from disciplinary specialization. As in interdisciplinary research itself the best evaluation may come from a team of evaluators with different areas of expertise.

Interdisciplinary evaluation will itself benefit from interdisciplinary research. Lyall et al. (2011) is one work which provides invaluable advice to referees and editors. And individual interdisciplinary evaluators will benefit from ease of access to relevant literatures in many fields. Our discussion of interdisciplinary evaluation thus provides further support for the development of an interdisciplinary approach to classification.[12]

The León Manifesto

Some relevant proposals regarding the future of knowledge organization emerged during the eighth conference of the Spanish chapter of the International Society for Knowledge Organization (ISKO). This conference, which took interdisciplinarity and knowledge organization as its theme, was held in the beautiful, lively atmosphere of the town of León, Spain, between April 18 and 20, 2007. These proposals accordingly were labeled 'The León Manifesto,' and are summarized in Table 1.3.

The Manifesto was published in *Knowledge Organization* 34(1): 6–8 (2007). It has been reproduced in several other venues, including the websites of ISKO Italy and ISKO Spain. It was also translated into Slovenian by Branka Badovinac and published in the printed journal 'Library News' of the National and University Library of Ljubljana.

---

[12] Though beyond the scope of this book, it should be appreciated that bibliometric analysis is of particular importance in the realm of interdisciplinary research. Diversity and network cohesion have been chosen as indicators for ID research measurement (Rafols and Meyer 2010). Elleby and Ingwersen (2010) recommend the study of citedness ratios in comparing interdisciplinary research with research evaluation in general.

Table 1.3 The León Manifesto

The current trend towards an increasing interdisciplinarity of knowledge calls for essentially new knowledge organization systems (KOSs), based on a substantive revision of the principles underlying the traditional discipline-based KOSs.
This innovation is not only desirable, but also feasible, and should be implemented by actually developing some new KOSs.
Instead of disciplines, the basic units of the new KOSs should be phenomena of the real world as represented in human knowledge.
The new KOSs should allow users to shift from one perspective or viewpoint to another, thus reflecting the multidimensional nature of complex thought. In particular, it should allow them to search independently for particular phenomena, for particular theories about phenomena (and about relations between phenomena), and for particular methods of investigation.
The connections between phenomena, those between phenomena and the theories studying them, and those between phenomena and the methods to investigate them, can be expressed and managed by analytico-synthetic techniques already developed in faceted classification.

A Brief Note on Digitization

We have focused our attention on interdisciplinarity in this chapter. We will find in what follows that our discussion of interdisciplinary KOSs intersects often with another important characteristic of the contemporary information environment: digitization. Card catalogues have been eclipsed by computer interfaces in libraries, and the Internet provides access to a host of information sources. Digitization is changing the way that scholars perform research (Meyer and Schroeder 2015). We will see that the sort of KOS that will best serve interdisciplinarity is far more feasible in the digital world than in the age of card catalogues (see Chap. 4). We will see that there are similar challenges in conversing across disciplinary boundaries and conversing across the diversity of databases available electronically, and will thus suggest that the recommended KOSs will facilitate search across diverse databases. We will see that the opportunities for information retrieval associated with digitization have stimulated the development of a new form of KOS, the ontology (Chap. 3). We will explore how the sort of KOSs recommended in this book might serve many of the purposes for which ontologies are developed (Chaps. 3 and 5). In particular we will examine its suitability for the Semantic Web (Chap. 8). And we will see in many places how a digital world increases the desire for interdisciplinary knowledge organization. We will in particular address the challenges of information overload (Chap. 8). In sum, then, digitization both facilitates and encourages the development of a KOS that will better serve inter-disciplinarity, while such a KOS in turn will address challenges and opportunities associated with digitization.

The Rest of the Book

This chapter has outlined the growing importance of interdisciplinarity. Along the way it has suggested some ways in which information science might respond. The next chapter is devoted to articulating in greater detail what interdisciplinary users of KOSs need. Chapter 3 then builds on that analysis to discuss the ideal nature of interdisciplinary KOSs.

Chapter 4 looks at the history of the field of knowledge organization through the lens of interdisciplinarity, and introduces the structure of two phenomenon-based KOSs. Its purpose is twofold: to show that the interest in both interdisciplinarity and phenomenon-based classification is longstanding, and to identify (and transcend) the reasons why previous efforts to develop interdisciplinary KOSs were unsuccessful. Chapter 5 then assesses the feasibility of creating KOSs of the sort indicated in Chaps. 3 and 4.

Scholars favoring a disciplinary approach often advocate 'domain analysis': the careful identification of the terminology employed in a field. It will often be noted in this book that domain analysis can be complementary to the pursuit of a general classification of the type advocated in this book; Chap. 6 then explores this complementarity in detail.

Chapter 7 speaks to how such systems could be developed in practice. The recommendations that this book will make are bold. It is thus essential that the book simultaneously address both the *desirability* and *feasibility* of designing and utilizing interdisciplinary KOSs. However, once these points are established, the rising importance of interdisciplinarity, in concert with the digitization of document classification, combines to generate a historical moment in which the development of a radically new system of document classification may be pursued.

Chapter 8 discusses how the recommended KOSs might prove to be advantageous both for information science and various types of user. Chapter 8 closes with a discussion of how the sort of classification recommended in this book might be adopted.

Chapter 9 reviews some of the theoretical concerns that information scientists favoring a disciplinary approach to knowledge organization have raised against the project outlined in preceding chapters, and discusses how these concerns are best addressed. Chapter 10 concludes the book and outlines avenues for further research.

Key Points

Information scientists should explore ways in which our systems for classifying ideas and documents could better facilitate interdisciplinarity. Scholars, students, and general users increasingly operate in an interdisciplinary fashion. By constructing KOSs that follow the basic guidelines set forth in the León Manifesto, we can potentially not only help interdisciplinarians find the information that they want, but can guide them to relevant information that they would not have thought to seek. Such a classification moreover can serve to clarify terminology and thus facilitate interdisciplinary communication. And interdisciplinary researchers—and importantly those who will evaluate such research—can benefit from enhanced access not just to the literature in diverse fields but also to the expanding literature on how to perform interdisciplinary research itself.

By placing interdisciplinarity within a social context, this chapter argues that society, not just the academy, will benefit from the development of KOSs better suited to interdisciplinarity. Interdisciplinary research is essential to coping with a wide range of societal challengers. The public interacts with scholars in many ways in addressing complex societal challenges, and thus also needs access to insights from diverse fields. The project of this book, to aid interdisciplinary scholarship, thus has important implications far beyond the academy. We will want to ensure in what follows that the approach to KOS to be pursued is accessible to the general user as well as to scholars.

It should also be emphasized that interdisciplinary understanding is possible. The present interest in interdisciplinarity has not emerged overnight but rather over a period of decades. Such a sustained interest would have been impossible if scholars and students had not found interdisciplinary exploration valuable. It must therefore be the case that individuals can communicate across disciplinary boundaries. This point may seem banal. But as we shall see in Chap. 9 especially, many scholars have used skepticism on this very point as a rationale for maintaining a discipline-based approach to knowledge organization.

References

Alrøe HF, Noe E (2014) Second-order science of interdisciplinary research: a polyocular framework for wicked problems. Constr Found 10(1):65–95

Apostel L (1972) Conceptual tools for interdisciplinarity: an operational approach. Interdisciplinarity. Problems of teaching and research in the Universities, Organization for Economic Cooperation and Development (OECD), Paris, pp 141–184

Association for Interdisciplinary Studies (AIS) (2013) About interdisciplinarity. www.oakland.edu/ais/

Augsburg T, Henry S (eds) (2009) The politics of interdisciplinary studies. McFarland Press, Jefferson, NC

Bartolo L, Trimble AM (2000) Heterogeneous structures database: vocabulary mapping within a multidisciplinary, multi-institutional research group. In: Beghtol C, Howarth LC, Williamson N (eds) Dynamism and stability in knowledge organization. Proceedings of the sixth international ISKO conference. Ergon Verlag, Würzburg, pp 118–123

Bates MJ (1996) Learning about the information seeking of interdisciplinary scholars and students. Libr Trends 45(1):155–164

Beers P, Boots P (2009) Eliciting conceptual models to support interdisciplinary research. J Inform Sci 35(3):259–278

Beghtol C (1995) 'Facets' as undiscovered public knowledge: S.R. Ranganathan in India and S. Guttman in Israel. J Doc 51(3):194–224

Bergmann M, Jahn T, Knobloch T, Krohn W, Pohl C, Schramm E (2012) Methods for transdisciplinary research: a primer for practice. Campus, Berlin

von Bertalanffy L (1968) General system theory: foundations, development, applications. Braziller, New York

Brome V (1963) The problem of progress. Cassell, London

Bulick S (1982) Structure and subject interaction. Marcel Dekker, New York

Burke P (2012) A social history of knowledge, 2: from the Encyclopédie to Wikipedia. Polity Press, Cambridge, UK

Carp R (2001) Integrative praxes: learning from multiple knowledge formations. Issues Integr Stud 19:71–121

Chakraborty T, Kumar S, Reddy MD, Kumar S, Ganguly N, Mukherjee A (2013) Automatic Classification and Analysis of Interdisciplinary Fields in Computer Sciences. In: International conference on social computing (SocialCom) 2013., pp 180–187

Civallero E (2010) UDC biology revision project: first stage: class 59 vertebrates. Extensions Corrections UDC 32:9–19

Cory KA (1997) Discovering hidden analogies in an online Humanities database. Comput Human 31(1):1–12

Craig BF, Peterson TR, Hamlyn EJ (2005) Interdisciplinarity and team dynamics. In: Sadalla E (ed) The U.S.—Mexican border environment. Dynamics of human-environment interactions. San Diego State University Press, San Diego, pp 371–385

Dahlherg I (1994) Domain interaction: theory and practice. Adv Knowl Org 4:60–71

Darbellay F, Moody Z, Sedooka A, Steffen G (2014) Interdisciplinary research boosted by serendipity. Creativity Res J 26(1):1–10

Davies R (1989) The creation of new knowledge by information retrieval and classification. J Doc 45(4):273–301

Eigenbrode SD, O'Rourke M, Wulfhorst JD, Althoff DM, Goldberg CS, Merrill K, Morse W, Nielsen-Pincus M, Stephens J, Winowiecki L, Bosque-Pérez N (2007) Employing philosophical dialogue in collaborative science. Bioscience 57(1):55–64

Elleby A, Ingwersen P (2010) Publication point indicators: a comparative case study of two publications point systems and citation impact in an interdisciplinary context. J Inform 4:512–523

European Commission (2009) ERA indicators and monitoring. Expert Group Report, October 2009. http://ec.europa.eu/research/era/pdf/eraindicators&monitoring.pdf

Foster AE, Ellis D (2014) Serendipity and its study. J Doc 70(6):1015–1038

Fox MJ, Olson H (2012) Feminist epistemologies and knowledge organization. In: Smiraglia RP, Lee H (eds) Cultural frames of knowledge. Ergon Verlag, Würzburg, pp 79–97

Fuchsman K (2012) Interdisciplines and interdisciplinarity: political psychology and psychohistory compared. Issues Integr Stud 30:128–154

Gibbons M, Limoges C, Nowotny H, Schwartzman S, Scott P, Trow M (1994) The new production of knowledge: the dynamics of science and research in contemporary societies. Sage, London

Glassick CE, Huber MT, Maeroff GI (1997) Scholarship assessed: evaluation of the professoriate. Jossey-Bass, San Francisco

Gnoli C (2006) The meaning of facets in non-disciplinary classification. In: Budin G, Swertz C, Mitgutsch K (eds) Knowledge organization for a global learning society: proceedings of the 9th ISKO conference. Ergon, Würzburg, pp 11–18

Gnoli C (2014) Boundaries and overlaps of disciplines in Bloch's methodology of historical knowledge. In: Babik W (ed) Knowledge organization in the 21st century: between historical patterns and future prospects. Proceedings of the 13th ISKO conference, Krakow. Ergon Verlag, Würzburg

Gordon MD, Awad NF (2008) The tip of the iceberg: the quest for innovation at the base of the pyramid. In: Bruza P, Weeber M (eds) Literature based discovery. Springer, Berlin, pp 23–38

Hurd JM (1992) Interdisciplinary research in the sciences: implications for library organization. Coll Res Libr 53(4):283–297

Ignaciuk A, Rice M, Bogardi J, Canadell JG, Dhakal S, Ingram J, Leemans R, Rosenberg M (2012) Responding to complex societal challenges: a decade of Earth System Science Partnership (ESSP) interdisciplinary research. Curr Opin Environ Sustain 4(1):147–158

Jacob S (2008) Cross-disciplinarization. A new talisman for evaluation? Am J Eval 29(2):175–194

Katz JS, Hicks D (1995) The classification of interdisciplinary journals: a new approach. Proceedings of the fifth international conference of the international society for scientometrics and informetrics. Learned Information, Melford

Kimmel SE (1999) Interdisciplinary information searching: moving beyond discipline-based resources. In: Fiscella J, Kimmel S (eds) Interdisciplinary education: a guide to resources. College Board, New York

Klein JT (1990) Interdisciplinarity: history, theory and practice. The Wayne State University Press, Detroit

Klein JT (1996) Interdisciplinary needs: the current context. Libr Trends 45(2):134–154

Klein JT (2010) A taxonomy of interdisciplinarity. In: Frodeman R, Klein JT, Mitcham C (eds) The Oxford handbook of interdisciplinarity. Oxford University Press, Oxford, pp 15–30

Klein JT, Newell WH (1996) Advancing Interdisciplinary Studies. In: Gaff JG, Ratcliff J, Associates (eds) Handbook of the undergraduate curriculum. Jossey-Bass, San Francisco

Knapp JA (2012) Plugging the 'whole': librarians as interdisciplinary facilitators. Libr Rev 61 (3):199–214

Kockelmanns JJ (1979) Why interdisciplinarity? In: Kockelmanns JJ (ed) Interdisciplinarity and higher education. The Pennsylvania State University Press, University Park, pp 123–160

Lattuca LR (2001) Creating Interdisciplinarity: interdisciplinary research and teaching among college and university faculty. Vanderbilt University Press, Nashville, TN

Lenoir Y, Klein JT (eds). (2010). Interdisciplinarity in schools: a comparative view of national perspectives. Special volume. Issues Integr Stud 28

León Manifesto (2007) Knowl Org 34(1):6–8. Available [with commentary] at: www.iskoi.org/ilc/leon.php

Looney C, Donovan S, O'Rourke M, Crowley S, Eigenbrode SD, Rotschy L, Bosque-Perez NA, Wulfhorst JD (2014) Using Toolbox workshops to enhance cross-disciplinary communication. In: O'Rourke M, Crowley S, Eigenbrode SD, Wulfhorst JD (eds) Enhancing communication and collaboration in interdisciplinary research. Sage, Thousand Oaks, pp 220–243

López-Huertas MJ (2010) Nuevo conocimiento, innovación y sociedad: Retos para la gestion de la información. In V Reunión Internacional de Gestión de la Información y Desarrollo, Florianópolis

Lyall C, Bruce A, Tait J, Meagher L (2011) Interdisciplinary Research Journeys. Bloomsbury Publishing PLC, Huntingdon, GBR

McCay-Peet L, Toms EG (2015) Investigating serendipity: how it unfolds and what may influence it. J Am Soc Inform Sci Technol 66(7):1463–1476

McDonald D, Bammer G, Deane P (2009) Research integration using dialogue methods. ANU Epress, Canberra

Meyer E, Schroeder R (2015) Knowledge machines: digital transformations of the sciences and humanities. MIT Press, Cambridge

Miksa FL (1992) The concept of the universe of knowledge and the purpose of LIS classification. In: Williamson NJ, Hudon M (eds) Classification research for knowledge representation and organization: Proceedings of the 5th international study conference on classification research, Toronto. Elsevier, Amsterdam, pp 101–126

Morin E (1995) Sobre la interdisciplinariedad. Revista Complejidad 1:0. http://www.pensamientocomplejo.com.ar/docs/files/morin%5Fsobre%5Fla%5Finterdisciplinaridad%2Epdf

Murphy J (2003) Information-seeking habits of environmental scientists. Issues Sci Technol Librarianship 38(Summer), http://www.istl.org/previous.html

National Academy of Science, the National Academy of Engineering, and the Institute of Medicine (2005) Facilitating interdisciplinary research. National Academies Press, Washington

National Science Foundation (2011) Rebuilding the mosaic. Report. http://www.nsf.gov/pubs/2011/nsf11086/nsf11086.pdf

Neurath O, Carnap R, Morris C (1937–8) International Encyclopedia of unified science. University of Chicago Press, Chicago

Newell WH (2001) A theory of interdisciplinary studies. Issues Integr Stud 19:1–25

Nicolescu B (1996) La Transdisciplinarité: Manifeste. Editions du Rocher, Mónaco

Nissani M (1997) Ten cheers for interdisciplinarity: the case of interdisciplinary knowledge and research. Soc Sci J 34(2):201–216

Nowotny H, Scott P, Gibbons M (2001) Re-thinking science: knowledge and the public in an age of uncertainty. Polity Press, Cambridge

Ørom A (2003) Knowledge organization in the domain of art studies: history, transition and conceptual changes. Knowl Org 30(3-4):128–143

O'Rourke M, Crowley S, Eigenbrode SD, Wulfhorst JD (eds) (2014) Enhancing communication and collaboration in interdisciplinary research. Sage, Thousand Oaks

Pahre R (1996) Patterns of knowledge communities in the social sciences. Libr Trends 45(2):204–225

Palmer CL (1996) Information work at the boundaries of science: linking library services to research practices. Libr Trends 45(2):165–191

Palmer CL (1999) Structures and strategies of interdisciplinary science. J Am Soc Inf Sci 50(3):242–253

Palmer CL (2001) Work at the boundaries of science: information and the interdisciplinary research process. Kluwer, Dordrecht

Palmer CL (2010) Information research on interdisciplinarity. In: Frodeman R, Klein JT, Mitcham C (eds) The Oxford handbook of interdisciplinarity. Oxford University Press, Oxford, pp 174–188

Phoenix C et al (2013) Paradigmatic approaches to studying environment and human health: (Forgotten) implication for interdisciplinary research. Environ Sci Policy 25:218–228

Popper K (2005) The logic of scientific discovery. Routledge, London

Porter AL, Rafols I (2009) Is science becoming more interdisciplinary? Measuring and mapping six research fields over time. Scientometrics 81(3):719–745

Qin J, Lancaster FW, Allen B (1997) Types and levels of collaboration in interdisciplinary research in sciences. J Am Soc Inf Sci 48(10):893–916

Rafols I, Meyer M (2010) Diversity and network coherence as indicators of interdisciplinarity: case study of bio-nanoscience. Scientometrics 82:263–287

Repko AF (2012) Interdisciplinary research: process and theory, 2nd edn. Sage, Thousand Oaks

Roa-Atkinson A, Velho L (2005) Interactions in knowledge production. A comparative study of immunology research groups in Colombia and Brazil. Aslib Proc New Inform Perspect 57(3):200–216

Romero-Lankao P et al (2013) ADAPTE: a tale of diverse teams coming together to do issue-driven interdisciplinary research. Environ Sci Policy 26:29–39

Root-Bernstein R (1989) Discovery. Harvard University Press, Cambridge, MA

Salter L, Hearn A (eds) (1997) Outside the lines: issues in interdisciplinary research. McGill-Queen's University Press, Montreal

Satija MP, Madalli DP, Dutta B (2014) Modes of growth of subjects. Knowl Org 41(3):195–204

Searing SE (1992) How libraries cope with interdisciplinarity: the case of women's studies. Issues Integr Stud 10:7–25

Shiri A (2009) Exploration of interdisciplinarity in nanotechnology queries: the use of transaction log analysis and thesauri. Paper presented to the 20th Annual ASIST SIG/CR Workshop: Bridging Worlds, Connecting People: Classification Transcending Boundaries. doi:10.7152/acro.v20i1.12883

Sievanen L, Campbell LM, Leslie HM (2011) Challenges to interdisciplinary research in ecosystems-based management. Conserv Biol 26(2):315–323

Smalheiser NR, Torvik VI (2008) The place of Literature-Based Discovery in contemporary scientific practice. In: Bruza P, Weeber M (eds) Literature based discovery. Springer, Berlin, pp 13–22

Smiraglia RP (2012) Introduction: theory, knowledge organization, epistemology, culture. In: Smiraglia RP, Lee H (eds) Cultural frames of knowledge. Ergon Verlag, Würzburg, pp 1–17

Song C-H (2003) Interdisciplinarity and knowledge inflow/outflow structure among science and engineering research in Korea. Scientometrics 58(1):129–141

Sparks S (2005) JISC disciplinary differences report. Rightscomm Ltd., London

Stokols D, Hall KL, Moser RP, Feng A, Misra S, Taylor BK (2010) Cross-disciplinary team science initiatives: research, training, and translation. In: Frodeman R, Klein JT, Mitcham C (eds) Oxford handbook of interdisciplinarity. Oxford University Press, Oxford, UK, pp 471–493

Sugimoto C, Weingart S (2015) The kaleidoscope of disciplinarity. J Doc 71(4):775–794

Swanson DR (1986) Undiscovered public knowledge. Libr Q 56(2):103–118

Swanson DR (2008) Literature based discovery: the very idea. In: Bruza P, Weeber M (eds) Literature based discovery. Springer, Berlin, pp 3–11

Swanson DR, Smalheiser NR, Bookstein A (2001) Information discovery from complementary literatures: categorizing viruses as potential weapons. J Am Soc Inform Sci Technol 52:797–812

Szostak R (2003) A schema for unifying human science: interdisciplinary perspectives on culture. Susquehanna University Press, Selinsgrove, PA

Szostak R (2004) Classifying science: phenomena, data, theory, method, practice. Springer, Dordrecht

Szostak R (2007) Modernism, postmodernism, and interdisciplinarity. Issues Integr Stud 26:32–83

Szostak R (2014a) Classifying for social diversity. Knowl Org 41(2):160–170

Szostak R (2014b) Classifying the humanities. Knowl Org 41(4):263–275

Szostak R (2014c) Skepticism and knowledge organization. In: Babik W (ed) Knowledge organization in the 21st century: between historical patterns and future prospects. Proceedings of the 13th ISKO conference, Krakow. Würzburg, Ergon

Szostak R (2014d) Communicating complex concepts. In: O'Rourke M, Crowley S, Eigenbrode SD, Wulfhorst JD (eds) Enhancing communication and collaboration in interdisciplinary research. Sage, Thousand Oaks, pp 34–55

Szostak R (2015a) Interdisciplinary and transdisciplinary multi-method and mixed methods research. In: Hesse-Biber S, Johnson RB (eds) The Oxford handbook of mixed and multi-method research. Oxford University Press, Oxford, pp 128–143

Szostak R (2015b) A pluralistic approach to the philosophy of classification. Library Trends 63(3):591–614

Warner J (2000) Can classification yield an evaluative principle for information retrieval? In: Marcella R, Maltby A (eds) The future of classification. Gower, Cambridge

Weingart P (2010) A short history of knowledge formations. In: Frodeman R, Klein JT, Mitcham C (eds) The Oxford handbook of interdisciplinarity. Oxford University Press, New York, pp 3–14

Wenzel V (2001) Complex systems in natural sciences and humanities. Scientometrics 52 (3):525–529

Wilson P (1968) Two kinds of power: an essay on bibliographic control. University of California Press, Berkeley

Workman TE, Fiszman M, Rindflesch TC (2014) Framing serendipitous information-seeking behavior for facilitating literature-based discovery: a proposed model. J Assoc Inform Sci Technol 65(3):501–512

Chapter 2
The Needs of Interdisciplinary Research

We begin this chapter by outlining a set of interdisciplinary information needs derived from our discussion in Chap. 1. We then discuss each of these in turn. We close the chapter by discussing how disciplinary scholars would be affected by the adoption of KOSs that met interdisciplinary needs.

Identifying Interdisciplinary Needs

The review of the nature of interdisciplinarity in Chap. 1 sets the stage for a detailed discussion in this chapter of what interdisciplinarians need from KOSs.[1] Though there is diversity in interdisciplinary practice it is still quite possible to identify key challenges that will face interdisciplinary scholars and students in general. These needs can be summarized in Table 2.1. They are also expressed figuratively in Fig. 2.1.

Needs Justification

Note that the first five desiderata outlined in Table 2.1 reflect both our understanding of what interdisciplinarians do *and* our understanding of the defining characteristics of the disciplines that interdisciplinarians need to navigate (on the latter see Table 1.2).

---

[1] There is no detailed model of interdisciplinary search practices (Palmer 2010, 182). We have thus pursued the strategy of first identifying what interdisciplinary researchers and students are trying to do, and then discussing what sort of information-seeking strategies are required.

© Springer International Publishing Switzerland 2016
R. Szostak et al., *Interdisciplinary Knowledge Organization*,
DOI 10.1007/978-3-319-30148-8_2

Table 2.1 Interdisciplinary needs

Interdisciplinarians will wish to know what has been said by all scholars (and indeed those beyond the academy) about a particular phenomenon (that is, the things or variables that we study) and especially about the relationships that might exist among two or more phenomena.
Interdisciplinarians will wish to know what theories have been applied to the phenomena and relationships that interest them.
Likewise interdisciplinarians will wish to know what evidence supports different theories, and this means knowing which methods have been applied to the phenomena and relationships that interest them and which data has been collected in exploring these things and relationships.
Interdisciplinarians will need to understand the meanings attached to particular terms.
Interdisciplinarians generally appreciate that each discipline has its own disciplinary perspective, and will thus wish to evaluate disciplinary insights in the context of that disciplinary perspective.[a] They will thus generally wish to know the disciplinary affiliation and outlook of authors, and also have access to works describing disciplines. [They will likewise need similar information regarding interdisciplinarity itself.]
We very briefly saw when discussing the León Manifesto, that it will be easier to facilitate the classification of diverse relationships if we pursue a synthetic approach to classification, such that a work can be classified by a combination of terms. We will develop this idea in future chapters. We can thus add 'synthetic' approach as an indirect interdisciplinary need.

[a]Recall that disciplinary perspective embraces a host of philosophical attitudes. We shall see in later chapters that users may wish to see works classified in terms of various perspectives—feminism, postmodernism, and so on—that an author brings to a work

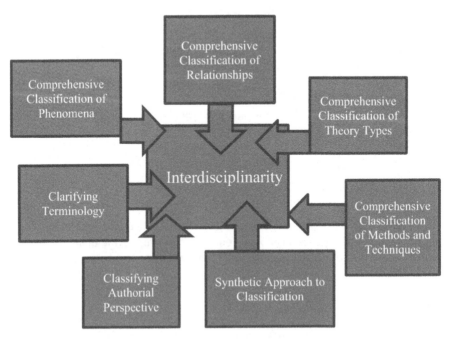

Fig. 2.1 Concept map of interdisciplinary knowledge organization. *Source*: Table 2.1

We do not mean to suggest that classification by theory, method/data, phenomena, concepts, and discipline are the *only* sorts of classification needed by scholars: like disciplinary scholars they will also care about such things as time and place and type of document. The desiderata of Table 2.1 are, however, by far the most important objectives currently ill-served by classificatory practice. As was suggested in our discussion of undiscovered public knowledge, classification schemes could, but generally do not, strive to capture within subject headings the key causal relationships investigated in a work. Only rarely are the theories or methods employed in a work captured in subject headings. And discipline-based classifications can employ terminology quite differently in different fields.

Davis and Shaw (2011, 31–2) list five types of general information need. These can each be related to the interdisciplinary needs identified above. The first is procedural (how to do things). For the interdisciplinarian this will include understanding multiple theories and methods. The second is substantive. This is where the interdisciplinarian wishes to find out what has been said about particular phenomena and relationships. The third is muddled, where the user is not sure what to seek. This is common in interdisciplinary practice for the researcher cannot know in advance what useful information might exist in other disciplines. They must thus be facilitated in searches both when they know what they are looking for and when they do not. The fourth type is verificative. The interdisciplinary researcher will be particularly curious as to whether similar causal arguments have been made in different fields, and what the evidence for these has been. The fifth is educational: the user may not understand what they find and need further resources in order to understand. One key source of misunderstanding is unclear terminology; classification can reduce ambiguity. Another is not understanding theories, methods, or disciplinary perspective; it is thus important to classify works in terms of these and guide user to works about them.

Mai (2008) concurs that the design of classifications should be grounded in an understanding of user needs. He worries that the descriptive literature on user behavior provides little guidance. He thus suggests that we perform 'cognitive work analysis': identify the constraints faced by particular user groups and then attempt to cope with these. Mai advises us to look first at the work environment, and then ask what sort of work is done, how is it organized, what strategies (for search especially) are involved, and what expertise is possessed by those doing the work. His approach thus supports the approach taken here of asking what interdisciplinarians do and how, and deducing their informational requirements on the basis of their work activities (see Szostak 2010). His particular five questions reinforce in turn the importance of knowledge organization to interdisciplinarity, and are summarized in Table 2.2. They also provide further justification for the specific needs of interdisciplinarians that were identified above.

It is also useful to revisit briefly our discussion of undiscovered public knowledge, for the needs identified in that literature bear a striking resemblance to those we have described above. Beghtol (1995) explored the implications of 'undiscovered public knowledge' for information science. Drawing on previous research by others, she noted five resulting problems:

Table 2.2 Cognitive work analysis of interdisciplinarity

Work Environment. Universities are generally organized around disciplines. The vast majority of scholars thus interact mostly with scholars with a shared disciplinary perspective. If they need or wish to look beyond their domain, they will need to rely either on the kindness of strangers or on useful guidance from the field of information science. Interdisciplinary scholars will be hobbled if they must master several domain-specific classifications or seek out many disciplinary experts for advice.
What Work is Done? A growing body of scholars defines themselves as interdisciplinary. This must mean that they do not take any one domain-specific terminology for granted, but must consciously master multiple domains. Even specialized researchers are expected to have some familiarity with how their research fits within the broader scholarly enterprise. We saw in Chap. 1 that interdisciplinary work involves investigating phenomena, relationships, theories, methods, perspectives, and terminology across disciplinary boundaries.
How is this Work Organized? An increasing number of scholars operate within interdisciplinary teams. These almost universally face 'translation' problems: scholars speak past each other because they use words in slightly different ways. Boundary work across disciplines is thus characterized by the use of 'pidgins': limited dialects that allow cross-disciplinary communication (Galison 1997; Klein 1990). Since pidgins are limited in scope, it would be difficult to classify all works relevant to such a cross-disciplinary endeavor in terms of the shared dialect. Conversation across all disciplinary boundaries would be better served by the sort of supra-language embedded in a general classification which does not employ different terminology in different fields.
What Strategies are Involved? In the absence of reliable guidance from information science, scholars wishing to pursue questions across disciplinary boundaries are forced to rely on a host of time-consuming and ineffective search strategies: seeking out scholars in other fields, chasing citations (the strategy recommended by Bates 1996, and Palmer 1996), following 'big names' in other fields, and so on (Palmer 1996).
What Expertise is Possessed? The vast majority of even interdisciplinary scholars received their training exclusively within one discipline (with perhaps a token course or two outside of their chosen discipline). They are thus not taught how to access information from outside their discipline, and perhaps even sub-discipline (though this is beginning to change). Nor are they taught any familiarity with the theories or methods or phenomena addressed by others. That is, scholars tend to know a lot about one thing, but have little or no training in how to connect that knowledge to related understandings in other fields. They rely on information science to facilitate this.

- Evidence that might refute a hypothesis is not recognized;
- Evidence that might add additional support to a hypothesis is likewise not appreciated;
- Analyses of missing links in a causal chain are ignored;
- Solutions to analogous problems are missed; and
- Unimagined correlations between concepts are not recognized.

It is notable that though these problems were identified in a quite different context, they point also toward the importance of relationships, methods/evidence/data, and concepts. Beghtol notes that the strategies generally recommended for uncovering 'undiscovered public knowledge' rely heavily on serendipity. Moreover they tend to be discipline-specific, whereas the likelihood of undiscovered public knowledge increases with interdisciplinary interaction

(Beghtol 1995, 195–6). The solution, it must seem, is to facilitate searches by phenomenon, relationship, theory, and method across disciplinary boundaries.

It is not just scholars pursuing big breakthroughs that need the sorts of information identified above. The vast bulk of scholarship involves the application of one or more scholarly theories and scholarly methods to the study of the relationships among one or more phenomena (see Szostak 2004). Scholars performing such research are naturally curious as to whether the theory and/or method they wish to apply to the study of their particular set of phenomena has been applied before. They thus wish to be able to search primarily by theory applied, method applied, and phenomena or relationship studied. Yet documents are generally classified exclusively by subject matter, by what a work is 'about.'

The needs addressed above also accord with Kleineberg's (2013) advice that we should capture the 'what,' 'why' and 'how' of arguments and documents. 'What' will be captured through phenomena and relationships; 'how' through methods and perhaps theory; 'why' through perspective in general. And our approach to identifying needs accords well with the pragmatic approach to knowledge organization urged by Hjørland and Nissen Pedersen (2005). They recommend 'classification in response to an objective' (584). We, like Spärck Jones (2005) to whom their paper is a response, respect their preference for a pragmatic approach. We also agree that classifications are to be judged, in large measure, by their congruence with the objectives of those who utilize them, and are thus best constructed with careful attention to those objectives. Indeed, the main contention of this book is that as scholarly research (and public policy analysis) becomes increasingly interdisciplinary, a—perhaps 'the'—key purpose of systems of classification is to facilitate interdisciplinary research and information sharing.

Extensions and Clarifications

We have naturally emphasized to this point the challenges faced by interdisciplinarians in searching. But once the interdisciplinary researcher has found relevant literature, they then need to understand it. Understanding terminology is important at the search stage—the interdisciplinarian needs to know what terms to search for—but also critical for then comprehending the literature. Information scientists should not forget that an appropriate classification clarifies the meaning of terminology. We will often return to this point in later chapters.

Since we will often have cause to discuss terminological ambiguity in this book, it is important to clarify our own terminology here. Strictly speaking a 'concept' is an idea. Concepts themselves cannot then be ambiguous. But humans attempt to signify concepts through the use of terms. Different individuals or groups may use different terms to describe the same concept or the same terms to describe different concepts. We strive in this book to speak of 'terms' rather than 'concepts' when ambiguity is emphasized. We follow common parlance, though, in referring to ambiguous 'complex concepts.'

We might also briefly note that successful 'search' itself depends on there being works to find. As Searing (1996) appreciates, library requisition budgets and responsibilities are generally divided by fields. An interdisciplinary work might be viewed as of tangential interest to all relevant acquisition librarians. If libraries were organized around phenomena rather than disciplines the value of interdisciplinary works would be more transparent.

Once the interdisciplinarian has (hopefully) identified a wide array of relevant literature, it will prove invaluable to organize this literature in terms of theories and methods applied. Interdisciplinary scholars will then wish to evaluate, build upon, and synthesize the insights they find. These steps need not trouble the information scientist greatly, except for the simple but critical requirement that works on how to perform interdisciplinary research can be readily identified by the interdisciplinarian. Despite recent efforts to consolidate this literature (Repko 2012; Bergmann et al 2012, AIS 2013) it is also scattered across many fields. A KOS designed for interdisciplinarity would thus provide easy access to the literature on interdisciplinarity. Since interdisciplinarity is itself a phenomenon, a KOS designed to facilitate search by phenomena would do this.

Last but not least the interdisciplinary scholar will wish to transmit their findings back to all relevant scholars. The interdisciplinarian will have to ensure that they employ terms in a manner that makes sense to diverse audiences. KOSs should then ensure that the work can be readily found by all relevant users, which of course reinforces the need for facilitating interdisciplinary searches.

The field of knowledge organization could try to meet the needs of interdisciplinarians in three ways (Kyle 1960):

- Adaptation of existent, discipline-based classifications to new uses;
- Creation of alternative hybrid classifications;
- Creation of new forms of classification.

This book will in general argue for at least hybridity if not complete novelty (see Chaps. 3 and 5). In order to establish that case we will, as we address each of the needs of interdisciplinarians in turn below, review how present systems of knowledge organization fail to meet those needs. It must then seem that only marginal changes to existing KOSs will not suffice. Given that the major KOSs in use today were all conceived decades ago when disciplines provided the dominant framework for the partitioning of knowledge, this result should not be surprising.

Classifying by Phenomena

Interdisciplinarians will obviously wish to identify works from various disciplines that address a particular phenomenon (thing that is studied). In turn, they will want their published research to be found readily by all other scholars interested in the same thing.

In present classification systems, though, documents are not classified according to some universal scheme of phenomena but according to the different terminology employed by diverse disciplines. As Hjørland and Nissen Pedersen (2005, 586) note, a single term can take on diverse meanings in the context of different disciplinary discourses. Thus even thesauri—which seek to identify the relationships among concepts (see below)—cannot flawlessly guide the scholar to relevant works in other disciplines. Works on the same phenomenon will be classified differently, and often using different terminology, depending on the discipline of the work. The 'Relative Index' of the Dewey Decimal Classification (DDC) guides cataloguers to the often dozen or more places that works on a given phenomenon might be classified; not only is this guidance imperfect but most library users are blissfully unaware of its existence. Likewise, subject catalogues provide a limited solution to this problem, in part because the logic of subject headings is opaque to most researchers (Julien et al. 2013). Full text searching is often thought to be the solution, but simply fails to identify works that utilize different terminology.

The fact that works about the same phenomenon can be found in many disciplines might be thought to be merely an inconvenience.[2] But of course the very reason that classifications were organized around disciplines rather than things in the first place was a recognition (often implicit) that each discipline organized its understandings in its own way (Langridge 1992; Svenonius 1997). And, in practice, quite different terminology is used in different disciplines (a challenge to keyword searching and also to subject searching if different controlled vocabulary is used across disciplines). The researcher will miss relevant works if they do not know what terms to search for. They could fall back on general works about disciplines, but this is a time-consuming strategy for identifying terminology. Moreover such a strategy presumes that they know at the outset which disciplines to investigate. Yet one of the challenges of interdisciplinary research is to identify relevant disciplines (Repko 2012). And as noted above the most useful information is often the most surprising, and this will usually be information the researcher would not have searched for (Palmer 2001). For all these reasons, the disciplinary base of current KOSs becomes more than an inconvenience but an active barrier that prevents scholars from finding relevant research in disciplines with which they are unfamiliar (see Palmer 2010).

As Bulick described as early as 1982, this disciplinary approach to classification has caused great confusion as disciplinary boundaries have shifted and interdisciplinary fields have emerged. Three broad types of problem occur: phenomena that are studied by more than one discipline are classified under different, often widely scattered, headings within a given classification; subjects that are inherently

---

[2] 'Since works on women's health are shelved in the *R*'s with other medical guides, literary criticism of the works of women authors shelved in the *P*'s by nationality and period, studies of female psychology in the *BF*'s, and so on, one cannot engage in the sort of browsing and serendipitous discovery that should ideally support interdisciplinary scholarship' (Searing 1992, 8). Arguably, though, browsing the shelves has become less important with digitization of both works and catalogues.

interdisciplinary have no obvious place; and subjects that combine existing subjects have no obvious place. This last problem, it might be noted, afflicts complex subjects even within disciplines. Existing KOSs necessarily grapple with these challenges. A synthetic non-discipline-based classification would face no difficulty.

Hoetzlein (2007, 73) discusses the example of 'energy':

> 'Many terms, such as that of energy, may easily appear in all of them [disciplines]. In the physical sciences, that is between chemistry, biology and physics, the concept has one and the same physical meaning but with different interpretations and formulations. In ecology the definition of energy may differ, but the idea must be linked to its more basic physical interpretation to fully appreciate it. In theology and philosophy the idea of energy has many other meanings, but these should be linked to the same singular concept as they provide a historical foundation for our modern definitions. Real relationships are lost when concepts, databases, and research areas become distinct. Only by connecting terms across disciplines is it possible to recover this understanding.'

Palmer (1996) outlined several further advantages of being readily able to track terminology across fields. Metaphorical use of a term from one field in another is often important for theory construction. Mapping terms across disciplinary boundaries can help us identify, and perhaps even predict, interdisciplinary knowledge structures. And she notes that we will want to track how meanings change as terms cross borders. We will devote much attention in this book to discussing how (and how best) to capture both similarities and differences in meaning.

Special note might be made of the problem of 'scatter': the fact that very similar works may be found in quite different places in a classification or physical library. User studies find that scholars in high-scatter fields (such as interdisciplinary scholars) consult multiple databases and have trouble keeping up with the literature (Hood and Wilson 2001). Cross-database keyword searching proves problematic for such researchers. They thus spend much time 'probing': searching for relevant information outside of their area of expertise. Nor can they be satisfied with just one reference from another field but appear to devote yet more time to verification (Palmer 2010, 181–3). They would clearly benefit if the interdependent literature they search for was not so widely scattered.

While the academy relies upon the complementary efforts of specialized and interdisciplinary researchers, even specialized researchers can benefit from familiarity with related work in other disciplines: this will not only suggest new avenues of research but remind them of the biases that could affect their disciplinary approach (Szostak 2004). Such knowledge would be much more likely if works on the same topic from different disciplines were classified and perhaps even shelved together (we address shelving decisions in more detail below).

In the contemporary world a further problem arises that plagues both specialized and interdisciplinary research. Searches for information increasingly span multiple digital databases; libraries, museums, archives, and private and governmental websites all possess valuable information organized in diverse ways.[3] Yet different

---

[3] It is increasingly important to access 'behind the scenes' records of scholarship (Lambe 2011). But this is generally held in archives or online databases rather than libraries.

databases employ quite different classification systems (Gnoli 2010). The lack of consistent controlled vocabularies across databases is a huge barrier to interdisciplinarity in particular, given the broader search interests of the interdisciplinarian (Kutner 2000). Landry (2004) has investigated the possibility of linking different subject heading lists and finds this feasible but time-consuming. The only common denominator that might allow seamless searches across multiple digital databases is the phenomena (and relationships) addressed in each, assuming these were given the same names across databases.[4]

The Semantic Web is an enterprise that aspires to allowing computers to navigate across diverse digital databases (Hart and Dolbear 2013). The key is to classify diverse databases in a common format such that a computer is able to draw inferences across databases. We shall see in later chapters that the approach to classification pursued in this book, with its emphasis on phenomena (and relationships), may support the Semantic Web.

Gnoli (2010) notes that we should classify the things we study, not just the documents that carry information about these. Knowledge organization should transcend libraries, after all, and allow, for example, museums and archives to better classify their contents. This again would require a classification grounded in things (phenomena) rather than disciplines. Museums, we shall see, have increasingly essayed to classify (some sorts of) objects. Notably they have eschewed the use of bibliographic classifications for this purpose. We will in later chapters explore the possibility that a phenomenon-based classification might serve the needs of both libraries and museums (and indeed archives and galleries).

In the foregoing we have stressed the obvious cost of the present system: that relevant information is not found or is found only with great difficulty. This means that interdisciplinary research is harder and less useful than it might be. Opportunities for productive synthesis of ideas are missed. There is a further cost: scholars often 'reinvent the wheel' through ignorance of previous work. This cost is borne not just by interdisciplinarians but by disciplinary scholars as well.

Classifying by Relationships Among Phenomena

As noted above, interdisciplinary research often examines links between phenomena that are investigated by different disciplines (see Fig. 2.2). The interdisciplinary researcher must first identify the set of relevant phenomena, and this task will be particularly difficult in the absence of a common classification of phenomena. Yet the problems identified in the previous section are only the beginning.

---

[4] In a different context, Boteram and Hubrich (2010) argue that a subset of relationships is needed to provide interfaces between different classification systems.

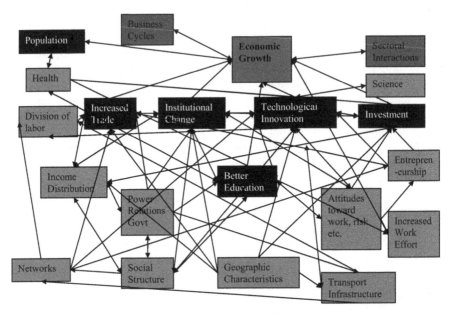

Fig. 2.2 The causes of economic growth 38. *Source*: Repko et al. (2014, 174) with permission of Sage Publishers

The Present Situation

Imagine that an interdisciplinarian is interested in a particular causal relationship: the effect of a certain pharmaceutical on a certain disease, a certain cultural attitude on a particular economic outcome, or a certain political institution on artistic production. We have seen in the previous section that tracking down all relevant works on any of these phenomena will be difficult. And in this case much of that effort will be wasted. The researcher will uncover many works on the drug that do not mention the disease and many works on the disease that do not mention the drug. It would be far better if the researcher could search directly for works that address the effect of the drug on the disease. [Of course the researcher might find that some of these other works are of some use, but that does not mean that the researcher should not be facilitated in identifying the works that most directly address their research interest.]

A work about how A affects B may be classed under just A or just B. It may be classed under both A and B if both are recognized subject headings, and the classifier recognizes that both are important. If so, a Boolean search—which allows the user to search by combinations of terms using 'AND' or 'OR' between terms— will uncover the work. But now the terminological problems identified in the preceding section are multiplied: in searching for a relationship the user needs to know all of the terminology that might be used to describe each concept in the relationship. Moreover, works that address how A influences B will be indistinguishable in a Boolean search from works that address how B affects A or works that simply happen to discuss A and B separately. All such works may be shelved with works on A or B. A work on how A, B, C, and D combine to influence E, F, G, and H will almost certainly not be classified under each of the relationships posited (though modern digital technologies make it quite feasible to do so). The ideal would be for the user to search for 'A causes/influences B' and be rewarded with all works that study whether A influences B. [We hasten to stress that the word 'cause' is used in the most general sense here to indicate any influence that A might exert on B.]

Classifiers have generally been satisfied with identifying the main thrust of documents. It is worth noting here that we could aspire to a classification of not just documents but the key insights that these contain. The latter will become increasingly enticing as open source publishing extends its reach. And such an exercise might be quite useful for the interdisciplinarian in particular. A specialized researcher will consult a constrained literature and absorb both the main and subsidiary arguments critical to their work. An interdisciplinarian might find that the most interesting insights from a particular discipline are not ideas that the discipline itself recognizes as particularly important. These subsidiary ideas will generally not be captured in the subject entries for the works in which they appear. But if works were exhaustively indexed in terms of a general classification of phenomena and relationships then even these ideas could be uncovered readily.

Despite the centrality of relationships to knowledge organization (and advancement in human understanding), existing KOSs fail to express these as usefully as they could (Green 2008, 154). As we shall see the norm is a singular subheading (s) rather than a subject heading that captures a relationship. It cannot be stressed too much that knowledge organization practice in this respect is quite at odds with scholarly practice. The vast bulk of scholarly research—both disciplinary and interdisciplinary—in fact addresses how one or more phenomena influence one or more others. This is also often the case for non-scholarly works of non-fiction (dogs biting mail carriers, gardeners growing flowers). And thus the easiest way of capturing the focus of a work would be in terms of the relationship(s) among phenomena being investigated. Yet the tradition in knowledge organization is to identify a work in terms only of one or more phenomena that are addressed.

As for works of fiction both general users and especially scholars would often like to search by causal relationship there as well (failed romance leads to suicide; mistaken identity generates friendship), but—beyond classification by genre such as western or romance—works of fiction are rarely if ever classified in terms of what happens within them (Šauperl 2013; Szostak 2014a; Beghtol 1994). Notably, Beghtol (1994, 113–5) found that there was 'no limitation' to what either literary scholars or literary authors might write about. Moreover, interdisciplinary scholars might be curious as to how (and if) any causal relationship they investigated was treated by authors of fiction. It thus seems that works of fiction also are best classified in terms of any possible relationship within a general classification.[5]

Web of Relations

If the researcher is able to identify all relevant works addressing the influence of A on B, they may thus be alerted to different ideas from different disciplines that when integrated provide a much better (more nuanced but also more comprehensive) understanding. This will be especially the case if they can readily distinguish different works in terms of the key arguments proposed (see below). Researchers will often be led to wonder about other possible influences on B: these again would be easily searchable and the results might also lend themselves to synthesis. Or, the researcher might become intrigued by the possibility of some causal chain, and find upon investigating studies of influences on A that much of the observed difference in the behavior of B can in fact be traced to factors that influence A. Or the researcher could be curious about feedback effects and find unrecognized parallels between the way B influences A and A influences B.

Olson (2007) discussed how users would often wish to follow such a web-of-relations. They might start out with an interest in A and B, but then become curious about influences on A or effects of B or just other phenomena associated with either of these. Importantly, Olson argued that a KOS which pursued a web-of-relations approach would better reflect feminist epistemology. For our purposes, we can well imagine that interdisciplinary scholars will often wish to pursue their curiosity from a phenomenon or relationship discussed in one discipline to a related phenomenon or relationship in another.

Börner (2006) suggests indeed that in the near future scholars might just add 'nuggets' or 'nodes' to the web of knowledge. That is, the present practice of writing stand-alone papers will be replaced by a practice of adding insights to a pre-existing structure. A scholar might, for example, provide evidence of a novel way in which a particular phenomenon affects another. Börner reviews various efforts over the last century to develop links between related bits of information (such as citation indices). New technology creates an opportunity to finally achieve this goal. But search engines are like inserting a needle in a haystack, and usually do not place search results in context: they 'fail to equip scholars with a birds-eye view of the global structure and dynamics of scholarly knowledge and expertise' (Börner 2006, 186). In a somewhat similar vein, Smiraglia and van den Heuvel (2013) seek to identify the most basic units of knowledge. They follow in the century-old steps

---

[5] Beghtol (1994, 143) notes that a synthetic approach is very useful in describing unreal things or processes such as (trees) (talking). She also (126) reports on research that suggests readers summarize fictional works in similar ways. She surveys many works that argue that it is both feasible and desirable to classify the relationships in fiction, though the precise classifications suggested are each problematic.

of Otlet, who also hoped to break works into their constituent parts and then re-combine these. They argue that works are comprised of ideas, and ideas are comprised of concepts which exist in relationship to each other and are represented by signs. This book also argues that works should be classified in terms of their ideas, and that these comprise relationships between things.

Such an approach has benefits beyond facilitating interdisciplinarity. Even within scholarly communities it can be difficult to keep up with all relevant literature. The inevitable result is that some books and papers are read by few if any scholars. This is especially likely if the author is not a leader in the field, and/or if the work does not have an obvious connection to the research interests of others. The danger, of course, is that other scholars may simply ignore the most novel published ideas. A better cataloguing system which recognized the ideas outlined in each work could render the scholarly enterprise much less wasteful of new ideas.

Moreover, scholars are often observed to 'talk past' each other by misunderstanding what each other is saying. Repko (2012) recommends mapping complex causal interactions in large part to clarify which particular causal arguments different authors are making. Classifying works in terms of the key causal relationships they contain will both facilitate interdisciplinary synthesis and reduce the likelihood that scholars will think they disagree when in fact they are addressing different relationships.

Types of Relationship

To this point we have stressed the importance of simply classifying works in terms of relationships. Further advantages would flow from taking another step and specifying types of relationship that might hold between A and B. Information scientists have indeed long speculated regarding the advantages of classifying the relationships that exist among things. Several complex schemes for doing so have been proposed (see Perrault 1994 for a summary), but none of these have been utilized in any major classificatory scheme (we are excluding for the moment consideration of thesauri which do adopt a limited set of relationships; see Chap. 3). Classificationists—those who develop classifications—have apparently decided that the proposed schemes do not deliver enough classificatory benefit to justify the cost of mastery by classificationist, classifier (those who place items within a classification), and user.

The reason might simply be that none of these preceding efforts started from an assessment of needs. As noted above, most scholarly works—and many if not most general works of both non-fiction and fiction—address how one or more things affect one or more other things. Thus, by far the most important relationships that must be investigated by the classificationist are those that involve some sort of causation or influence. Any proposed scheme for classifying relationships that does not devote the bulk of its attention to causal relations will of necessity fail to maximize the value versus cost ratio of employing the classification. Recall that the word 'causal' is used in the broadest sense to refer to any instance where (it is alleged that) one thing exerts some influence on another; the word 'causal' in no way implies that this influence need be large and certainly not that it is the only influence on the thing being affected, nor that there is any simple deterministic process at work.

Even scholars who disdain words such as 'cause' or even 'influence' often speak of how one thing affects another (for example, how a work of art moves an audience). And this implies that the classificationist needs not just to signal the directions of influence posited in a particular work—though this on its own would be an important step—but to capture all of these different types of cause/influence. In Chap. 5 we will address the feasibility of distinguishing a wide variety of relationships. These include direct causation, creation, cooperation, conflict, constraint, control, partial influence, mediation, selection, damage, and destruction (see Perrault 1994), and many others (see Szostak 2012). We can recognize for now that searches by 'type of influence' would be particularly important in uncovering analogous arguments made across distinct literatures (a form of 'undiscovered public knowledge').

Philosophers, it might be noted, debate the grounds on which we make causal statements. When we see a child kick a ball, we infer from the movement of the child's leg and the subsequent movement of the ball that the child caused the ball to move. But arguably we have no solid basis for making this inference, but rather have chosen to organize our perceptions around the idea of causation (Hume 2000). The information scientist need not enter this debate. Traditionally we have classified works with regard to what they are 'about' without feeling any need to pass judgment on the veracity of subject matter: we can classify works on astrology without feeling that we thereby endorse astrology. Likewise we can classify the idea 'child kicks ball' without endorsing any particular philosophical attitude toward causation.[6]

The importance of causal relationships, broadly defined, has often been stressed in the knowledge organization literature.[7] The excellent survey by Bean et al. (2002) speaks of three broad types of relationship: equivalence, hierarchical, and associative. They note that there is no agreement on types of associative relationship, but laudably focus their attention on cause-effect relationships. Zeng et al. (2011) provide what they believe is an exhaustive list of types of associative relationship that should be—but often are not—captured in subject authority files. One of their ten types is hierarchical (whole/parts), and another two can generally be captured by the non-causal relator 'of' (object/field of study and concept/properties). The rest are each a type of or component of a causal relationship:

---

[6] We need to embrace—and perhaps distinguish—different types of causation/influence identified by philosophers: individual instances (child kicks ball), causal laws (the laws of thermodynamics), and causal possibilities (aspirin can reduce headaches).

[7] Most documentary reports, although usually dealing with phenomena, do so from the viewpoint of a particular activity, so both aspects are needed in order to state its "subject" (Vickery 2008).

cause/effect proper, the action/process that an agent undertakes (speedometer measures), the result of that action (cloth woven), the agent that is affected (student taught), counter-agent (pesticides control pests), raw material (wine is made from grapes), and properties of actions (communicates well). Although there is thus recognition of the need for a classification of causal relationships, the only recent effort to develop such a classification seems to be Szostak (2012).

While the focus here is on causal linkages, the strategies for classification advocated here could be applied as well to other sorts of relationships among phenomena such as comparisons or analogies. Both interdisciplinary and specialized scholars often draw comparisons and analogies; indeed interdisciplinarity in the humanities is particularly associated with analogy or metaphor. A user who wishes to search for works on the basis of analogies and/or metaphors will not want to search for works on causal relationships, and vice versa. We thus should carefully distinguish different types of associative relationship.

Summing Up

We will return to issues of feasibility in Chap. 5. It is useful to close by reiterating what interdisciplinary scholars (but also many other types of user) need in terms of relationships. Ideally, the interdisciplinary scholar interested in the influence of A on B (or less commonly some other type of relationship between A and B) would like to be able to search in the handful of ways outlined in Table 2.3.

Existing classification systems are imperfect in all of these respects (Cousson 2009). Even in faceted[8] classifications (with the notable exceptions of the Integrative Levels Classification [ILC] and Basic Concepts Classification [BCC]), the same phenomenon is placed in different (discipline-based) main classes, is often labelled by different terms when it occurs in different disciplinary main classes, and is not infrequently represented by different notational symbols when occurring in different disciplinary main classes (Gnoli 2007). Works describing how A influences B are often classified under one or the other, or under both with no indication of the direction of influence. If compound notation is provided, this may also differ by class, with causal facets having different notations in different disciplines, hence not being retrievable by a cross-disciplinary search for causal relationships: as above a work on culture and poverty will be treated differently by discipline. Moreover, existing faceted classifications all treat causal links within a class (agent facets) quite differently from causal links across classes (influence phase relationships): this practice makes it difficult to search for a particular type of

---

[8] Faceted classifications take a synthetic approach, and seek to identify the key attributes of a work. They are contrasted with the more common enumerative approach which seek to enumerate a large set of often complex subject headings. This distinction is further explored at the start of Chap. 3. See Integrative Levels Classification (2004) and Szostak (2013) respectively. See also Chap. 4 below.

Table 2.3 Interdisciplinary search of relationships (A to B)

Users should be able to search by A, where all works about A are identified by a unique search term A*.
Users should be able to search by B, where all works about B are identified by the search term B*. Since works can only be placed physically in one place, the usual prescription is that works on B influenced by A be placed with other works on B. Thus an added desideratum for printed holdings would be that all works about 'determinants of B' would be physically collocated. [Users interested in A in our example will have to move about the shelves to find the work on A affecting B.]
Users should be able to search for the relationship from A to B. This usually has to be extracted at present by a Boolean search for A *and* B (which will not distinguish desired works from those that address A and B in some other fashion): this approach is clumsy and often not possible because works are not classified under all key subjects. If Boolean 'AND'ing is not employed, the search will locate huge numbers of works that address A in some fashion or B in some fashion but do not relate A to B. Note that in a library of printed documents all works on how A affects B should ideally be filed in close proximity (though perhaps not next to each other; see the following bullet point).
There will often be different ways that A might affect B. The researcher may be able to learn much about the focus of works in this respect if these are classified in terms of the theories (and to a lesser extent methods; see below) applied in a particular work. Nevertheless, it would be useful if different types of causation/influence could be distinguished. Works about B might then be subdivided with respect to different types of causal influence on B.

influence which might occur both within and across classes. Notably, the Bliss Classification (BC2) provides general rules for how links can be drawn across classes, but also provides specific instructions at many points in its schedules regarding how particular links can be made; since these deviate from the general rules, similar influence phase relationships will be treated differently depending on whether general or specific rules are to be followed. Furthermore, its non-expressive notation cannot be exploited for automatic searches. [We are told that the editors of the Bliss Classification are working on these challenges, and find them easier to address in a digital age than when Bliss was first developed.] This distinction is abolished in the *freely faceted classification* invoked by Austin (1976; see also Gnoli and Hong 2006), although no such general scheme was actually produced before the recent ILC project (ILC 2004). Last but not least, existing classifications all focus the bulk of their attention on concepts expressed in terms of nouns and noun phrases containing adjectives; there is much less development of (nominalised) verbal forms, such as "producing" or "damaging," (though some verbs such as 'communicate' are treated in the noun form: 'communication') but it is verbs that describe different types of influence.

A Typical Example

Typical examples of the challenges of classifying complex subjects come from experience with classifying the BioAcoustic Reference Database (Gnoli et al. 2008). One representative paper in this database (Reijnen and Foppen 1994) is entitled 'The Effects of Car Traffic on Breeding Bird Populations in Woodland, 1: Evidence of Reduced Habitat Quality for Willow Warblers (*Phylloscopus trochilus*) Breeding close to a Highway.' This paper reports on a study investigating possible causal links between a technological installation (a highway on which traffic produces noise) and an organic phenomenon (the size and health of a bird population). It is thus representative of a type of interdisciplinarity very common in contemporary research. Taken separately, such phenomena could be thought as the subjects of completely different disciplines, engineering and biology respectively. However, the main contribution of the paper is not providing standard information *about* this bird species, nor *about* highways. Rather it is the assessment of some influence of one of them on the other one. This is emphasized in its title by the words "Effects" and "Evidence". Note that the latter term expresses the fact that not only are the effects of the highway noise upon the bird species discussed, but new data are presented to support the hypothesis that they actually occur. In linguistic terms, what is relevant is thus not just the 'theme' of the paper—that is, what it is about—but its 'rheme'—the new information that it provides on the theme (Hutchins 1977).

Classifying by Theory Applied

Interdisciplinary research in practice tends to be problem-oriented. That is, an interdisciplinary project might tackle a complex societal issue such as inner-city poverty, seeking to analyze all relevant causal links (in isolation and in interaction) and drawing on all relevant theories and methods in doing so. Of course, no one research project can aim for exhaustive coverage in all of these respects, and thus even interdisciplinary analyses can be incomplete.[9] Skeptical concerns regarding the possibility of enhancing scholarly understanding may thus not be entirely alleviated by familiarity with interdisciplinary practice (Szostak 2014b). Yet the strategy of integration can potentially be applied across all research, integrating all available insights and identifying areas where additional research is necessary. It can thus yield a coherent understanding of how the world in its entirety operates: this will most often not be a simple understanding encapsulated in one theory but a complex understanding where a diverse body of theories casts light on different (and likely overlapping) parts of the puzzle.

Interdisciplinary scholarship thus urges integration across different theories, as well as across different methods and disciplinary perspectives. In this way, the

---

[9] Szostak (2002) developed a 12-step process for interdisciplinary analysis. It was argued that even though these steps could not all be followed exhaustively in any project, it was very important for researchers to reflect on what had been omitted. Szostak (2009) is organized around these 12 steps. Newell (2007) outlines a slightly different but complementary approach. Repko (2012) synthesizes these and other approaches, and shows how these can be applied.

partial insights of diverse communities of scholars (and insights from beyond the academy) can be combined into a more accurate and holistic analysis of any complex issue or theme. That is, the answer is not generally to be sought in one overarching theory (or ideology or method) but rather through recognizing the strengths—and weaknesses—of a variety of theories, and then integrating the best of these.

Interdisciplinary scholars are thus guided to ask what range of theories has been applied to the study of a particular phenomenon or (more likely) a particular type of relationship among certain (classes of) phenomena. They may in a particular research project need to focus on only a subset of these. Or they may wish to embrace all relevant theories. Alternatively, they may wish to focus on just one theory. In any of these cases it will be invaluable to be able to identify works in terms of the theory or theories that are applied. If a particular theory has not been applied to the particular phenomenon or relationship of interest, the interdisciplinarian may wish to search for the theory's application to other questions that are similar in certain respects: that address similar phenomena or similar types of relationship.

While interdisciplinarians are usually problem-oriented, they could also be interested in testing theories. This will be especially the case for those interdisciplinarians who still hope that some general theory will explain (or at least provide insight into) a large set of causal relationships. Such an interdisciplinarian will then wonder to what set of relationships a particular theory has been applied, and how successful the various applications of this theory have been in accounting for these relationships. Note in this regard that one of the key scholarly tasks is to identify the range of applicability of a particular theory: to which phenomena and relationships does a theory seem to apply? This is a task that natural scientists have often pursued more diligently than human scientists, but it is a task that all scholarship should embrace. In the absence of such an effort it is all too easy to assume that a theory that seems powerful in one application is universally powerful or alternatively to extrapolate from one example where a theory had little explanatory power to conclude that it is useless.

Present Practice in General Classifications

Works are *not* usually classified at present in terms of the theories or methods employed in a piece of research. Theories and methods are classified only when a work is about theory or method, not when these are applied. Weinberg (1988) famously noted that researchers in general are poorly served by classifications (indeed indexing languages of any type) of documents solely in terms of what these are 'about': novices search for books 'about' a particular topic, but scholars seek works that express certain 'ideas.' They seek works that apply particular scholarly perspectives (Weinberg stressed theories but addressed methods) to particular subjects:

'Whereas the student or layman is looking for literature on or about a topic, the scholar/ researcher's information need is, in most cases, substantially different. This group of users deals in ideas and theories, and wants to know whether specific ideas have previously been expressed in the literature. For example, a historian may have a new explanation for the cause of the Civil War, and going to this heading in a subject catalog or periodical index is not likely to answer precisely the question "Has anyone ever expressed this theory in print before?"' (Weinberg 1988, 3).

Palmer (1996) also urges the classification of documents in terms of theory and method applied. It is notable that while Palmer specifically addressed the needs of interdisciplinarians, Weinberg's concern was for all scholars. Knapp (2012) appreciates likewise that 'Scholars of all kinds of fields, interdisciplinary or not, could benefit from a system that classified knowledge in terms of methods and theories.'

Even the classification of works about theories can be problematic for the interdisciplinarian. Different disciplines intend quite different causal processes by the same nomenclature: for example, Hjørland and Nissen Pedersen (2005) noted that the term 'activity theory' can be used in three distinct senses. Even more troubling are cases where quite similar theories or techniques go by quite different names in different disciplines. In such cases, researchers cannot readily identify all relevant works about a particular theory or technique. The disciplinary specialist may only need to engage with one version of a theory operating under one name, or may be acquainted with a handful of related theories and the names by which they are known. The interdisciplinarian will often be confused by different theories operating under the same name and ignorant of applications of a single (type of) theory applied under different names in different contexts. As with phenomena, the interdisciplinarian thus needs some sort of general classification of theories that clearly identifies all instances of the same type of theory. We will explore in Chap. 5 the feasibility of developing and applying such a classification of theory types.

Summing Up

In sum, interdisciplinarians in particular but scholars more generally are interested in asking the following questions:

- What theory types and methods have been applied to the study of a particular set of phenomena in the past?
- To what set of phenomena has a particular theory type or method been applied?
- What problems have been encountered in these endeavors? (This question cannot be entertained until the more basic questions are answered.)

An Example That Adds a Wrinkle

How should disagreements between mainstream and alternative medicines be handled? A domain-specific approach would classify these two literatures separately (Hjørland and Nissen Pedersen 2005, 592). The interdisciplinary impulse is to facilitate awareness across these two fields. Though Hjørland and Nissen Pedersen are open to the idea of classification by theory and method applied, and they recognize the advantage of juxtaposing different perspectives, their basic approach ensures that the literatures of these different communities of scholars are classified separately. Only if documents are classified with respect to a general classification of theories and methods can a researcher easily locate works within one or the other tradition. Likewise, given the different terminologies used within the two fields, searches by causal link will turn up both perspectives on the link in question only if documents are classified in terms of a common set of phenomena (and of course if both literatures are classified together). Given the differences in terminology between the domains of mainstream and alternative medicine, separate classifications will ensure that practitioners of one type of medicine will have difficulty accessing relevant information from the other, assuming that they are motivated enough to look at the alternative classification in the first place. A unified classification puts alternative perspectives at their fingertips, but distinguishes these so that the researcher can also choose to ignore them. In this example, the classification of works in terms of theory and method applied would allow users to easily distinguish mainstream approaches to a particular disease from alternative approaches. It is thus a useful complement to the approach of classifying works in terms of a common list of phenomena.

Classifying by Method Applied

The arguments made in the preceding sections regarding theory can be applied with equal force to the case of methods. Interdisciplinary scholars will want to know which methods have been applied to the study of which causal relationships. While each discipline tends to value only one or two methods, the interdisciplinarian sees complementary strengths and weaknesses in each of the dozen methods employed by scholars (Szostak 2004 classified the key strengths and weaknesses of the dozen methods employed by scholars). One of the key challenges of interdisciplinary research teams is coming to appreciate the methods employed by other team members (Palmer 2010, 182). Given that no method is perfect, interdisciplinarians advocate the 'triangulation' of results achieved by employing different methods. Triangulation is the technique used by land surveyors of identifying a precise location by taking readings from different locations and seeing where these intersect. With respect to methods it involves evaluating and balancing the results obtained from different methods. Interdisciplinary scholars will thus wish to know what methods have been applied to a particular problem. In their efforts to evaluate the strengths and weaknesses of each method, they will also wish to know to what problems (and how successfully) each method has been applied.

The use of multiple methods is especially important when different theory types are compared. Scholarly understanding advances by comparing theoretical explanations, and seeing which is most important along a particular link (but not necessarily dismissing other theories as completely unimportant). If only one method is used in such a test, the results will generally be biased toward whichever theory that method is particularly well suited to investigating. This result is particularly noteworthy, for disciplines tend to choose a mutually supportive set of theory and method (and phenomena), and can be blissfully unaware of or hostile to contradictory evidence produced using other methods. Such close-mindedness is not conducive to enhancing our understanding of the complex world we inhabit.

The literature on interdisciplinarity overlaps with but is distinct from the literature on mixed-methods research (Szostak 2015). Mixed-methods research can be practiced even within a discipline, as when sociologists blend quantitative and qualitative analysis. The literature on mixed methods research celebrates the advantages of using multiple methods within the same research project. This is sometimes done as above to facilitate the comparison of results across methods. Alternatively, the results of one method may be utilized as inputs into the application of another (as when survey results are subjected to statistical analysis). In either case the mixed methods researcher will be curious about previous applications of the methods engaged. The advantages of classifying works in terms of method applied thus are not limited to interdisciplinary research.

A choice of method has implications for the types of data one will engage. And thus searches across different theory types and methods would be hugely important in identifying commonalities or differences across disciplines in the evidence for similar hypotheses. Nevertheless it may be useful at times to identify the type of data employed in a work. Note that data is here used in its widest sense so that interview transcripts and indeed any written, oral, or visual text could be considered data.

Hjørland (2012) speaks approvingly of 'evidence-based practice' and wonders what sort of judgment the classificationist and classifier might employ in order to guide users to the most reliable resources. While the phrase 'evidence-based practice' is itself fairly innocuous (though some postmodernists might disdain any recourse to evidence), and could/should refer to evidence of any sort gathered by any method, in practice those who employ the phrase (especially in the medical field) tend to value only the evidence acquired through use of the experimental method. Yet both those who favor a broad definition of evidence and those who favor a narrow definition can benefit from a classification of works in terms of method employed. Those who value only experiments can seek only works that have employed experiments (and indeed particular techniques in experimental design that might be particularly valued). The interdisciplinary researcher should appreciate that no method is perfect and thus potentially value works that employ multiple methods. They will thus benefit from a classification that signals any method and technique employed. Of course, all users can benefit from some indication of how well a particular method was employed in a particular work. Such judgments are likely beyond the scope of classification itself, but digital libraries might try to link individual works to critiques or commentaries of these. And of course if researchers have ready access to treatments of the method itself (and especially common weaknesses in its application) they will be in a better position to themselves judge if it has been applied properly.

Clarifying Concepts

As noted earlier, one of the main sources of difficulty in interdisciplinary searches is that the terms by which concepts are designated have different meanings across disciplines. The same concept thus may have different names, and—more confusingly—different concepts may be designated by the same name. But this problem of terminology affects the interdisciplinarian far beyond issues of search. Interdisciplinarians struggle to understand the works that they uncover. 'Studies across interdisciplinary fields have indicated that most interdisciplinary researchers need to be familiar with the terminology of other disciplines in order to understand the literature they consult and to carry out their research projects;' this need for 'translation' comprises one of the most difficult and laborious components of the interdisciplinary research process (Palmer 2010, 183).[10] Interdisciplinary teams struggle to understand each other. Interdisciplinarians struggle to communicate their research results to diverse audiences.

An example may be useful here. When economists speak of 'investment,' they mean only expenditures on buildings or machines that are used to produce goods or services. An accountant uses 'investment' in a manner more similar to common parlance to refer to any expenditure intended to earn a financial return through time. Buying a bond is investment to the latter but not the former. Such instances of differing definition are common. Yet disciplinarians will not feel any need to define words that they use all the time.

Scholars of interdisciplinarity have thus long worried about how to cope with ambiguity. O'Rourke et al. (2014) is devoted to transcending communication challenges in interdisciplinary research. In the editorial introduction the editors note that 'Researchers trained in different disciplines often use different vernaculars and belong to different disciplinary cultures, creating the need for translation on multiple levels ... Linguistic differences can lead collaborators to use the same term for different concepts, such as *dynamic* or *triangulation*, impairing communication by creating both false disagreement and false agreement' (2014, 2). Scholars have observed that 'pidgins' or 'creoles' are often created along disciplinary boundaries so that scholars from those disciplines can interact (Galison 1997; Klein 1996; Baird and Cohen 1999). Notably scholars from third disciplines would still struggle.

The implication for information science deserves to be stressed: *Any success achieved by knowledge organization systems (KOSs) in clarifying the meaning of*

---

[10] Palmer notes that while vocabulary is central to the challenge of translation so also are 'research conventions and culture.' These will be addressed below under 'disciplinary perspective.'

terminology will not only aid user search but will significantly alleviate the communication problems that plague interdisciplinary research. Lambe (2011) thus maintains that the first duty of classification is to clarify concepts in order to facilitate conversation. Scholars of knowledge organization should not take ambiguity for granted but should appreciate that we have some significant ability to reduce it through our own efforts.

How can this be done? Szostak (2014c) discusses how breaking complex concepts—terms for which there are not shared understandings across groups or individuals—into basic concepts can facilitate interdisciplinary communication. This is a strategy we will explore later in this book. It is worth noting that this strategy will prove useful both in the development of a comprehensive classification as well as in directly aiding interdisciplinary communication.

The very act of classification itself can also support clarity in terminology. Placing a concept within a logical hierarchical classification establishes clearly what sort of thing it is and what sort of thing it is not, and often the sorts of subsidiary elements of which it may be comprised. Wittgenstein (1953) famously argued that the best way to define a concept was to provide examples of it (game: chess, soccer, poker). He did not appreciate that a classification that provided an exhaustive set of examples would provide a very precise definition. This is, admittedly, an extensional definition by enumeration, rather than an intensional definition by essential features as had long been sought by philosophers. But as we will observe more than once in this book the practical field of knowledge organization should focus on the degree to which it can in practice reduce ambiguity rather than whether its strategies address philosophical concerns. We will find in later chapters that the sort of classification urged in this book is better able than the general classifications most used in the world to insist on logical subdivision within its classificatory hierarchies. We can note here that if hierarchy is abused by including items that are not logical subclasses then hierarchy is no longer able to serve to clarify the meaning of terminology.

In sum, the existing level of ambiguity in cross-disciplinary communication is not inevitable, but reflects the lack of a general classification that employs both a common vocabulary of basic concepts and a logical hierarchical structure throughout. This is not to say that classification is the exclusive source of or solution to ambiguity, but that careful logical classification in terms of basic concepts is perhaps the most powerful tool for reducing ambiguity.

Note here that scholarly concepts almost all refer to the phenomena studied or relations among them, the theories used to examine these, or the methods employed in their study, since these are the key elements of scholarly discourse (Wallace and Wolf 2006, 4–5; Repko 2012; Szostak 2007). It thus stands to reason that the comprehensive classifications of phenomena and relationships, theories, and methods that were urged above must of necessity alleviate some of the terminological ambiguity that plagues interdisciplinarity.[11]

---

[11] This argument is consistent with Stone's (2014) contention that the key to successful interdisciplinary communication is an ontological emphasis on real objects in the world that we perceive in similar ways rather than the epistemological emphasis on ways of knowing favored by disciplines.

Questions of feasibility will be addressed later in the book. But it should be noted at the outset that information scientists have often shied away from the task of alleviating conceptual ambiguity. Hjørland and Nissen Pedersen (2005, 586) advocate *only* an entirely inductive approach to classification whereby concepts are identified in use within particular scholarly domains. Such an approach, as we shall see in Chaps. 3, 6, and 7, has much merit. But to urge information science away from attempting to reduce cross-disciplinary ambiguity is unfortunate. Other information scientists have been more positive. Palmer (2001, 131), for example, notes that interdisciplinarians want information scientists to translate jargon across disciplinary boundaries.

Disciplinary Perspective

Why is interdisciplinary conversation so difficult? One reason, conceptual ambiguity, was addressed above. But there is a second serious source of difficulty. Disciplinary researchers absorb a host of disciplinary assumptions in the course of their education: epistemological, ethical, ideological, theoretical, and methodological. They may often not be conscious of these buried assumptions. Yet they interpret what others say through the lens of these assumptions. Since scholars from other disciplines will not have grounded their utterances in the same set of assumptions, misunderstanding is common. Sometimes the misunderstanding is clear at the time. Commonly in such situations the respondent wonders how on earth the utterer could have said something so at odds with the respondent's view of how the real and/or scholarly worlds should or do work. More insidiously, the misunderstanding may not be obvious at first, and erstwhile collaborators carry on for some time under a mistaken impression of shared understanding. The solution advocated in O'Rourke et al. (2014) and elsewhere for this sort of misunderstanding is to have collaborators share and compare and discuss their assumption sets.

Moreover, in their efforts to integrate insights from different disciplines interdisciplinary researchers are urged to evaluate these insights in terms of the overarching disciplinary perspective of the discipline. This is only possible if the researcher can readily identify what constitutes a given disciplinary perspective. Repko (2012) provides brief descriptions of the perspectives of the major disciplines, but researchers will often want more detail on these and/or information on smaller fields, including emerging interdisciplines. They will thus want to be able to search for works on (elements of) the disciplinary perspective of various fields (as well as on the nature of disciplines in general). They will otherwise misunderstand much of what they hear and read.

There is little value in having ready access to works on disciplinary perspective if we do not identify the disciplinary home of the authors of works. As noted in

Chap. 1, interdisciplinarity exists in a symbiotic relationship with specialized research. It should thus not be surprising that the interdisciplinarian does not seek to erase all vestiges of disciplinarity from KOSs:

> 'Studying a thing in isolation and studying it in context are two halves of modern scholarship, and neither may be safely neglected. The structure of knowledge representation must continue to shift to reflect this balance' (Iyer 1995, 27).

Of course, diversity exists within any discipline, and interdisciplinary scholars stress the dangers of stereotyping scholars. Yet it is still useful to know a scholar's disciplinary home. Even very interdisciplinary scholars still tend to betray some of the assumptions inherent in their disciplinary training. By the same, token, however, it will also be useful to be able to signal when a work takes a genuinely interdisciplinary approach, either through the purposive efforts of a single scholar or due to collaboration.

It would indeed be useful to move beyond simply recognizing the disciplinary (or interdisciplinary) home of authors and attempt to identify also other elements of the guiding perspective of the authors of a work. We have already addressed two key elements of disciplinary perspective above: theories applied and methods applied. Many geographers feel that their discipline should be identified by map-making, and many economists would associate their discipline with rational choice theorizing. Whatever the value of these views, the point here is that identifying a work in terms of theory applied or method applied may carry more valuable insight about that work than whether it is classified as (or shelved with) economics or geography or some other discipline. And we could thus imagine further aiding both interdisciplinarians and disciplinarians in the twin tasks of identifying and evaluating literature by classifying works in terms of still other elements of disciplinary perspective such as, for example, epistemological or ideological or ethical outlook. The possibility of addressing authorial perspective in these additional sorts of ways will be addressed in Chap. 5.

What About Disciplinarians?

Before moving on, it is worth noting that the vast bulk of disciplinary or specialized research also involves the investigation of causal links: economists worry about how changes in the money supply affect business cycles, chemists study how one chemical reacts with another to create yet another, and so on. Dahlberg (1994) thus stressed the importance of subjects and predicates in all disciplines. Causal links within disciplines are easier to search for within existing classification systems than causal links across disciplines simply because each phenomenon is generally given only one place within the disciplinary main class. Yet this solves only part of the problem. Causal links are still not generally indicated as such: the researcher may thus still have to troll through a vast literature on A and B to find works on how A influences B. Even when some attempt is made to index a work in terms of related concepts it is not always obvious what the work addresses: does a document indexed under 'teachers,' 'students' and 'behavior' deal with the influence of teachers' behavior on students, or the reverse? (Austin 1976). And different types of influence are only rarely distinguished, so again the user may retrieve many works that are not quite what they are looking for. These problems *may* be manageable if the researcher is interested in a small set of phenomena, and/or there are a limited number of types of influence among these that have been studied. Yet the fact remains that even disciplinary scholars will benefit from more careful treatment of causal relationships.

Moreover, users of any bibliographic classification do not just have 'information needs' but often more general 'knowledge (or understanding) needs.' That is, they are usually not searching for one isolated piece of information, but rather are seeking to expand (or test) their understanding. Drawing connections among different bits of information is crucial to their success. KOSs thus need to facilitate the drawing of connections (Thellefsen et al. 2013).

Specialized disciplinary researchers also sometimes examine the internal nature or functioning of one phenomenon. Such research is easier to cope with within any classificatory approach: it will be classed (and shelved) under the phenomenon investigated. Even here, a synthetic approach which can identify which particular characteristics of a phenomenon are being investigated will be helpful.

Specialized disciplinary researchers will also benefit if works are coded in terms of theories and methods applied. Not only will such modes of classifying works help scholars to identify the works in which they are most interested but it will also expose them to, and so stimulate them to look at, alternative approaches to understanding the phenomena or relationships that they are studying.

How will disciplinarians fare if disciplinary structures are replaced by a phenomenon-based general classification? Disciplinarians will benefit from being readily acquainted with research on particular linkages performed in other disciplines. They may, though, be much more interested in works generated within their own discipline. It is, of course, quite possible to continue to code works by the disciplinary home of the author. And the desirability of doing so was urged above. Researchers can then search only within their discipline for works on a particular causal link. Palmer (1996) notes that digitization (and hypertext in particular) allows us potentially to design access to resources suited to different users: a disciplinary researcher can thus be guided exclusively to disciplinary resources if they so choose.

This solution, though, may depend on scholars from different disciplines organizing their understandings in similar ways; if not, disciplinarians may find themselves lost in a general classification that cannot cater to their particular way of seeing/organizing the world. Wesolek (2012) worries in particular that a general classification might define classes more broadly than a domain analysis would. But this is hardly inevitable. And if it were the case for some classes, Wesolek's problem might be solved by identifying sub-classes of greater interest to certain disciplines (he worries, for example that sociologists may be more interested in studying loan sharks as a financial institution than are economists).

Advocates of domain-specific classifications argue that we can only cope with the ambiguous nature of language by classifying works domain by domain: only then can users share an understanding of what the terms used to classify documents mean. One advantage, then, of a discipline-based general classification is that the terminology of each domain can be catered to (but with the result necessarily being that it is more difficult to search across domains). It is an empirical question as to how great the ambiguity problem is for a general classification. If the problem is large, the ideal solution may involve domain-specific classifications, each of which is translated into a phenomenon-based general classification (see Szostak 2010). But recall that a general classification that employs the same vocabulary and hierarchical structure throughout can itself reduce ambiguity. The cost imposed on the disciplinarian cannot be properly evaluated until the comprehensive classification is in place.

While the disciplinarian faces both challenges and opportunities in adapting to the sort of classification advocated by the León Manifesto (2007), the opportunities could well outweigh the challenges. This is especially the case once it is appreciated that the scholarly need for information science is inversely related to the degree of specialization. As already noted in Chap. 1 a very specialized scholar does not much need knowledge organization. They quickly learn which journals and conferences are most likely to yield the information that they need for their studies. As they expand their gaze beyond their narrow area of specialization knowledge organization becomes ever more important. If it is accepted that every scholar should have some appreciation of how their area of specialization fits within the broader scholarly enterprise, then the benefits of a general phenomenon-based classification far outweigh, for *all* scholars, the costs of adapting to such a classification.

Key Points

First and foremost, we have seen that existing classification systems serve interdisciplinarity poorly. Second, interdisciplinarians need the resources offered by information science more than do disciplinary researchers. It follows that KOSs need to be developed to better serve interdisciplinarity.

In particular interdisciplinarians need to search by:

- The phenomena addressed in a work.
- The relationships among phenomena addressed in a work.
- The theory(s) applied in a work.
- The method(s) applied in a work.
- The disciplinary (or interdisciplinary) perspective of authors [Note that interdisciplinary researchers will also need easy access to general works on disciplines and interdisciplinarity.]

If information scientists could provide general classifications of these elements they would at the same time serve a further important function of clarifying concepts. This is important, for, at present interdisciplinarians struggle not just to find works but to understand these due to differences in terminology across fields.

References

Association for Interdisciplinary Studies (AIS) (2013) About Interdisciplinarity. http//www.oakland. edu/ais/

Austin DW (1976) The CRG research into a freely faceted scheme. In: Maltby A (ed) Classification in the 1970s, a second look. Bingley, London, pp 158–194

Baird D, Cohen MS (1999) Why trade? Perspect Sci 7(2):231–254

Bates MJ (1996) Learning about the information seeking of interdisciplinary scholars and students. Libr Trends 45(1):155–164

Bean CA, Green R, Myaeng SH (2002) Preface. In: Green R, Bean CA, Myaeng SH (eds) The semantics of relationships. Kluwer, Dordrecht, pp vii–xvi

Beghtol C (1994) The classification of fiction, the Development of a system based on theoretical principles. Scarecrow Press, Lanham, MD

Beghtol C (1995) 'Facets' as undiscovered public knowledge: S.R. Ranganathan in India and S. Guttman in Israel. J Doc 51(3):194–224

Bergmann M, Jahn T, Knobloch T, Krohn W, Pohl C, Schramm E (2012) Methods for transdisciplinary research: a primer for practice. Campus, Berlin

Börner K (2006) Semantic association networks: using semantic web technology to improve scholarly knowledge and expertise management. In: Geroimenko V, Chen C (eds) Visualizing the semantic web, 2nd edn. Springer, Berlin, pp 183–198

Boteram F, Hubrich J (2010) Specifying intersystem relations: requirements, strategies, and issues. Knowl Org 37(4):216–222

Bulick S (1982) Structure and subject interaction. Marcel Dekker, New York

Cousson P (2009) UDC as a non-disciplinary classification for a high school library. Proceedings of the UDC seminar 2009: classification at a crossroads. Extensions Corrections UDC 31:243–252, http://arizona.openrepository.com/arizona/handle/10150/199909

Dahlberg I (1994) Domain interaction: theory and practice. Adv Knowl Org 4:60–71

Davis CH, Shaw D (2011) Introduction to information science & technology. ASIST Monograph Series, Medford, NJ

Galison P (1997) Image & logic: a material culture of microphysics. The University of Chicago Press, Chicago

Gnoli C (2007) Progress in synthetic classification: towards unique definition of concepts. UDC seminar: the Hague. Extensions and Corrections to the UDC 29. http://arizona.openrepository. com/arizona/handle/10150/105614

Gnoli C (2010) Classification transcends library business. Knowl Org 37(3):223–229

Gnoli C, Hong M (2006) Freely faceted classification for Web-based information retrieval. New Rev Hypermedia Multimedia 12(1):63–81

Gnoli C, Merli G, Pavan G, Bernuzzi E, Priano M (2008) Freely faceted classification for a Web-based bibliographic archive: the BioAcoustic Reference Database. Repositories of knowledge in digital spaces: proceedings of the eleventh German ISKO Conference, Konstanz. Ergon, Würzburg

Green R (2008) Relationships in knowledge organization. Knowl Org 35(2/3):150–159

Hart G, Dolbear C (2013) Linked data: a geographic perspective. CRC, Boca Raton, FL

Hjørland B (2012) Is classification necessary after Google? J Doc 68(3):299–317

Hjørland B, Nissen Pedersen K (2005) A substantive theory of classification for information retrieval. J Doc 61(5):582–595

Hoetzlein R (2007) The organization of human knowledge: systems for interdisciplinary research. Masters thesis, Media Arts and Technology Program, University of California Santa Barbara

Hood WW, Wilson CS (2001) The scatter of documents over databases in different subject domains: how many databases are needed? J Am Soc Inform Sci Technol 52(14):1242–1254

Hume D (2000) An enquiry concerning human understanding. Clarendon Press, Oxford, UK, Edited by Tom L. Beauchamp

Hutchins WJ (1977) On the problem of 'Aboutness' in document analysis. J Inform 1:17–35

Integrative Levels Classification (ILC) (2004) ISKO Italia. www.iskoi.org/ilc/

Iyer H (1995) Classificatory structures: concepts, relations and representation. Indeks Verlag, Frankfurt/Main

Julien C-A, Tirilly P, Dinneen J, Guastavino C (2013) Reducing subject tree browsing complexity. J Am Soc Inform Sci Technol 64:2201–2223

Klein JT (1990) Interdisciplinarity: history, theory and practice. The Wayne State University Press, Detroit

Klein JT (1996) Crossing boundaries: knowledge, disciplinarities, and interdisciplinarities. University of Virginia Press, Charlottesville

Kleineberg M (2013) The blind men and the elephant: towards an organization of epistemic contexts. Knowl Org 40(5):340–362

Knapp JA (2012) Plugging the 'whole': librarians as interdisciplinary facilitators. Libr Rev 61 (3):199–214

Kutner LA (2000) Library instruction in an interdisciplinary environmental studies program: challenges, opportunities and reflections. Issues Sci Technol Librarianship 28. www.library. ucsb.edu/istl/00-fall/

Kyle B (1960) Classification: adopt, adapt, or create?: A discussion point. Aslib Proc 12 (9):317–320

Lambe P (2011) KOS as enablers to the conduct of science. Paper presented at the ISKO-UK conference. http://www.iskouk.org/conf2011/papers/lambe.pdf

Landry P (2004) Multilingual subject access: the linking approach of MACS. Catalog Classif Q 37 (3-4):177–191

Langridge DW (1992) Classification: its kinds, elements, systems and applications. Bowker-Saur, London

León Manifesto (2007) Knowl Org 34(1):6–8. Available [with commentary] at: www.iskoi.org/ilc/ leon.php

Mai J-E (2008) Actors, domains, and constraints in the design and construction of controlled vocabularies. Knowl Org 35(1):16–29

Newell WH (2007) Decision-making in interdisciplinary studies. In: Morcol G (ed) Handbook of decision-making. Marcel Dekker Publishers, New York, pp 245–264

Olson H (2007) How we construct subjects: a feminist analysis. Libr Trends 56(2):509–541

O'Rourke M, Crowley S, Eigenbrode SD, Wulfhorst JD (eds) (2014) Enhancing communication and collaboration in interdisciplinary research. Sage, Thousand Oaks

Palmer CL (1996) Information work at the boundaries of science: linking library services to research practices. Libr Trends 45(2):165–191

Palmer CL (2001) Work at the boundaries of science: information and the interdisciplinary research process. Kluwer, Dordrecht

Palmer CL (2010) Information research on interdisciplinarity. In: Frodeman R, Klein JT, Mitcham C (eds) The Oxford handbook of interdisciplinarity. Oxford University Press, Oxford, pp 174–188

Perrault JM (1994) Categories and relators: a new schema. Knowl Org 21(4):189–198

Reijnen R, Foppen R (1994) The effects of car traffic on breeding bird populations in Woodland, 1: evidence of reduced habitat quality for Willow Warblers (Phylloscopus trochilus) breeding close to a highway. J Appl Ecol 31:85–94

Repko AF (2012) Interdisciplinary research: process and theory, 2nd edn. Sage, Thousand Oaks

Repko AF, Szostak R, Buchberger MP (2014) Introduction to interdisciplinary studies. Sage, Thousand Oaks

Šauperl A (2013) Four views of a novel: characteristics of novels as described by publishers, librarians, literary theorists, and readers. Catalog Classif Q 51(6):624–654

Searing SE (1992) How libraries cope with interdisciplinarity: the case of women's studies. Issues Integr Stud 10:7–25

Searing SE (1996) Meeting the information needs of interdisciplinary scholars: issues for administrators of large university libraries. Libr Trends 45(2):315–342

Smiraglia RP, van den Heuvel C (2013) Classifications and concepts: towards an elementary theory of knowledge interaction. J Doc 69:360–383

Spärck Jones K (2005) Some thoughts on classification for retrieval. J Doc 61(5):571–581 [Originally published, 1970]

Stone DA (2014) Beyond common ground: a transdisciplinary approach to interdisciplinary communication and collaboration. In: O'Rourke M, Crowley S, Eigenbrode SD, Wulfhorst JD (eds) Enhancing communication and collaboration in interdisciplinary research. Sage, Thousand Oaks, pp 82–102

Svenonius E (1997) Definitional approaches in the design of classification and thesauri and their implications for retrieval and for automatic classification. In: Knowledge organization for information retrieval: proceedings of the sixth international study conference on classification research, London. FID, The Hague, pp 12–16

Szostak R (2002) How to do interdisciplinarity: integrating the debate. Issues Integr Stud 20:103–122

Szostak R (2004) Classifying science: phenomena, data, theory, method, practice. Springer, Dordrecht

Szostak R (2007) Modernism, postmodernism, and interdisciplinarity. Issues Integr Stud 26:32–83

Szostak R (2009) The causes of economic growth: interdisciplinary perspectives. Springer, Berlin

Szostak R (2010) Universal and domain-specific classifications from an interdisciplinary perspective. In: Gnoli C, Mazzocchi F (eds) Paradigms and conceptual systems in knowledge organization: proceedings of the 2010 conference of the international society for knowledge organization, Rome. Ergon Verlag, Würzburg, pp 71–77

Szostak R (2012) Classifying relationships. Knowl Org 39(3):165–178

Szostak R (2013) Basic concepts classification. https://sites.google.com/a/ualberta.ca/rick-szostak/research/basic-concepts-classification-web-version-2013

Szostak R (2014a) Classifying the humanities. Knowl Org 41(4):263–275

Szostak R (2014b) Skepticism and knowledge organization. In: Babik W (ed) Knowledge organization in the 21st century: between historical patterns and future prospects. Proceedings of the 13th ISKO conference, Krakow. Würzburg, Ergon

Szostak R (2014c) Communicating complex concepts. In: O'Rourke M, Crowley S, Eigenbrode SD, Wulfhorst JD (eds) Enhancing communication and collaboration in interdisciplinary research. Sage, Thousand Oaks, pp 34–55

Szostak R (2015) Interdisciplinary and transdisciplinary multi-method and mixed methods research. In: Hesse-Biber S, Johnson RB (eds) The Oxford handbook of mixed and multi-method research. Oxford University Press, Oxford, pp 128–143

Thellefsen M, Thellefsen T, Sørensen B (2013) A pragmatic semeiotic perspective on the concept of information need and its relevance for Knowledge Organization. Knowl Org 40(4):213–224

Vickery BC (2008) The structure of subject classifications for document retrieval. Butterworths, London

Wallace RA, Wolf A (2006) Contemporary sociological theory: expanding the classical tradition, 6th edn. Harper-Collins, New York

Weinberg BH (1988) Why indexing fails the researcher. Indexer 16(1):3–6, http://people.unt.edu/~skh0001/wein1.htm

Wesolek A (2012) Wittgensteinian support for domain analysis in classification. Libr Philos Pract 1 (1):1–10, http://digitalcommons.unl.edu/cgi/viewcontent.cgi?article=1933&context=libphilprac

Wittgenstein L (1953) Philosophical investigations. In: Anscombe GEM, Rhees R (eds) trans Anscombe GEM. Blackwell, Oxford

Zeng ML, Zumer M, Salaba A (2011) The functional requirements for subject authority records. International Federation of Library Associations and Institutes Report. DeGruyter, Berlin

Chapter 3
The Nature of Knowledge Organization Systems to Serve Interdisciplinarity

Chapter 2 closed with a list of the desired attributes of knowledge organization systems (KOSs) for interdisciplinarity. This chapter opens with a brief survey of KOSs, and then asks what sort of KOS could provide these desired attributes. In particular, it provides arguments for the theses that:

- A classification is called for that is general in coverage, and employs the same terminology and structure throughout. There is still considerable scope for domain analysis.
- Both induction and deduction should be employed in its development.
- This classification should allow any two concepts to be freely linked.
- The classification should capture as much as possible of the unique character of a work or the ideas that it contains.
- The classification should be governed by transparent rules in order to facilitate computer-based searching.

We close the chapter by reflecting on whether existing KOSs can be adapted to serve interdisciplinarity, or whether something radically different is called for.

Knowledge Organization Systems

There are various kinds of KOSs, and various approaches to subject search (Golub 2014). These include classification schemes, subject heading lists, thesauri, keywords, folksonomies, and ontologies. The most ubiquitous KOS is likely the classification scheme. North American library users will have generally encountered two of these, the Library of Congress Classification (LCC; used in large university libraries) and the Dewey Decimal Classification (DDC; used in most public libraries and smaller universities). Some public libraries and most bookstores use BISAC (Book Industry Standards and Classifications), a classification system of the association of booksellers. In Europe the Universal Decimal Classification

© Springer International Publishing Switzerland 2016
R. Szostak et al., *Interdisciplinary Knowledge Organization*,
DOI 10.1007/978-3-319-30148-8_3

(an offshoot of the DDC that has evolved in quite different directions) is common, though DDC and LCC are also widely used. Some other general classifications can be found: the Bliss Classification is employed in a few British libraries, and the Colon Classification is used in some Indian libraries. Only the DDC and LCC have a large bureaucracy that can both update the classification as new subjects emerge, and provide libraries with classifications of most works they might obtain. In addition to these 'general' classifications that attempt broad coverage, there are a host of specialized classifications that serve particular fields.

The general classifications above are sometimes termed 'universal' classifications. The word 'universal' might then be understood as merely a synonym for generality in coverage. For many in the field of information science, though, 'universal' implies that people come to see the world in the same way (Szostak 2014c). Since the idea of disciplinary perspective is a cornerstone of interdisciplinary analysis (see Chap. 1), we would hardly wish to leave the mistaken impression that we aspired to a unity of perspective. The word 'universal' is thus eschewed in this book in favor of 'general' or 'comprehensive.'

Most classification systems historically have been 'enumerative': they have organized hierarchically all of the subjects they seek to classify. An alternative approach is to allow some sort of synthetic constructions such that a work might be classified in terms of combinations of simple subjects. All major classifications have allowed some degree of synthesis. For example, it is common (though not universal) to have a schedule of geographical places (countries, regions, cities, and so on) that can be combined with a more general subject: *Tourism—France*. Ranganathan in the 1930s proposed 'facet analysis' (see Ranganathan 1967), whereby the subject of a book would be described in terms of combinations of key characteristics.[1] The Colon Classification takes a facet approach. The Bliss Classification, though originally enumerative, also pursues a faceted approach. More recently two of this book's authors have developed the Integrative Levels Classification and the Basic Concepts Classification (described in Chap. 4), that take different approaches to facet analysis and were each designed to serve the needs of interdisciplinary scholars. Though all faceted classifications make arrangements for synthetic combinations across domains—termed 'phase relationships' by Ranganathan—it is only the last two of these systems that are designed with an expectation that synthesis across disciplines will be the norm.

General users may associate classification systems with shelf placement. They are used, especially in North America, for this purpose. But the more general purpose of classifications is to index knowledge so that relevant items can be

---

[1] Causal relationships were only one type of connection for which Ranganathan recommended synthetic notation ('phase relationships'). Another occurred when the subject matter of one discipline was applied to another. Such connections are also captured by classifying works in terms of theory and method applied. Ranganathan also discussed possible ways in which concepts might be related definitionally; this concern is also addressed elsewhere. Rowley and Hartley (2008) and Marcella and Newton (1994, 60) are among many information scientists who have urged the use of synthetic notation.

retrieved by users. In a digital environment, organization and retrieval remain important but shelving ceases to matter. We will occasionally refer to questions of shelf placement in this book but will focus our attention on the more general organizational and retrieval goals of classification systems. In particular, our concern is whether a particular classification guides interdisciplinary scholars and students (but also their disciplinary counterparts) to relevant information. It can be noted here that different libraries can employ the same classification but make different shelving decisions.

Classification schemes are closely associated with subject heading lists. Only a fraction of the headings in the Library of Congress Subject Headings (LCSH) are associated with an LCC class. Still, users can search by any of these headings and locate works that were classified in terms of that subject. Note that subject heading lists involve a 'controlled vocabulary': if the subject heading is 'automobiles' one cannot search by 'cars.'

An alternative to subject searching is keyword searching. In the contemporary world people are familiar with keyword searching from exploring the internet. One does not generally employ a controlled vocabulary on the internet but searches by whatever term one wishes. One then risks missing documents that only employ the term 'automobile' if one searches by 'car' (though some search engines may suggest alternative searches). More generally, keyword searching is observed to limit the range of material discovered (Palmer 2010, 174). Users performing keyword searches in libraries may mistakenly assume that they are performing a full-text search as on the internet (that is, that the computer is searching for any uses of the search term in the text of the documents the library contains). In fact keyword searches in libraries can generally only search over terms in library records such as title and subject headings. Notably, one-third of the results from keyword searching in library databases are from subject headings assigned to works (Zeng et al. 2014).

Keyword search is popular, especially in the internet age: it is familiar and easy. But we have already seen one problem: that works using slightly different terminology will be missed. This is a problem of 'recall,' the proportion of relevant documents that are retrieved. There is also a problem of 'precision': the proportion of retrieved documents that are relevant. Keyword searches, especially full-text keyword searches, will retrieve large numbers of documents, many of which are of no value to a particular user. These problems of recall and precision may be limited if there are many documents that might satisfy a user's needs. Recall and precision can be enhanced through 'Boolean' searching: one can in most databases search for combinations of terms utilizing 'AND' or 'OR' command between search terms. But Boolean searching also has its limits: in particular it will not distinguish 'history of philosophy' from 'philosophy of history' or indeed any document that addresses both history and philosophy. Hoetzlein (2007), for example, describes searching for 'robots that draw' on the internet and retrieving many documents about drawings of robots and other combinations of robots and drawing. If there are few documents that will serve the user's needs, or if the user needs to find several documents that will each address part of their information need, the user may be much better served by subject searching. It will then be invaluable to develop classification systems and subject heading lists that are easy to use.

One challenge in utilizing classifications or subject heading lists is the controlled vocabulary. Thesauri have been developed to (further organize knowledge and) alleviate this challenge. The term 'Thesauri' has a very specific meaning within information science. Thesauri will, most obviously, identify synonyms: the user will be told to employ 'automobile' rather than 'car' in their subject search. But thesauri also identify hierarchical relationships: the user can be advised that they could search for a variety of types of car (narrower terms or NT), or alternatively that they could search more generally for 'vehicles' (broader terms or BT). Thesauri also generally refer to 'related terms' (RT) such as 'automobiles' and 'driving.' Thesauri can be thought of as mapping the relationships between terms. Thesauri often also include 'scope notes' that provide definitions of terms (classifications, notably the DDC, also include extensive scope notes). We will see in later discussions of thesauri that there are proposals to identify different types of association, as well as degrees of agreement in synonyms and different types of hierarchical relation.

Thesauri thus provide both an entry point to classifications and a means to the clarification of the meanings of terms employed in a classification. Yet thesauri at present are generally only constructed for particular fields of study: disciplines or clearly-defined interdisciplines such as gender studies. Yet some of these—such as the Art and Architecture Thesaurus produced by the Getty Museum or *Nuovo Soggettario* (in Italian)—are very broad in coverage, suggesting that a comprehensive thesaurus might be possible, at least in principle.

The use of controlled vocabulary may privilege certain individuals or groups. It is thus important to ensure that terms in general use are employed and that the terminology employed by all potential users is captured in thesauri. One more 'democratic' approach is to allow users to 'tag' documents with their own preferred vocabulary. Efforts to develop 'folksonomies' grounded in 'tagging' have naturally faced challenges in that individual tags are often idiosyncratic. It might nevertheless be possible to incorporate some of the connections observed in tagging into thesauri.

In our own pursuit of terminological clarity, we should discuss briefly our use of the terms 'concept' and 'term' in this book. We utilize 'concept' to refer to a particular idea. The looser word 'term' signifies language that attempts to signify a concept. Concepts themselves are not necessarily ambiguous but humans are limited in their ability to capture concepts in words, and thus terms are ambiguous. We will, though, follow common usage and speak of 'complex concepts'—terms for which there is a considerable degree of differences in understanding across groups—and 'basic concepts'—terms for which there is a much lesser degree of cross-group ambiguity.

There are still other types of KOS. Only one other will be of interest in this book. This is the ontology. Ontologies (as defined in information science or computer science) provide precise names and definitions of terms and carefully describe the sort of relationships that are allowed to exist between terms. Glushko (2013, 202) defines ontology as a network of relationships. That is, ontologies involve creating a logical structure for language expression. An ontology is thus more formal than a typical classification system. Information scientists have become increasingly interested in formal ontologies in recent years (Almeida 2013; DeRidder 2007;

Gnoli 2011b; Masolo et al. n.d.). Though the ontological project can be traced to at least Aristotle, the contemporary desire to allow computers to process meanings has been a key motivator of ontological research (and thus the high degree of precision sought). We will discuss in this and later chapters some of the challenges in ontology development. Since each concept must be carefully defined in terms of a particular logical structure, and relationships carefully stipulated, creating ontologies is a slow, time-consuming, and controversial practice (see Masolo et al. n.d.). It will be argued that the sort of classification urged in this book (supplemented by an appropriate thesaurus) might serve at least some of the purposes of ontology.

Comprehensive Classification and Domain Analysis

The most obvious implication of the analysis in Chap. 2 is that interdisciplinarity will be best served by a comprehensive classification of phenomena and the relationships obtaining among them. Only then can the interdisciplinarian readily search for relevant works on a particular subject across all fields of inquiry. Since theories, methods, and the other elements of perspective are also phenomena, a comprehensive classification of phenomena will also facilitate searches in terms of theory, method, and perspective. Last but not least, such a classification would serve to clarify the meaning of the terms employed, and would thus facilitate interdisciplinary conversation.

Many writers in the field of Knowledge Organization stress instead the pursuit of 'domain analysis': the careful classification of the concepts within some 'domain' (e.g. Hjørland 2002). A recent interchange of articles between Birger Hjørland and Rick Szostak in the *Journal of Documentation* (Hjørland 2008; Szostak 2008) thus articulated two contrasting views of classification:

1. A view which urges the development of a general phenomenon-based classification that would facilitate the access of especially interdisciplinary scholars to insights generated by all communities of scholars.
2. A view that terminology is ambiguous and thus that it is best to classify documents only within particular domains employing terms as scholars within the community in question are found to understand these.

Scholars of knowledge organization have long debated the relative merits of these two views. Yet these two positions might be seen as complements rather than mutually exclusive alternatives (see Kleineberg 2013).[2] Indeed interdisciplinary scholarship itself would urge us toward 'both/and' analysis rather than 'either/or' analysis: that is, to seek to integrate the best of contrasting views rather than

---

[2] Wesolek (2012) asserts incorrectly that Szostak opposes domain analysis. Szostak had opposed only an exclusive reliance on domain analysis. Wesolek does appreciate that Szostak sought to balance Hjørland's inductive approach with a deductive comprehensive analysis.

conclude that one is entirely misguided (see Repko 2012). Since these two views are both widely held within the Knowledge Organization (KO) literature, it is important that this possible complementarity be carefully elucidated so that the KO community can work together toward shared goals rather than be diverted into fruitless controversies.

Clarifying the Nature of Domain Analysis

It is first necessary to discuss the nature of domain analysis. Smiraglia (2012) notes that the term 'domain' is not well defined in the knowledge organization literature. It is often assumed to be equivalent to discipline. But in fact the definition of domain is internal to the field of knowledge organization: 'A domain is best understood as a unit of analysis for the construction of a KOS' (Smiraglia 2012, 114). Domains should share an epistemology (an understanding of how understanding is best pursued), have a coherent ontology (understanding of the nature of the world), and share a culture and understanding of concepts. Importantly Smiraglia stresses that 'domain' is actually a matter of degree, and thus of judgment: 'The closer the agreement the higher the degree of "domain" accordance' (Smiraglia 2012, 113). A certain group, or the body of documents they produce, can thus be considered to be a domain if there is 'enough' shared understanding for the purpose of classification. It then becomes tautologically true that the field of knowledge organization should limit itself to domain analysis: it would make no sense to seek a common classification if there were not 'enough' commonality in understanding. But the empirical question remains of exactly when enough 'agreement' exists for the purposes of KOS.

Interdisciplinary scholarship—or at least problem-oriented interdisciplinary scholarship of the type described in Repko (2012), Bergmann et al (2012), and AIS (2013)—might be considered to be a domain. As we saw in Chap. 1 there is arguably a shared epistemology, ontology, and culture. The community is striving for a shared understanding of its own terminology (see the Definitions section of AIS 2013 or the extensive glossary in Repko 2012). Of course, the efforts of this community to integrate understandings generated in disciplines must confront terminological ambiguity external to the discourse of interdisciplinarity itself. But 'redefinition' is then employed as a strategy to establish a shared understanding of what one or more terms mean. That is, the interdisciplinary scholar is urged, when faced with different meanings attached to the same term by different groups of scholars, to identify a common meaning for one or more terms that the relevant disciplines could potentially agree upon (see Repko 2012). Various authors in Repko et al. (2012) successfully employ the strategy of redefinition.

We will in Chap. 6 discuss how the domain analysis of academic communities can be performed in concert with the pursuit of a comprehensive classification of the type advocated in earlier chapters. In this we follow Dervos and Coleman (2006,

57), who suggested [at the biennial conference of the International Society for Knowledge Organization] that 'we first identify the terms and their competing definitions from the many branches of knowledge, and then work consensually towards acceptance of the fundamental ones such that they are sharable and applicable across interdisciplinary domains.' Dervos and Coleman felt that such a strategy was in accord not only with the interdisciplinary imperative but with the literature on domain analysis. It is noteworthy that their advice parallels that provided in Repko (2012).

As we have seen, 'domain' is often equated with 'discipline.' It is worth considering then the arguments of Dogan and Pahre (1990) and Dogan (1996) that the contemporary academy is characterized by the fragmentation of disciplines into distinct specialties, and their recombination or 'hybridization' with fields from other disciplines. In the light of this analysis it becomes particularly unclear where domain analysis is best performed: discipline, disciplinary field, hybrid field, or something else? The best answer is perhaps to appreciate that each possible choice exhibits a different kind of 'domain-ness.' We will in Chap. 6 explore in detail the domain analysis of the interdisciplinary field of gender studies: this will inform us regarding the strategies of domain analysis, the challenges facing one group of interdisciplinary scholars, and how domain analysis can facilitate interdisciplinarity.

In sum, then, the literature on domain analysis need not be taken to imply that there is any necessary barrier to the pursuit of a comprehensive classification that employs the same terminology and structure throughout. Rather domain analysis can facilitate the development of such a classification. It is thus disappointing that domain analysis is more often urged than practiced: excepting one special issue there have only been a handful of applications of domain analysis ever published in the journal Knowledge Organization (a couple of these by one of the authors of this book), and the bulk of domain analyses found elsewhere pursue citation analysis (in order to identify domains) rather than any sort of epistemological investigation (Smiraglia 2012).

Linking Domain Analysis to Comprehensive Classification

Every one of the needs outlined in the previous chapter will remain problematic in the absence of a general classification of phenomena. If the analysis of discipline-like domains were to be pursued exclusively within information science, then interdisciplinary researchers might be faced with a bewildering array of domain-specific classifications that they needed to engage in order to find relevant information in different disciplines. Information scientists might then struggle to provide conversion (mapping) tables or thesauri or some other device to facilitate users' movements from one domain-specific classification to another. This would seem to be an even more daunting exercise for information science than the development of a single general classification which employed the same terminology and structure throughout. Mapping between classifications is a very time-consuming enterprise, especially if different hierarchical structures are employed in different classifications. Some strategies exist for mapping by machine (e.g. Martin and Shen 2008), but these are neither easy nor unproblematic. A likely outcome would be that only some pairs of domains would be linked directly by a translation table. The point to stress in this chapter is that such translations would serve the needs of interdisciplinarians much less well. They would still have to know which disciplines to search, and would have to struggle with multiple terminologies.

Moreover, there are advantages for domain analysis itself in being linked to a general classification (Wåhlin 1974). In developing a domain-specific classification, information scientists may often find it useful to declare how a particular term is *not* used (this group treats term X differently from common usage elsewhere). Domain-specific classifications, then, neither will nor should be developed in isolation. Gnoli (2011a) discusses how domain-specific classifications could be linked to the Integrative Levels Classification (ILC).

But does a general classification need domain analysis? Indeed it does. How else can both classificationist and classifier be confident that the terminology employed in the general classification adequately captures the meaning of works and ideas emanating from particular domains? After all, a general classification is only useful if it can guide users from every discipline to works in every discipline. And it is not possible to ensure this outcome without linking domain and general analysis. Chapter 6 will explore how this can best be done in practice.

It was argued in the preceding chapter that knowledge organization could potentially decrease the ambiguity of language and thus directly facilitate interdisciplinary understanding. The degree to which ambiguity can be lessened by classification is hidden from us by the simple fact that most library users do not understand how library catalogs are organized. If library users understood the logic behind some comprehensive classification, they would find the terminology used in that classification much less ambiguous. Of course few users may wish to master an entire classification, even if it were logically structured (though our schools might be more willing to teach such material if a general classification existed that was easy to understand). But as long as a computer can be programmed with the logical structure of an entire classification, a search interface can take a user from any search item to an outline of how the user's interests are reflected within the organization of knowledge (DeRidder 2007; see below). One valuable entry point for a user might well be from the terminology employed in a domain-specific classification.

There is a further source of complementarity. Gnoli (2007) argued that classification systems are best grounded in both ontology (an understanding of what things exist in the world and how these are related) and epistemology (an understanding of how scholars study things). The domain-specific approach leans heavily on epistemology: it seeks to ground classifications in an understanding of how scholars in that domain operate. Comprehensive classifications can and should have an ontological base. Yet most comprehensive classifications rely on disciplines as a classificatory device and are thus to a considerable extent largely epistemological in approach. The sort of classification advocated in this book is grounded in ontology, for it is grounded in the phenomena (things) that exist in the world.[3] Yet as noted above the details of such a system are worked out with careful attention to how scholars study things.[4]

The Need for Both Induction and Deduction

Philosophers of science—at least those who believe that scientific understanding can advance—recognize that scientific understanding advances best when both induction and deduction are employed. A purely deductive enterprise can easily become un-tethered from reality, while a purely inductive enterprise can too easily miss the connections among diverse observations (Gower 1997, 254). Information science too can benefit from a mix of induction and deduction. Rowley and Hartley (2008) have indeed argued that information science has generally been inductive in orientation—classificationists surveyed the works to be classified and went from there—and applaud efforts to deductively ground classifications in a theoretical understanding of the structure of knowledge.

Deduction can be defined here as exclusively applying general rules in order to identify subclasses within a classification. Induction instead involves exploring the world and identifying the elements that need to be classified. Deduction provides a logical structure; induction ensures that everything has a place. Both have something to contribute, but each also has weaknesses. The scholarly project is largely predicated on an understanding that deductive reasoning alone will miss much that is important in the world. And exclusive reliance on induction may provide little guidance on which observations deserve to be treated together, or indeed on how best to structure the relationships between terms. A system such as LCC that relies too heavily on finding a place for every work to fit will deviate from a logical structure; a system that does not look at how scholars are actually utilizing terminology will inevitably lump together quite different

---

[3] Hjørland (2013) worries that classifications differ by ontology, and thus there is no one best ontology. Yet his conclusion stresses that we should ground classifications in scientific understanding within different fields. The approach recommended here aspires to do precisely that. The question as to how well these domain-specific understandings of the world fit within a comprehensive ontology is an empirical question. There is certainly considerable consensus around the existence of at least some types of things and relationships. We are nevertheless guided to reduce opportunities for conflict.

[4] Most of the headings for a thesaurus in women's studies could be terms used in a general classification (López-Huertas and Torres Ramirez 2007). The authors worry that employing such a structure does not accurately reflect what is considered important in the field. But it might be possible to construct a thesaurus that prioritized the terminology of the field while providing links to the terms in a general classification.

types of work.[5] Especially (but not exclusively) with respect to the most specific (lower-level) entries in a hierarchical classification, there is simply no substitute for examining how scholars conceptualize the things they perceive in the world and how they organize their conceptualizations. The recent *Nuovo Soggettario*, or Italian subject indexing system, pursued exactly this strategy of developing logical hierarchies but ensuring that all elements encountered inductively had a place (Cheti and Paradisi 2008). Developers of a general classification can thus usefully try to integrate the insights of domain-specific classifiers (and vice versa).

Given their concern regarding the feasibility of defining the essence of concepts, Hjørland and Nissen Pedersen (2005) are naturally skeptical of the possibility of deriving a classification deductively from first principles. They emphasize instead the autonomous development of classifications: by looking at documents produced by a particular community of scholars and seeking commonalities one can develop classifications that adequately serve that class of documents. Such a strategy has many merits but it also presents difficulties. One potential problem is that the sorts of shared understandings that Hjørland and Nissen Pedersen hope to discover inductively evolve (sometimes rapidly) through time, and thus their classifications will soon fail to provide appropriate guidance. Indeed the very boundaries and characteristics of the academic communities or disciplines that would be the focus of their efforts change through time (see Klein 1990 or Salter and Hearn 1996). The fact that disciplines, unlike the phenomena they study, can only be induced at a point in time rather than deduced (see Chap. 1), renders these a problematic base on which to build a classification.

From the perspective of this book, there is an even greater problem with an entirely inductive approach. Hjørland and Nissen Pedersen (2005) argue that their inductive approach is only suited to the classification of the literatures of individual scholarly communities. This book suggests that this need not be the case. To be sure, a greater variation in meanings will be found as one searches across a wider sample of literature. Potentially at least, large enough differences in meaning could result in different classifications. Notably, though, when López-Huertas investigates the interdisciplinary field of gender studies inductively, she finds that roughly half of the concepts employed are borrowed from other disciplines 'with the same form and apparently the same sense as they have in their original realm' (2006, 333; see Chap. 6). The 32 % of terms developed independently within gender studies, and especially the remainder that are developed through interaction with other disciplines, may also share similar meanings in different realms.

Hjørland and Nissen Pedersen (2005) are guided, as is much recent research in information science, by a laudable desire to reflect the differences in perspective that characterize modern scholarship. Yet their recommended strategy serves to

---

[5] Beghtol (2003) noted that literary warrant—the idea that a place must be found for all works in a bibliographic classification—guides information science to build its classifications upon those developed by scholars. But scholars develop classifications in the first instance to aid research on the frontiers of understanding, and these "naïve" classifications need not be ideally suited to organizing information for retrieval.

create barriers between communities with different perspectives. The scholarly project can only benefit from different worldviews if there is communication between communities. The approach recommended in this book is also grounded in the recognition of different scholarly perspectives, but allows these to be more readily juxtaposed and thus integrated.

Spärck Jones (2005 [1970]) developed a three-dimensional typology of classifications. Classes could be either ordered or non-ordered, exclusive or overlapping, and monothetic (objects share one property) or polythetic (objects share some, though not necessarily all, of a set of properties). Spärck Jones argued that the choices made in these three respects when classifying should reflect both classification theory and the objectives of a particular classification; in general one would evaluate the latter in terms of the former. Exclusive reliance on Hjørland and Nissen Pedersen's (2005) inductive approach of looking for co-occurrence of terms within a domain would produce a non-ordered, overlapping, and polythetic classification. Such classifications are necessarily grounded in the discourse of one academic community and will be difficult to decipher by scholars from outside that community.

The objective of serving interdisciplinary scholarship is best realized by a classification that is primarily:

- Ordered. Phenomena and methods should be sorted and organized hierarchically. Theories are classified in terms of a handful of key characteristics.
- Exclusive. Phenomena, theories, and methods can generally be defined precisely enough to ensure exclusivity. In practice, some limited overlap may occur.
- Monothetic. Phenomena are defined wherever possible either in terms of their internal essence or function.

While the approach to classification recommended in this book is thus quite different from that in Hjørland and Nissen Pedersen (2005), it flows not from the rejection of their inductive approach but from harnessing this to a compatible deductive approach.

Experience shows, as reported by Mayr (1981), that in most cases a sound foundation of a KOS in the objective structure of the phenomena it models, as unveiled by the current results of scientific investigation, will also result in efficiency for information retrieval as a consequence, while the opposite is not always true. Therefore, KOS developers should always try to follow logical and scientific principles, even when aiming at solving more specific needs. In developing a comprehensive phenomenon-based classification, then, we should strive to reflect as much as possible consensus that might exist among scholars about how the world we study is organized.

Yet there are also several advantages of induction for the project of this book. The feasibility of a deductively derived classification can be tested and improved upon by the use of inductive methodology. Induction can ensure that some phenomena, theories, or methods are not inadvertently excluded. Induction also allows us to further clarify the precise meanings of individual phenomena, theories, and methods. Induction could also usefully establish whether some elements in the classification often/always co-occur with others. And of course induction provides critical insight into the precise meaning attached to particular concepts by different groups and individuals.

Linking Any Two Concepts

We saw in Chap. 2 the importance of relationships among phenomena. If interdisciplinarians are to be able to search for information on relationships among any two phenomena that are of interest to them, then a KOS must allow any two phenomena to be linked. Likewise, if users wish to search for a combination of relationship, theory applied, and method applied, then the KOS must facilitate such searches.

Note that a user can only find a work through a KOS if the work is classified in the way that the user wishes to search. If the user wishes to search by relationships, then the work needs to be classified in terms of relationships. Boolean searches are possible in most databases, but, as noted in Chap. 2, will fail to uncover relationships effectively because works are not classified reliably in terms of the phenomena involved in a relationship, and not classified at all in terms of relationships themselves.

The desideratum is simple. Works that address a particular relationship (and most do) should be classified as (A) (exerts particular effect on or has particular relationship with) (B). [The citation order would be reversed for shelving purposes, so that the work would be shelved under B.] Works that address several relationships should be classified in terms of all of these. [Works that address hundreds of relationships will require some special treatment of course.] The first and last terms will be handled by the comprehensive classification of things urged above. A KOS thus also needs:

- A classification of relationships
- A notational system that facilitates classification in terms of a combination of phenomena and relationships. [This system should in particular allow the direction(s) of influence to be clearly indicated.]

As discussed in Chap. 2, if the user will be able to readily search for any relationship, it follows that all relationships must be treated in the same way throughout a classification. That is, the user should not be expected to know that some set of relationships is treated in one way but a different set is treated in a different way. Yet this is the case in all KOSs in use today. In enumerative schemes, the difference is stark: some relationships are treated as classes and can be searched for if one knows the class name, others can be approximated by Boolean searches, and others are simply impossible to search for. Faceted schemes, which in general are more amenable to linking distinct topics, tend to have different rules for linking topics that lie within a discipline from the rules for linking topics across disciplines. This need not be the case: freely faceted classifications (such as the Integrative

Table 3.1 Logical arguments for allowing free combination

1. The vast majority of scholarly (and many if not most non-scholarly) works explore how one or more phenomena (things) affect one or more others. This is especially true for interdisciplinary works, but applies also to specialized research.
2. The best way to classify such works is through combinations of things and relationships. If a book is about dogs biting mail carriers, the ideal subject entry is '(mail carriers) (bitten by) (dogs).' The classification system then captures the unique insights of particular works.
3. This is best done by allowing things and relationships to be freely linked in both classification and search.

Level Classification [ILC] and the Basic Concepts Classification [BCC]) allow for the same relationships to be employed across the classification.

It is worth summarizing the set of logical arguments underpinning the foregoing argument. This is done in Table 3.1.

Such an approach was extremely difficult in an era of card catalogues. It is thus perhaps not surprising that it was eschewed in the classification systems that have come to dominate the world's libraries. But it is entirely feasible in the digital age. The sort of classification we are urging for interdisciplinarity is also thus one that is well-suited to a digital age.

Capturing the Unique Contributions of a Work

It is a principle of knowledge organization that we should want the subject entry for a work to be co-extensive with what is understood to be the actual subject of the work (Foskett 1996, 127). 'In the best of all possible worlds, a bibliographic record for an item serves as a sufficiently informative document surrogate that enables accurate assessments of relevance' (LaBarre and Tilley 2012, 688). We would argue here that the characteristics of an ideal KOS for interdisciplinarity will lead the KOS to accord with this important principle. As noted above, the vast bulk of scholarly research investigates how one or more phenomena influence one or more others. This is likely also the case for most general non-fiction works: these discuss such relationships as how gardeners can grow flowers, how parents can raise children, and how people can achieve happiness or success. A system that allowed such research to be classified in terms of the phenomena studied and the relationships posited among these would provide the best possible mechanism for subject-based information retrieval.

Smiraglia (2001) investigates the nature of a work in detail, drawing on the literature not only of information science but also philosophy, linguistics, sociology, and other fields. He concludes that the nature of a work lies in the ideas that the work conveys. Works thus have an 'inherent nature as communicative signifying objects' (54). FRBR (Functional Requirements for Bibliographic Records), the standard for bibliographic classification, also treats a work as an abstract entity

Table 3.2 Addressing rhemes

Sometimes the main claim of a work may be that A affects B in an important way. [That is, it does not just investigate possible connections but reaches a conclusion that there is a causal relationship. Only the latter is a 'rheme' within Hutchins' terminology.] Thus the simple act of coding causal links captures some rhemes. It also captures at least one element of the most common type of rheme '(A) (affects in manner X) (B).'
Sometimes the main claim of a work may involve an assertion that theory X does (or does not) explain some change in B. Classifying works in terms of theories applied may thus provide some insights into the rheme of particular works.
Likewise some works are primarily methodological in nature, the rheme being that 'Method Z allows us (or not) to investigate changes in B.' Classifying works by method applied may thus provide some access to that sort of rheme.

(Smiraglia 2001, 47). Smiraglia does not, though, specify the precise nature of 'ideas.' We would suggest that a work's ideas are best represented in a classification by the causal arguments that it makes, and the theories, methods and perspectives that it applies.

Classificatory practice has not followed the emphasis of Smiraglia on 'ideas.' A work that describes how a particular drug affects a particular disease will generally be classed primarily under the disease and secondarily under the drug. No mention may be made of how exactly the drug works. The author of the study may well feel that the most important element of the work is its explication of how the drug works. Yet this element may not be expressed in the subject classification at all. The author will often also be particularly proud of the precise research protocols pursued but these also will not generally be captured.

In other words, as we saw in Chap. 2, classification tends to focus on the 'theme' rather than the 'rheme,' where the rheme can be understood as what is novel about a work (Hutchins 1977). While novices *may* often wish to search by theme,[6] scholars are likely to be as or more interested in the rheme of a work. The proposed classification approaches the issue of rhemes in a variety of ways. These are summarized in Table 3.2.

As useful as these approaches are, it is still of central importance to identify the core element of most rhemes: the claim about how exactly A affects B. This can only be achieved by classifying 'types of influence.' This involves dealing with predication. While there are important distinctions between the linguistic structure of sentences and the logical structure of information, it is nevertheless true that the rheme of most works can be approximated by a sentence of the form 'A does Z to B.' Existing classification systems emphasize noun-type descriptors. Thus when verb-like terms are included they are expressed in the form of a noun: fusion rather than fusing, comparison rather than comparing. It is thus more difficult to achieve a

---

[6] Olson (2007) notes that users often wish to search for syntagmatic relationships, such as embroidered Christmas ornaments, but the bulk of effort in information science has focused on paradigmatic relationships (those that always hold). General users as well as interdisciplinary scholars will clearly benefit from a synthetic approach.

sentence-like structure than if verb-like terms were included. It is thus desirable to investigate how relationships, which are often best signaled by verbs, might be better treated in a novel classification.

Just as interdisciplinarians (and disciplinarians) will benefit from a unique classification of all the phenomena involved in a causal link, they will also benefit from a general list of the types of influence involved in causal links, rather than having the same relationship treated differently in different parts of the classification. Scholars can more easily master and understand a general class of types of influence rather than a large set of overlapping and idiosyncratic verbs. More importantly, scholars may often wish to search for the same sort of influence across many different situations (as noted in Chap. 2). The field of communication studies in fact does just that: it studies the act of communicating across a wide array of circumstances (Cesanelli 2008). Communication is one causal process that does get treated within existing general classifications, though of course as the noun 'communication' rather than the verb 'communicate.' Acts of communication studied outside of the field of communication studies will be classified differently from those performed by communication studies scholars. Yet the field of communication studies has expanded its scope into areas such as new media studies. This increases the likelihood that very similar works can be found in quite different places in existing classifications. Still, the treatment of communication is better than that of many other causal relationships. Scholars may be interested in studying 'supervising,' 'paying,' or 'conflicting with' across many distinct causal linkages, but will find it exceedingly difficult to do so.

Even faceted classifications do not facilitate searches in terms of relationships as well as they might. Since the Bliss Classification (BC2) unpacks each facet only within main classes, a general list of relationships is not generated, apart from that of facet categories. The Colon Classification (CC) does a somewhat better job. In the (oft-ignored) seventh edition of CC, much of what had been the energy facet in the (much more often referenced and applied) sixth edition is transferred to the matter facet, leaving a set that more closely resembles types of influence (verbs). Moreover, a general list of relationships that can be used with the same notation across all main classes is generated. It includes the following verbs: 'create, produce, operate, infer, identify, mix, impregnate, collect data, test, design, absorb, teach, survey, review, standardize, aid, sponsor, and mediate.' Yet even CC7 still maintains lengthy lists of class-specific verbs (Satija 1989, 15–6). 'Prevention' gets consideration under both medicine and agriculture. The education class hosts a set of verbs with more general applicability: 'select, administer, enroll, assess, and even accredit.' The agriculture class contains some verbs that may have limited applicability elsewhere ('sow, plow'), but also several that clearly do ('treat, cut, store, clean, sort'). And even the more specific verbs might be thought of as special cases of more general verbs: 'sow' is a way of starting a growth process, while 'plow' is a manner of churning/mixing applied to soil.

It should also be noted that classifying works with respect to theory and method applied is useful both for users with strong theoretical and methodological preferences (who can be spared the inconvenience of consulting works they will disdain)[7] and those who are interested (as interdisciplinary researchers should be; Repko 2012) in integrating across different theories and methods. For both specialized and interdisciplinary users, then, theory and method applied are both important signals of the relevance of a work.[8]

Smiraglia notes, following deconstructionist thought, that author and reader may disagree about the key ideas conveyed in a work. [And Cleverdon and Keen 1966 famously found that indexers often attribute different subjects to a work.] It should be emphasized that this is a problem for all efforts at bibliographic classification, not just the approach recommended in this book. Yet the KOS recommended in this book requires only that either classifier or author identify key causal arguments the author thought he or she was making as well as theories and methods applied. This should be possible for most (at least non-fiction) works.

Works often have multiple instantiations. When does a work change enough that it deserves to be treated as a new work? Smiraglia argues that the answer lies in whether the ideas a work conveys have changed 'enough.' Though it may not be possible to give a precise definition of 'enough,' the approach here indicates that we should explore whether causal arguments, theory, or method have changed.

Smiraglia (2001) places an important caveat on the foregoing analysis. The ideas in a written or oral work are necessarily conveyed in words. It is not possible to completely separate content from the style of presentation. Indeed many works (think, say, of the Gettysburg Address) are remembered as much or more for their style as their content. It will thus be useful to attempt to classify works in terms of style *in addition to* the elements stressed above. This is a challenging task. Some descriptors might be fairly easy to apply: humor, satire, sarcasm. Others would present a greater challenge: rhetoricians disagree about the full set of rhetorical strategies (Harris 2013 lists 60) that can be employed in a work, and how each might be identified. Smiraglia raises his caveat with respect to all works, not just interdisciplinary works, and so the need to capture "style" is tangential to the main thrust of this book. But since 'style' overlaps significantly with 'authorial perspective' (and 'genre;' see Szostak 2014a), Smiraglia's caveat does provide another justification for exploring ways of classifying works by authorial perspective.

Transparent Rules for Computer-Based Searching

As noted above, much of the value of the sort of classification system proposed above will be lost if users have difficulty navigating it. To maximize ease of navigation by users there should be:

---

[7] Davis and Shaw (2011, 32–3) appreciate the existence of a confirmation bias whereby users often seek information that accords with their point of view.

[8] Questions regarding if/how to signal how well particular theories or methods are applied are beyond the scope of this book. Szostak (2014b) explores some possibilities.

- A simple organizing structure for the classification so that a computer can be programmed to navigate the system in response to any search request;
- Thesaurus-like sets of synonyms and semantic relationships that will guide users to appropriate search terminology.

Users need not master the logic behind a new system as long as they have access to a computerized search tool that is grounded in that logic (DeRidder 2007, 227). But computers cannot successfully deal with organizing structures that do not strictly follow certain logical rules. They can however master a complex but logical organizing structure. Computers can then be programmed to provide users with a detailed analysis of where their search terms fit within all relevant hierarchies and/or the full set of causal (or other) relationships that might be pursued. Note that most of the classification systems employed in the world today were developed before the advent of computers and were thus not designed with computerization in mind. They can, of course, be adapted for online use (Svenonius 1983). But this is not the same as being designed from the outset with computers in mind, and thus with a strict emphasis on following strict logical rules as much as possible.

Many characteristics enumerated above (and elsewhere) should serve to facilitate the task of appropriately computerizing a classification. These are summarized in Table 3.3.

The experience of SYNTOL (Syntagmatic organization language), an early effort led by Jean-Claude Gardin to develop a classifier-assisted computer program for indexing and retrieval of works in any domain, is instructive. The developers of SYNTOL discovered very early that compound indexing solely in terms of things led to too many 'false drops' (works that did not address the user's query were identified) in retrieval, presumably because users sought some particular relationship between two things. They found that even adding poorly specified relationship terms greatly facilitated retrieval; context generally clarified what otherwise could have been ambiguous (though note that the system was generally applied to domain-specific collections) (Gardin 1965, 53–5). As we shall see later, the (much better funded and developed) Unified Medical Language System (UMLS) also operates successfully with 54 semantic relationships (National Library of Medicine 2014).

Digitization has provided both challenges and opportunities for the field of knowledge organization. On the one hand, the popularity of free-text searching allows and encourages many users to eschew systems of subject classification (and often libraries themselves) entirely. But the very fact of terminological ambiguity (discussed above) means that free-text searching is itself problematic: the user finds many resources that are not useful and misses many that are. The sister field of information retrieval (and allied fields in computer science) has thus increasingly come to question the 'bag of words' assumption (that is, the assumption that search terms are independent) that has underpinned most search algorithms, and is exploring ways to enhance retrieval through appreciating the linkages that may exist across search terms (see Wallach 2006). That is, scholars of information retrieval see advantages in searching for linked sets of search terms. It is thus possible that

Table 3.3 Advantages of the recommended KOS for computer navigation

Classification takes place in terms of phenomena and relationships rather than disciplines. As we have seen, this will mean that each work has one obvious place in a classification (though a decision will need to be made of which phenomenon or relationship to prioritize for shelving purposes); The logical hierarchies of phenomena will make it easy to show users where a query fits hierarchically.
Most works are classified as relationships between phenomena. This reflects an understanding that most research investigates relationships (especially causal) among phenomena. By instantiating a web of relations, users can be shown how they could follow their curiosity to related works.
Detailed classifications of methods and theory types will allow works to be precisely classified in terms of the theories and methods applied as well.
Main classes should reflect integrative levels (that is, levels of complexity; see Chaps. 4 and 7). The theory of integrative levels claims that the natural world is organized in a series of levels of increasing complexity: from physical particles and molecules, through biological structures, to the most sophisticated products of human thought (e.g. Feibleman 1954). There is thus a logical order to main classes.
Phenomena need to be classified hierarchically in a logical manner. As Mazzocchi et al. (2007) have shown, extant classifications are often forced to abuse logical hierarchy: recycling is treated as a subset of garbage because there is no other obvious place to put what is clearly a relationship. Ideally a classification would strictly distinguish narrower terms that reflect types of the broader term from narrower terms that reflect parts of the broader term.
A synthetic approach should also be taken to representing the 'properties' of a thing. This is of course one of the primary aims of facet analysis: a core set of qualifiers is utilized across all phenomena (and perhaps relationships). The result is a classification that not only is efficient in its allocation of notation but is much more useful to the user. We thus follow Metcalfe, who had distinguished between 'specification' (basically, types of a thing), which should be handled by the creation of a hierarchy of subject headings, and 'qualification' (everything else: process, aspect, form), which should be addressed through linked notation (this distinction is emphasized in Foskett 1996, 127). The user may at times find it valuable to search by qualifier (how is 'beautiful' applied to different phenomena?). More generally, the user can combine nouns and adjectives in search rather than ascertain a particular combination favored by a classificationist. We discuss the classification of properties in Chap. 7.

the sort of approach urged above may encourage a rapprochement between the once-connected but now distinct fields of knowledge organization and information retrieval.[9]

The Semantic Web deserves special attention here. The idea of the Semantic Web is that computers should be able to navigate across databases (Hart and Dolbear 2013 provide a very readable overview of the Semantic Web). Notably, it is not hoped that computers will divine the nature of a particular resource through full-text searching. Rather, resources are supposed to be coded in a manner that allows computers to draw inferences across different databases containing documents on related subjects. Computers will only be able to draw connections across databases if the terminology used when databases are coded for the Semantic Web

---

[9] Hjørland (2012) explores the possibilities for knowledge organization in a world "after Google." He appears to appreciate the value of some sort of general classification in meeting this challenge.

is common or at least interoperable through KOSs, especially in the form of controlled vocabularies (Golub 2014). There is perhaps an irony in the fact that this latest stage in digital evolution depends on some sort of controlled vocabulary: the terminology used for coding any one database must at the very least be explicitly translated into terminology used elsewhere. For the field of knowledge organization the lesson should be clear: KOSs may have a critical role to play in the Semantic Web but only KOSs that are readily navigated by computers. Since the sort of classification that we have urged for interdisciplinarity involves a common controlled vocabulary across all fields it may prove to be particularly well-suited to the digital environment of the future. We shall find in later chapters that the synthetic approach that we have urged is also well suited to the Semantic Web.

Shelving Issues

Since catalogs and—increasingly—documents are available online, we naturally focus in this book on digital rather than physical searching for documents. Users— both scholarly and general—are much more likely these days to search electronically than to browse library shelves looking for relevant material. But browsing the shelves has not disappeared as a search practice. We should thus devote some attention to the implications of the above analysis for shelving.

There is obviously an advantage to shelving works in accordance with the sequence of classes stipulated by a phenomenon-based classification. Browsing shelves organized in this manner would, in particular, increase the possibility of uncovering 'undiscovered public knowledge' (on which see Chap. 1). Yet there is obviously a potential cost to the disciplinarian in not having the same easy access to shelves devoted entirely to their discipline. They may have to wander a bit more in order to find the same number of disciplinary works. This cost may be small if all works are clearly marked with an indicator of disciplinary perspective where needed.

Notably, the classificationist need not make the shelving decision. If works can be organized by different dimensions of their subject content, then individual libraries could make quite different decisions as to which dimension of a given compound subject is to serve as the basis for organizing documents on the shelves. Most obviously, they could continue to prioritize disciplines rather than phenomena (though as interdisciplines multiply this will seem less and less advantageous). Less obviously they could even shelve works in terms of theory or method applied. And if a library is classifying works according to relationships, the librarian has scope for deciding which of the phenomena involved is most useful from the point of view of that library's particular patrons.

Shelving works in a large library (though not a bookstore or some small libraries) generally involves the use of a compact notation which indicates where a work should be placed on the shelves. We can note here three characteristics that might be useful in adding notation to the classification recommended in this book:

- Expressive notation should be used to the greatest extent possible. The user will better appreciate how notation is derived if it is expressive, and the classifier will find it much easier to classify if notation is memorable.[10]
- Short notations should be used for simple subjects. In this way compound notation becomes feasible even for very complex subjects. Note that UDC uses linked notation extensively, and is often criticized for unwieldy notation. Much of the problem stems from very long notation for simple subjects (because UDC builds upon DDC7). UDC may also sometimes put more detail in the call number than is required (Foskett 1996, 186.) [The latter may reflect a problem in the protocols for applying UDC, not the classification itself.]
- There should be devices for expanded notation as needed, especially for classes that grow and change through time (authors, countries, theories). The Integrative Levels Classification (ILC) employs empty digits (that is, has the reserved character z allowing for insertion of additional notation where needed) (ILC 2004).

Adapt or Innovate?

López-Huertas (2007, 5) observes that 'a perspective change like the one proposed for inter- and transdisciplinarity is going to deeply affect some of the models, claims and methods traditionally established.' The inadequacy of existing KOSs to treat interdisciplinary knowledge has already been observed and emphasized by several authors, including Beghtol (1998), who has made reference to the focus on phenomena in JD Brown's Subject Classification.

Existing classification systems stress disciplines, tend to ignore relationships, ignore theories and methods applied for the most part, and provide different instructions to classifiers in different parts of the classification. Some of the changes urged above might readily be incorporated into existing classifications. These might, in particular, start classifying works in terms of theory and method applied (or even other elements of disciplinary perspective). Yet even this can only be done (at least well) if we first develop a general classification of theories and methods. And this arguably is best done as part of a broader effort to classify phenomena. There may even be some considerable value in adding some classification of 'types of relationship' to existing classification systems, though such a classification is best used in concert with a comprehensive classification of phenomena (Szostak 2012a, b).

Classifying works in terms of relationships among a common and comprehensive set of phenomena is a major break from traditional practice in KOS, and one that by definition can only be accomplished by first developing such a classification of phenomena, and then allowing any two concepts to be combined within the

---

[10] See Ranganathan (1967) on seminal mnemonics.

classification on the basis of a given classified set of relationships. Such a classification could free users (and classificationists and classifiers) from the disciplinary limitations of existing general classifications (León Manifesto 2007; Szostak 2008, 2011). At the same time it allows us to readily classify objects and insights as well as works, and provides the best means of providing simultaneous access to multiple databases. This is not something that can be done by tweaking an existing classification.

There may, though, be some scope for a hybrid classification. Cousson (2009) suggests that UDC could be organized around phenomena rather than disciplines. Broughton (2010) discusses both the challenges and advantages of revising the UDC schedules so that complex entries are treated as compounds of simpler terms. Szostak (2011) shows how a large section of the Dewey Decimal Classification (DDC) can be translated into the terminology of a comprehensive classification of phenomena. Works might readily be classified in terms of both classifications, and both might then be used as search tools.

Thesauri

Palmer (2010, 185) urges the development of cross-disciplinary thesauri (and ontologies) to support interdisciplinary research. A general thesaurus, if feasible, would be a tremendous boon to interdisciplinarians. A thesaurus could—especially if linked to a general classification—guide a user to the synonyms that are employed in that classification, and also point the user to related terms. This would be the case even if such a thesaurus somehow indicated that a certain term took on a particular meaning in one field(s) but a different meaning in another. Shiri (2012) surveys a vast literature on the shape and role of thesauri, with a focus on digital environments. Thesauri have been found to aid users both in free-text and controlled vocabulary searching. Shiri (2012) urges interoperability among thesauri and the development of switching languages between thesauri. He appreciates that interoperability is becoming increasingly important with the development of the Semantic Web. Though he stops short of urging a general thesaurus, he appreciates the advantages of being able to move seamlessly across thesauri. He also appreciates that thesauri can and should be directly linked to classifications. Thesauri could help users most obviously at the initial stage of a search, by translating the terms in which they are interested into the terminology employed in a classification (thesauri can also aid free-text searching by suggesting multiple search terms), but they can also play a role later in searches as the user encounters new terminology. Shiri naturally urges increased machine-readability of thesauri. It will be useful to explore as we proceed the possibility of a comprehensive thesaurus to accompany the comprehensive phenomenon-based classification envisioned above. Some classification schemes, including ILC, already provide sets of synonyms or quasi-synonyms in the captions of their classes, which can be of help in implementing this functionality.

Our emphasis on relationships above suggests another desideratum with respect to thesauri. The RT relationship employed within most thesauri encompasses a diverse range of different types of relationship. If it is useful to distinguish different types of relationship within a classification system, it will likewise be useful to distinguish these in thesauri. Such a practice would facilitate machine navigation of thesauri. This approach has indeed been recommended by several information scientists in recent years. Vickery (2008) argues that thesauri are unstructured because of the vagueness in related terms (RT), and articulates a dozen more precise terms that could replace RT. Soergel et al. (2004) discuss how thesauri could be 'expanded' into ontologies by making RTs more precise. Olson (2007) notes that the thesaurus construction standard, ANSI/NISO Z39.19, provides for a limited set of allowed related term (RT) relationships: process/agent, process/counteragent, action/property, action/product, action/target, cause/effect, concept or object/property, concept or object/origins, concept or object/measurements, raw material/product, and discipline or field/object or practitioner; and also antonyms (plus a few arcane exceptions). The standard allows these to be explicitly indicated on a local basis. We might instead insist that these and others are always designated. The latest ISO standards for thesauri are intended to encourage interoperability, and urge subdivisions not just of related terms but also of terms related by equivalence relationships (close synonyms versus precise synonyms versus some overlap in meaning) and of those terms standing to one another in hierarchical relationships (so that 'part of' is distinguished from 'type of' and 'geographically contained in;' see Dextre Clarke 2011). Weisgerber (1993) had argued that enhanced thesauri could alleviate many problems faced in interdisciplinary search.

Thesauri tend to focus on nouns, ignore some verbs and translate other verbs into nouns ('clean' becomes 'cleaning'), and treat adverbs and adjectives at best as constituents in noun phrases rather than separately. The analysis above implies that verbs, adjectives, and adverbs deserve more attention if we are to pursue a synthetic approach to classification in which these distinct elements are to be freely combined. A classification of relationships would be a particularly useful input into thesaurus construction (see Zeng et al. 2011 and Green et al. 2002). In sum, a comprehensive thesaurus which distinguished different types of RT and equivalence and hierarchy, and encompassed nouns, verbs, adverbs, and adjectives would provide the best possible entry point to the comprehensive phenomena-based classification suggested above.

Ontologies

The development of ontologies in the twenty-first century bears some resemblance to the development of classification systems over a century ago: many competing systems exist grounded in conflicting principles. It would thus be difficult at present to ground a general classification in an ontology. From the perspective of interdisciplinarity, a comprehensive and widely accepted ontology would help to further clarify the meaning of concepts in general and the concepts employed in classification systems in particular. There is also some similarity in the emphasis on relationships among phenomena in both ontologies and in the approach to classification recommended in this book. It is thus worthwhile to reflect on the nature and feasibility of such an ontology as we move forward.

The approach taken in this book may be seen as a middle ground between present classifications and formal ontologies: it calls for adherence to logical rules in developing hierarchies of things and relationships, but does not demand that concepts be defined precisely in terms of some logic. Indeed, we have repeatedly noted that some degree of ambiguity may be unavoidable but is acceptable for the purposes of classification. It is thus possible to structure a comprehensive classification of phenomena *right now* rather than waiting for the full development of a comprehensive ontology in the future; it could be that as ontologies are developed and some consensus is achieved on which ontology is best suited to the needs of information science, ontological insights will allow further clarification of concepts.[11] In other words, the approach of this book is consonant with that of ontologies, but by demanding less precision than ontologies it provides, at least for the foreseeable future, a more practical way of structuring a general classification. In turn, efforts to develop comprehensive classifications of phenomena and relationships could usefully inform efforts to develop ontologies.[12]

Contemporary interest in ontologies largely reflects the desire to encourage interoperability of databases, and in particular to facilitate the development of the Semantic Web. As noted above, the sort of classification that is called for to serve the needs of interdisciplinarity may also be well-suited to the needs of the digital age. It is perhaps not surprising that a classification that facilitates the crossing of boundaries between disciplines might also serve to facilitate the transcendence of boundaries between diverse databases: the pursuit of a common controlled vocabulary is useful in both cases. Given this potential synergy it is worth exploring in later chapters the degree to which the approach to classification advocated in this

---

[11] It should be noted that there are multiple upper level ontologies following different sets of axioms (and ontologists such as Masolo et al. n.d., aspire merely to link these and identify their sources of difference—which notably include preferences over different degrees of compounding), and thus the path through ontology to a general classification is at this point unclear (see Masolo et al. n.d., for a comparison of several upper-level ontologies). [The National Centre for Ontological Research in the United States does aspire to instill certain logical principles that would facilitate cross-ontology communication.] Moreover it should be appreciated that some ontologies would exclude logically many documents/ideas from consideration (e.g. the past may be thought to be unreal). The sort of logical argument that ontologists engage (such as how abstract things such as numbers can be said to exist without existing at any particular point in time) are often of little import to the classificationist.

[12] Topic maps (Melgar Estrada 2011) are yet another approach that could potentially benefit from an exhaustive classification of phenomena and causal relationships.

book achieves the goals for which ontologies are developed, particularly with respect to the Semantic Web.[13]

Key Points

A KOS designed for an interdisciplinary world will be characterized by:

- A comprehensive classification of phenomena (including theories, methods, and elements of disciplinary perspective) and relationships, which will be developed in concert with domain analysis;
- Application of both induction and deduction in its development;
- The possibility that any two or more concepts can be freely linked;
- The capture of as much as possible of the unique contributions of a work or the insights that it contains;
- Transparent rules for developing hierarchies and linking concepts, in order to facilitate computer-based searching;
- Access ideally through a comprehensive thesaurus that addresses nominal, verbal, adjectival, and adverbial notions alike in its terminology;
- Congruence with many of the goals of formal ontologies, thus allowing it to serve as a basis for ontology development.

These are, notably, characteristics not found for the most part in the classification systems used most widely in the contemporary world.

References

Almeida MB (2013) Revisiting ontologies: a necessary clarification. J Am Soc Inform Sci Technol 64(8):1682–1693

Association for Interdisciplinary Studies (AIS) (2013) About interdisciplinarity. http://www.oakland.edu/ais/

Beghtol C (1998) Knowledge domains: multidisciplinarity and bibliographic classification systems. Knowl Org 25(1/2):1–12

Beghtol C (2003) Classification for information retrieval and classification for knowledge discovery: relationships between "Professional" and "Naïve" classifications. Knowl Org 30(2):64–73

Bergmann M, Jahn T, Knobloch T, Krohn W, Pohl C, Schramm E (2012) Methods for transdisciplinary research: a primer for practice. Campus, Berlin

Broughton V (2010) Concepts and terms in the faceted classification: the case of UDC. Knowl Org 37(4):270–279

Cesanelli E (2008) Classificare il dominio della comunicazione secondo la teoria dei livelli di integrazione. E-LIS. http://eprints.rclis.org/14632/

---

[13] Almeida (2013) argues that the purpose of ontology is to capture the nature of a work, not just its subject. We have seen above that the sort of classification urged here should capture the nature of a work.

Cheti A, Paradisi F (2008) Facet analysis in the development of a general controlled vocabulary. Axiomathes 18(2):223–241

Cleverdon CW, Keen EM (1966) Factors determining the performance of indexing systems. Vol. 1: Design, Vol. 2: Results. Aslib Cranfield Research Project, Cranfield, UK

Cousson P (2009) UDC as a non-disciplinary classification for a high school library. Proceedings of the UDC seminar 2009: classification at a crossroads. Extensions Corrections UDC 31:243–252, http://arizona.openrepository.com/arizona/handle/10150/199909

Davis CH, Shaw D (2011) Introduction to information science &technology. ASIST Monograph Series, Medford, NJ

DeRidder JL (2007) The immediate prospects for the application of ontologies in digital libraries. Knowl Org 34(4):227–246

Dervos D, Coleman A (2006) A common sense approach to defining data, information, and metadata. In: Budin G, Swertz C, Mitgutsch K (eds) Knowledge organization for a Global Learning Society. Proceedings of the ninth international ISKO conference, Vienna. Ergon, Würzburg, pp 51–58

Dextre Clarke SG (2011) ISO25964 A standard in support of KOS interoperability. In: Gilchrist A, Vernau J (eds) Facets of knowledge organization: proceedings of the ISKO UK second biennial conference, London. Emerald, Bingley, UK, pp 129–133

Dogan M (1996) The hybridization of social science knowledge. Libr Trends 45(2):296–314

Dogan M, Pahre R (1990) Creative marginality: innovation at the intersection of social sciences. Westview, Boulder, CO

Feibleman JK (1954) Theory of Integrative Levels. Br J Philos Sci 5(17):59–66, Reprinted in Theory of subject analysis (1985) Chan L M et al (eds) Libraries Unlimited, Littleton. pp 136–142

Foskett AC (1996) The subject approach to information, 5th edn. Library Association Publishing, London

Gardin J-C (1965) SYNTOL. Graduate School of Library Service, Rutgers, the State University, New Brunswick, NJ

Glushko RJ (ed) (2013) The discipline of organizing. MIT Press, Cambridge, MA

Gnoli C (2007) Ten long-term research questions in knowledge organization. Knowl Org 35 (2/3):137–149

Gnoli C (2011a) Animals belonging to the emperor: enabling viewpoint warrant in classification. In: Landry P, Bultrini L, O'Neill ET, Roe SK (eds) Subject access: preparing for the future. De Gruyter, Berlin, pp 91–100

Gnoli C (2011b) Ontological foundations in Knowledge Organization. Scire 17(2)

Golub K (2014) Subject access to information: an interdisciplinary approach. ABC-Clio, Santa Barbara

Gower B (1997) Scientific method: an historical and philosophical introduction. Routledge, London

Green R, Bean CA, Myaeng SH (eds) (2002) The semantics of relationships. Kluwer, Dordrecht

Harris RA (2013) A handbook of rhetorical devices. http://www.virtualsalt.com/rhetoric.htm

Hart G, Dolbear C (2013) Linked data: a geographic perspective. CRC, Boca Raton, FL

Hjørland B (2002) Domain analysis in information science. Eleven approaches—traditional as well as innovative. J Doc 58(4):422–462

Hjørland B (2008) Core classification theory: a reply to Szostak. J Doc 64(3):333–342

Hjørland B (2012) Is classification necessary after Google? J Doc 68(3):299–317

Hjørland B (2013) Theories of knowledge organization—theories of knowledge. Knowl Org 40 (3):169–181

Hjørland B, Nissen Pedersen K (2005) A substantive theory of classification for information retrieval. J Doc 61(5):582–595

Hoetzlein R (2007) The organization of human knowledge: systems for interdisciplinary research. Masters thesis, Media Arts and Technology Program, University of California Santa Barbara

Hutchins WJ (1977) On the problem of 'Aboutness' in document analysis. J Inform 1:17–35

Integrative Levels Classification (ILC) (2004) ISKO Italia. www.iskoi.org/ilc/

Klein JT (1990) Interdisciplinarity: history, theory and practice. The Wayne State University Press, Detroit

Kleineberg M (2013) The blind men and the elephant: towards an organization of epistemic contexts. Knowl Org 40(5):340–362

LaBarre K, Tilley CL (2012) The elusive tale: leveraging the study of information seeking and Knowledge Organization to improve access to and discovery of folktales. J Am Soc Inform Sci Technol 63(4):687–701

León Manifesto (2007) Knowl Org 34(1):6–8. Available [with commentary] at: www.iskoi.org/ilc/leon.php

López-Huertas MJ (2006) Thematic map of interdisciplinary domains based on their terminological representation. The gender studies. In: Budin G, Swertz C, Mitgutsch K (eds) Knowledge Organization for a Global Learning Society. Proceedings of the Ninth International ISKO conference, Vienna. Ergon, Würzburg, pp 331–338

López-Huertas MJ (2007) Comment on the León Manifesto. www.iskoi.org/ilc/leon.php

López-Huertas MJ, Torres Ramírez I (2007) Gender terminology and indexing systems: the case of woman's body. Libri 57:34–44

Marcella R, Newton R (1994) A new manual of classification. Gower, Aldershot, UK

Martin TP, Shen Y (2008) Soft mapping between hierarchical classifications. In: Bouchon-Meunier B, Marsala C, Rifqi M, Yager RR (eds) Uncertainty and intelligent information systems. World Scientific, Singapore, pp 155–167

Masolo C, Borgo S, Gangemi A, Guarino N, Oltramari A(n.d.) Ontology Library. Laboratory for Applied Ontology - ISTC-CNR. http://wonderweb.semanticweb.org/deliverables/documents/D18.pdf

Mayr E (1981) Biological classification: toward a synthesis of opposing methodologies. Science 214:510–516

Mazzocchi F, Tiberi M, De Santis B, Plini P (2007) Relational semantics in thesauri: some remarks at theoretical and practical levels. Knowl Org 34(4):197–214

Melgar Estrada LM (2011) Topic maps from a Knowledge Organization perspective. Knowl Org 38(1):43–61

National Library of Medicine (2014) Semantic relationships. http://www.nlm.nih.gov/research/umls/new_users/online_learning/SEM_004.html

Olson H (2007) How we construct subjects: a feminist analysis. Libr Trends 56(2):509–541

Palmer CL (2010) Information research on interdisciplinarity. In: Frodeman R, Klein JT, Mitcham C (eds) The Oxford handbook of interdisciplinarity. Oxford University Press, Oxford, pp 174–188

Ranganathan SR (1967) Prolegomena to library classification, 3rd edn. SRELS, Bangalore

Repko AF (2012) Interdisciplinary research: process and theory, 2nd edn. Sage, Thousand Oaks

Repko AF, Newell WH, Szostak R (eds) (2012) Case studies in interdisciplinary research. Sage, Thousand Oaks

Rowley JE, Hartley R (2008) Organizing knowledge, 4th edn. Ashgate, Aldershot, UK

Salter L, Hearn A (eds) (1997) Outside the lines : issues in interdisciplinary research. McGill-Queen's University Press, Montreal

Satija MP (1989) Colon classification, 7th edn. Ess Ess Publications, New Delhi

Shiri A (2012) Powering search: the role of thesauri in new information environments. ASIS&T Monograph series, Medford, NJ

Smiraglia RP (2001) The nature of "a work": implications for the organization of knowledge. Scarecrow Press, Lanham, MD

Smiraglia RP (2012) Epistemology of domain analysis. In: Smiraglia RP, Lee H (eds) Cultural frames of knowledge. Ergon Verlag, Würzburg, pp 111–24

Soergel D, Lauser B, Liang A, Fisseha F, Keizer J, Katz S (2004) Reengineering thesauri for new applications: the AGROVOC example. J Digit Inform 4(4)

Spärck Jones K (2005) Some thoughts on classification for retrieval. J Doc 61(5):571–81 [Originally published, 1970]

Svenonius E (1983) Use of classification in online retrieval. Libr Resour Tech Serv 27:76–80

Szostak R (2008) Classification, interdisciplinarity, and the study of science. J Doc 64(3):319–332

Szostak R (2011) Complex concepts into basic concepts. J Am Soc Inform Soc Technol 62 (11):2247–2265

Szostak R (2012a) Classifying relationships. Knowl Org 39(3):165–178

Szostak R (2012b) Toward a classification of relationships. Knowl Org 39(2):83–94

Szostak R (2014a) Classifying the humanities. Knowl Org 41(4):263–275

Szostak R (2014b) Skepticism and Knowledge Organization. In: Babik W (ed) Knowledge Organization in the 21st century: between historical patterns and future prospects. Proceedings of the 13th ISKO conference, Krakow. Ergon, Würzburg

Szostak R (2014c) How universal is universality? [Letter to the editor]. Knowl Org 41(6):468–470

Vickery BC (2008) The structure of subject classifications for document retrieval. http://www. iskoi.org/ilc/vickery.php

Wåhlin E (1974) The AR-complex: adapted systems used in combination with a common reference system. In: Wojciechowski JA (ed) Conceptual basis of classification of knowledge: proceedings of the Ottawa conference. Verlag Dokumentation, Pullach, pp 416–449

Wallach H (2006) Topic modelling: beyond 'bag of words'. In: Proceedings of 23rd international conference on machine learning. Pittsburgh

Weisgerber DW (1993) Interdisciplinary searching: problems and suggested remedies. A report from the ICSTI group on interdisciplinary searching. J Doc 49(3):231–254

Wesolek A (2012) Wittgensteinian support for domain analysis in classification. Libr Philos Pract 1 (1):1–10, http://digitalcommons.unl.edu/cgi/viewcontent.cgi?article=1933&context=libphilprac

Zeng ML, Zumer M, Salaba A (2011) The functional requirements for subject authority records. International Federation of Library Associations and Institutes Report. DeGruyter, Berlin

Zeng ML, Gracy KF, Žumer M (2014) Using a semantic analysis tool to generate subject access points: a study using Panofsky's theory and two research samples. Knowl Org 41(6):440–451

Chapter 4
Phenomenon Versus Discipline-Based Classification

Previous chapters have developed an argument that interdisciplinary scholarship (in particular) would benefit from an approach to classification grounded in phenomena rather than disciplines. It might seem that such a recommendation represents a strong break with traditions in the field of classification research. Yet this is not the case. This chapter begins with a discussion of the historical emergence of discipline-based classifications. It then proceeds to examine a tradition within the field of knowledge organization of urging a phenomenon-based approach, and illustrates contemporary projects that are advancing in this direction. It discusses why such KOSs have not previously been widely adopted.

Disciplinary Libraries

In previous centuries, libraries were often organized by disciplines. In many contexts, this only required a very broad organization, consisting of few main classes, as the number of volumes was relatively limited, so that each one could be found within its broad group quite easily. For example, some rooms of Giacomo Leopardi's house in Recanati are covered by shelves where, at the beginning of the nineteenth century, the young poet famously used to spend many hours studying alone. On the top of each shelf is an oval sign with Roman numbers and corresponding disciplines, like sacred history, secular history, literary history, theology, and so on. The disciplines clearly reflected the culture of the time. However, this kind of system is still used in many libraries of relatively small size, both public and private, as well as in many bookshops.

From the nineteenth century on, as public and academic libraries grew to include increasingly large numbers of volumes, it became necessary to organize and catalog them in more detail. Librarians like Antonio Panizzi in London and Charles Ammi Cutter in Boston developed explicit rules for cataloging. At Amherst College, in Massachusetts, Melvil Dewey devised his Dewey Decimal System (DDC) to

© Springer International Publishing Switzerland 2016
R. Szostak et al., *Interdisciplinary Knowledge Organization*,
DOI 10.1007/978-3-319-30148-8_4

express the subject of any book as part of a rich hierarchy of disciplines and subdisciplines. This system allowed for potentially infinite specificity, and was also adopted with minor modifications in Europe for the Universal Decimal Classification (UDC). Other classificationists developed their own schemes on the basis of similar principles.

Classification thus meant arranging disciplines, as opposed to directly listing the objects of knowledge, expressed by controlled terms, as was done in dictionary entries and verbal subject heading systems. While by the Library of Congress Subject Headings one can express the fact that a book is about *animals*, by UDC one can say that it belongs to class *59* standing for 'zoology,' a subdivision of class *5* 'natural sciences' (a similar analysis holds for the Library of Congress Classification (LCC), DDC, and others). Indeed, these classifications are said to be based on *aspect*, the scientific perspective by which the subject matter is treated, rather than on the very phenomena discussed in the text (Broughton 2004, 18; Slavic 2007). Disciplinary classifications have remained the standard approach in twentieth-century libraries: probably this was due to an inertial process boosted by the economic advantages of sharing existing, well-known systems, especially by deriving ready-made classified records from the catalogs of such big institutions as the Library of Congress or the British Library.

This chosen path has had important consequences. Not all books dealing with animals will be grouped in class *59*. Indeed, books on animal breeding will instead be filed under *636* animal husbandry, being part of agriculture, in turn part of applied sciences; books on animal health will be filed under *614.9* veterinary hygiene, a part of medical sciences; animals as a means of transport will be filed under *656.1* road transport, part of communication industries; not to mention that paintings of animals will be filed under *75* painting, part of the arts. In other words, the phenomenon of animals will be scattered in many parts of the scheme, depending on the disciplinary perspective by which it is treated in each case. Current handbooks for classifiers explicitly state that this practice is the regular one to be adopted.

However, as we explore a disciplinary tree in more and more detail, we usually reach a point where the subclasses are illustrated by terms referring to phenomena rather than disciplines. Zoology in UDC is divided into the subdisciplines of animal physiology, ethology, systematic zoology, and so on; systematic zoology includes *599* zoology of mammals, whose technical disciplinary names 'mammalogy' or 'theriology' would be hardly known by non-experts; going on, a subclass like *599.4* will be described more often as the class of bats than as that of chiropterology, and the further subdivisions of bats would probably lack any name for a corresponding subdiscipline. We have thus gradually moved from names of disciplines to names of phenomena.

Current UDC principles are based on facet analysis, a method not yet available when the first editions of the UDC were published. It has become the UDC practice (although not published in detail yet) that the first digits of a class represent subdisciplines, while the following digits represent the object facet of that discipline. That is, in the case of zoology, the groups of animals forming its object of study: *599.4* would thus properly mean 'systematic zoology of bats' rather than 'chiropterology.' On the other hand, no symbol makes it clear at which point in notation we move from a subdiscipline to its object facet, while the number of digits expressing subdisciplines may well vary from one class to another. Also, assuming that systematic zoology is the last disciplinary subdivision, followed by its objects, implies that there is no notational space remaining for further specifying kinds of systematic zoology (that is, to identify subdisciplines in more detail) should this be needed in the future.

The sort of implicit structures described above reflect progressive adaptations over time to systems with a very long history, and that were originally conceived with a disciplinary, non-faceted structure. Although for many practical cases DDC and UDC work well (no doubt, better than no standard classification at all), they cannot be taken as a reference when discussing the best principles needed for interdisciplinary knowledge organization.[1]

The choice of disciplines as the structural basis of the major bibliographic classifications comes from their history of following an academic approach. It is usually justified by the rationale that scholars will find it convenient to have grouped together all books sharing the same disciplinary approach, rather than all books sharing the same objects of study. Clearly, indeed, taking one of the two as the primary subdivision will make the other scattered in different points of the collection. Librarians have generally assumed that scattering disciplines in order to group phenomena would be a major disadvantage for their users. Is this true? We have doubted this conclusion in preceding chapters.

What is surely true is that researchers are now *used* to finding documents grouped by discipline. So the disciplinary approach in the organization of knowledge can make them feel more comfortable with this established order of knowledge. Knowledge organization tends to represent existing, consolidated orders, rather than playing a more active role by suggesting new orders. For the purposes of interdisciplinarity, this is clearly an obstacle to the creation of innovative paths across different areas of knowledge.

Furthermore, the usual approach tends to privilege academic disciplines over domains of interest to general users. In real life, many users are less interested in Germanic literature than they are in reading a romantic novel situated in the nineteenth century, or an account of a journey across Asia; many need less to learn about motor engineering than to look at the features of a car they are considering to order through a website. Leisure is an important part of life that is poorly accounted for by traditional knowledge organization, although people increasingly use information sources regarding it (Hartel 2003). So disciplinary knowledge organization risks being useful only for a limited segment of users—

---

[1] Research on the updating and development of traditional schemes can happily advance in parallel with more general and speculative research on new systems: indeed, one of the authors is proud to work for the UDC Editorial Board.

maybe even the segment less in need of it, as researchers often know about the basic references in their own field already, as has often been observed.

Economic historians use the phrase 'path dependence' to refer to the importance of contingency in history. Typewriter manufacturers settled on a keyboard layout in the nineteenth century that made sense at a time when mechanical realities limited typing speeds (there is even some speculation that manufacturers may have been trying to slow typing speeds to reduce the frequency of jammed keys). It may be that a keyboard layout with the most-used letters in the middle could accelerate typing speeds significantly, but more than a century of training people on the old keyboard makes the switch difficult. It is not impossible to change paths: there is software that allows computers to utilize a different keyboard layout, and over time people might be trained on a different configuration. Likewise we may yet see the development of electric cars, but this transformation is made difficult by the century of development of technology and infrastructure to serve gasoline-powered automobiles (whereas in 1900 it was unclear which technology was superior).

The insight for information science is that once a path is chosen it develops its own momentum. Paths may be changed, but not easily. A classification system, once in place, tends to cope with new subjects in the manner that requires the least change to the system (see Chap. 7). Changes to a system that has long been in use must mean that works classified in the old way either become hard to find or must be reclassified into the new system. The conditions—disciplinary hegemony and reliance on card catalogues—that encouraged discipline-based classification in the nineteenth century have changed, just as the conditions that supported the 'QWERTY' keyboard layout have changed. If we had inherited a keyboard with the "a" and "e" in the middle, we would take this for granted. Likewise we might well have spent the last century happily fleshing out the sort of classification urged in this book.

Previous Attempts at Classifying by Phenomena

Despite the predominance of disciplines, the alternative approach of classification by phenomena was already clear in the early times of modern library classification to Paul Otlet, the pioneer of many advanced ideas in information science:

> The objects of knowledge [...] can be considered from two points of view. From the first point of view they can be envisaged as complete in themselves, as autonomous, as a totality, as a concrete whole. From the second point of view, they are envisaged in terms of their relations with other objects or as parts of an abstract entity. [...] To be complete, a classification should, therefore, enumerate both the objects and the points of view and choose as the basis of classification a sequence of one or the other as needs be. (Otlet 1896)[2]

---

[2] We are indebted to Thomas M. Dousa for pointing us to this source and its relevance.

Still, in practice Otlet employed the disciplinary option, which was ready-made in the DDC adopted as the main source for his UDC. A few years later, Julius Otto Kaiser (1911, para 209) recommended that users of his Systematic Indexing verbal system should focus on the phenomena studied and avoid '-ology' terms, although he did not apply this suggestion to classification.

Another early explorer of alternatives to canonical disciplines was British librarian James Duff Brown. Already a century ago, he proposed a Subject Classification, in which the main filing classes were 'concrete subjects' rather than disciplines, although the latter were still taken as main classes. This choice was aimed at placing all works dealing with one object, such as roses or coffee, in the same place independently from the 'standpoints' by which the object was considered. Subjects could then be subdivided by a Categorical Table anticipating to some extent (as was the case with Kaiser) the facets later introduced by Ranganathan. Brown's Subject Classification was also original in allowing for notational synthesis of subjects taken from different main classes, thus facilitating interdisciplinarity (Brown 1906; Beghtol 2004). Brown's system is no longer used today, but is an interesting precursor of non-disciplinary classifications.

The non-disciplinary option was then investigated in more direct and deep ways by the Classification Research Group (CRG), a sort of club of original thinkers in the domain of classification who regularly met in London from the 1950s. After developing various faceted systems focused on special domains, the CRG was granted funding by NATO in order to investigate the possibility and basic structure of a new general faceted classification system. Some members, including Foskett, Kyle, Farradane, Austin and Coates, supported the idea of building the system on main classes of entities, properties and activities, rather than on disciplines. Although unusual in classification, this was common in verbal subject heading lists and now in thesauri, a new kind of KOS inspired by linguistic tools like Roget's 1852 *Thesaurus of English words and phrases*. Indeed, terms listed in thesauri, like descriptors in alphabetical subject headings, refer to such individual concepts as (especially) objects, processes or events, rather than to disciplinary fields.

CRG members drafted main classes for their new general system, and discussed its basic principles in papers (Austin 1969; CRG 1969) as well as in their meeting bulletins:

> Mr. Farradane [...] said that he thought it had been accepted that the logical way to build a classification was to start from the individual concepts and build the classification through study of the relationships between them. To revert to accepting disciplines as main classes and classifying by subdivision would lead back to old confusions, since the content of 'disciplines' changes with time while the objects to which they relate, the natural entities and man, do not. [...] In non-scientific subjects the real problem was one of definition—to determine what the writer really meant by the words used. [...] Disciplines can be *derived* from various ways of observing and presenting phenomena, and some might prove to be those proposed by Mr. Langridge, but this cannot be accepted *a priori*. (CRG 1973)
>
> Coates thinks that it is dangerous to regard a structure based on division by disciplines as superior to any other; historically, people devising schemes of classification have always begun by looking at disciplines and have compromised by looking at literature. But

disciplines are always disorderly and the general feeling of the Group was that there is not agreement on what constitutes a discipline. Langridge, however, pointed out that it is essential to distinguish between fundamental disciplines, which can clearly be recognized, and their main subdivisions, which is where the area of disagreement arises. (CRG 1978)

The new CRG approach was quite revolutionary, in that notation for a document was not just taken from a hierarchical list of classes, but could be obtained by combination of single concepts, each representing an entity or a property or an activity, by means of *operators* specifying the kind of relationship between them. 'Washing of bottles' could thus be represented as *V67(5)Z96* by connecting notations for bottles and for washing through the effect operator *5*.

Of course, combination in itself is also possible with disciplinary classifications. Ranganathan's *subject device* allowed the classifier to specify a disciplinary class by another disciplinary class written in brackets after it. Also, two disciplinary classes could be in *phase relationship*, to express meanings like 'comparison between philosophy and religion,' or 'influence of geography on history,' or 'application of mathematics to aircraft engineering.'[3] UDC especially makes extensive use of combinations between concepts from different disciplinary classes. For example, ethics as a part of philosophy can be combined with such concepts as smoking, suicide, or abortion to class books discussing ethical views on these subjects. However, these concepts have to be taken in turn from a given disciplinary class, which implies a certain disciplinary meaning: if abortion is found under medicine, the combination will mean 'ethics of abortion-as-a-medical-practice,' and if suicide is found under law, the combination will carry a legal aspect with it. In these systems, it is not possible to refer to suicide or abortion as simple objects in themselves, expressing their connotations only by the occasional combination. What would be needed for this is what Farradane called a *place of unique definition*, identifying a concept according to its nature rather than under one disciplinary perspective or another. This can only be achieved with a classification of phenomena.

Unfortunately the CRG project came to an end without producing any final version of the system. Members more supportive of the disciplinary approach, like Mills and Langridge, applied the previous research to the construction of another disciplinary system (the second edition of the Bliss Classification); although this classification also provided initial classes for phenomena treated in an interdisciplinary way, these have never been developed (Gnoli 2005). However, the idea was there. Derek Austin was hired by the British Library, where he implemented a verbal system based on the same principles to combine concepts by operators, the Preserved Context Index System (PRECIS; see Austin 1984): a very advanced tool

---

[3] Satija (1979) appreciates that interdisciplinary studies have made multi-phased subjects inevitable. He briefly deals with their provision in several classification schemes. Though the Colon Classification is equipped through its phase relations to deal precisely with such subjects, there are only two phases in a complex class. He suggests that through a logical extension of the phase relation rules, however, the class number for a complex class of any order may be synthesised in Colon.

based on linguistic theory and general systems theory which was applied for years to the British National Bibliography.

The CRG was not alone. De Grolier (1962) surveyed dozens of efforts at that time (including the CRG) in many countries to develop 'general categories of phenomena.' For example, Gardin in France started first in archaeology and tried to develop general categories for defining, say, the shape of a knife handle, or decorations on pottery, then moved on to pictures and texts, and developed a classification of verbs. De Grolier attributes these various efforts to the introduction of 'machines' which meant that complex terms needed to be broken into simpler terms, hierarchy should be reduced, and there should be increased emphasis on relations between terms (de Grolier 1962, 10). Yet he notes that such efforts—he refers to the CRG in particular—were hard to combine into a general classification (99). De Grolier had tried to convince UDC to adopt a couple dozen general relator terms, including one for causation, but they balked, likely because such terms infused the schedules. Perrault (1969) also urged the integration of relationship terms into UDC. Donker Duyvis of UDC noted that it is easy to subdivide but difficult to give broader meaning to an existing division in a schedule (de Grolier 1962, 42). De Grolier concluded that it was not possible to renovate existing schemes beyond a certain point (de Grolier 1962, 20–1). A common auxiliary table for *Relations, Processes and Operators* has been introduced into UDC more recently (McIlwaine 2007, 87) but involves lengthy notations and is not applied widely.

Meanwhile, other classificationists were coming to similar conclusions concerning the definition of main classes by phenomena instead of disciplines. Ingetraut Dahlberg (1974, 1978) agreed with Farradane that with disciplinary systems 'difficulties were experienced whenever the same objects were treated by different disciplines,' and so resolved 'to separate the main objects and their aspect fields (subject fields, disciplines) from each other establishing thus the first two fundamental categories.' Her Information Coding Classification first lists ten classes of general objects, and then derives disciplines by applying a set of nine perspective categories to each of them. Her work thus foreshadows the approach recommended in this book not just with respect to classifying phenomena but perspective also; it differs though in still stressing disciplines (Dahlberg 2009). Martin Scheele (1977, 1983) tested a Universal Faceted Classification of phenomena where 'all notations are freely combinable among one another.' While discussing a project of classification for community information, Robin A.B. Bonner (1982) remarked that people needing to know what to do when their spouse dies are not interested in disciplines but in practical information, ranging across political sciences, religion, psychology, economics, medicine, and so on (much like in present-day e-government websites). A.A. Shpackov (1992) developed a Universal Classification of objects and their attributes as separate from research approaches. Brian Vickery (2008) suggested that 'there could be two schedules, one listing phenomena in all their variety, the other listing "viewpoints" (or preferably, activities) in all their variety, so that each set of concepts has the same freedom. Each human activity can then, in principle, be applied to any phenomenon (e.g. we can sell anything).' All these voices encourage classificationists to separate the dimension of phenomena from that of perspectives, whatever their preferred order. This is also recommended in the León Manifesto already mentioned in Chap. 1, which indeed emerged from a conference focused on interdisciplinarity in knowledge organization.[4]

Why Not Before?

If a KOS focused on phenomena is as useful as was suggested in Chaps. 2 and 3, why has it not already been developed and applied? Of course, this question can be asked of any innovation before it is successful. Yet the fact that general biblio-graphic classifications have not classified documents in the past in terms of theory and method applied, or in terms of a general classification of phenomena studied, suggests that these enterprises might be (too) difficult. We have seen above that many classificationists worked toward the development of phenomenon-based general classifications, and so ignorance of the very possibility of such an approach to classification cannot be the explanation. Weinberg (1988) herself, despite her concerns, made no recommendations for change, feeling that efforts to classify in terms of theory and method applied would be too complicated. However, several alternative explanations can be provided. These are listed in Table 4.1.

The last point merits further discussion. As noted in the Preface, this book is aimed at both information scientists and scholars of interdisciplinarity. It might be thought that the latter may have little interest in the details of KOSs. They can appreciate the interdisciplinary needs outlined in the first two chapters but may be quite happy to leave the details of their satisfaction to others. But KOSs are a major—in all likelihood *the* major—barrier to interdisciplinarity. And KOSs are complex creations. We will in this book outline the broad nature of desired KOSs and suggest a variety of specific strategies for their achievement. But the development of such KOSs will necessarily involve a host of detailed decisions, and these are best addressed by scholars with expertise in both knowledge organization and interdisciplinary studies. As we outline the contours of contemporary attempts to develop such classifications in this and later chapters, interdisciplinary scholars can reflect on how they might facilitate the development of these KOSs.

In sum the fact that it has not been done before is in no way an indication that it cannot be done in the future. This historical moment, characterized both by a widespread desire to facilitate interdisciplinarity and by rapid advances in digiti-zation (and particularly the development of the Semantic Web) creates an oppor-tunity for the development of something new. We have seen above that scholars of

---

[4] We do not survey here all of the contemporary authors or conferences which have voiced an attitude favorable to a phenomenon-based approach. Some of these voices of support are referenced on the website of the Integrative Levels Classification at http://www.iskoi.org/ilc/ref. php.

Table 4.1 Reasons that phenomenon-based classifications do not yet exist

As noted in the preceding section, it was simply too demanding to provide multiple entry points to the subject of a work in an age of card catalogues. Digitization makes it straightforward to classify (and search for) a work (or insight) along multiple dimensions.
Focus was mainly on the physical arrangement of volumes on shelves in a helpful linear sequence, so that a single dimension had to be chosen from the multidimensional subject of each work. With digitization the relative importance of shelving decisions has declined. Faceted classifications attempt to capture multiple dimensions of a work, while appreciating that one dimension must be privileged for shelving purposes.
While interdisciplinarity has been urged since the rise of disciplines in the eighteenth and nineteenth centuries, it has only become widely accepted within the academy in the last couple of decades (see Repko 2012; Klein 1990; Weingart 2010). That is, the general classifications in widespread use today were developed at a time of disciplinary hegemony (we borrow this phrase from Augsburg and Henry 2009).
Inertia is a powerful force in document classification (see above). We argued in Chap. 3 that the changes proposed in this book could not be accommodated by minor tweaks to existing systems. [Note in this regard that the systems proposed in this book rely heavily on linking concepts, and thus hold out the hope that novel areas of scholarly research can generally be accommodated by invoking linkages between existing concepts so that the elements of the classification will not require alteration as new subjects of study are brought within its purview.]
We will introduce in Chaps. 5, 6, and 7 several important strategies that are critical for the development of such a classification.
There may well be a need for interdisciplinarity in document classification itself. Both classificationist and classifier need little knowledge of the content of the documents they address if they will classify these only in terms of how the documents fit into a narrow disciplinary conception of subject matter. If instead these will be classified in terms of a general classification of phenomena, and in terms of theory and method applied, more careful content analysis—or collaboration between information scientists and other scholars—will be called for.[a]

[a]The inductive approach advocated by Hjørland and Nissen Pedersen (2005) and others represents one promising strategy for developing better classifications based on more careful analysis of texts. But as those authors freely admit, a multi-domain classification is unattainable with their approach. Knapp (2012) suggests that some form of crowd-sourcing might be employed to clarify the terminology in a general classification. Golub et al. (2014) argue that tagging works much better if participants utilize a controlled vocabulary. Bawden (2008) addresses the general question of whether information science should be interdisciplinary

knowledge organization have urged and explored the possibility of a comprehensive phenomenon-based classification throughout the last century (and more). Our work has built upon their efforts. We are fortunate to operate in a more propitious environment.

The Integrative Levels Classification Project

Classification by phenomena as separate from disciplines is being experimented with today in the Integrative Levels Classification (ILC) research project. This initiative, involving several researchers in various countries including two authors of this book, is mainly inspired by the work of the Classification Research Group

Table 4.2 Perspective facets in ILC

Notation	Facet
0	As for [perspective]
00	As attested in [document]
01	As known in [epoch]
02	As known in [place]
03	As studied by [method]
04	According to [theory]
05	Studied by [discipline]
06	As known in [culture]
07	Applied to [activity field]
08	Illustrated by [modality]
09	Conveying [communicative function]

briefly described above, though also informed by more recent literature in knowledge organization and original ideas.

The structure of a general classification scheme, conceived in a way similar to the CRG one but with new classes, categories and notational system, has been developed. Main classes, represented as lower case letters, are phenomena sorted by increasing level of organization, according to the integrative levels theory variously presented in twentieth century philosophy: from basic forms and physical quantities, through molecules, living beings, minds and societies, until the most complex technological and cultural products of the human spirit (the ILC main classes are reprised in Table 7.2 where the theory of integrative levels is discussed). Each class has its own subclasses (further letters) and facets (introduced by digits) (ILC 2004; Gnoli 2006; Gnoli et al. 2011).

The perspective dimension can be represented in the form of perspective facets (starting by *0*). These include communicative function, modality, activity field of application, discourse community, discipline, theory, method, place, epoch, and document (see Table 4.2). Thus the phenomenon *mqvo* 'birds' (a subclass of *m* organisms) can be combined with a particular discipline: *mqvo05tu* 'birds, studied in agronomy;' a particular method: *mqvo03et* 'birds, studied by telemetry;' a particular epoch: *mqvo01e* 'birds, as known in the Middle Ages,' and so on (Szostak and Gnoli 2008).

Of course, several combinations at a time are possible, to express very specific topics like those typical of scientific papers: ILC is freely faceted (Gnoli and Hong 2006), meaning that any concept can be combined with any other, like in *mqvt36vbh05tu03et* 'birds, affected by hunting, studied in agronomy, by telemetry.' The same phenomenon can thus occur in very different contexts, like *xs8mqvo* 'films, representing birds.' A search for birds in a digital environment will retrieve both documents, as well as any other in which birds appear in some combination or alone.

Disciplines themselves are listed in ILC at level *y* of knowledge phenomena: *ysq* 'linguistics,' *ytu* 'agronomy,' etc. Although usually expressed as perspective facets in the study of some phenomenon, they can well be taken as the main theme when this is needed: a book focusing on agronomy as a discipline cultivated in Asia can be indexed as *ytu2k*. Thus, ILC effectively allows works to be classified either by phenomenon or by discipline, according to the collections and needs at hand. The León Manifesto claims that in the interest of interdisciplinary research phenomena should usually be given priority.

ILC still is an ongoing, experimental project. While details of its schedules are being considered and further developed, sample collections are indexed with it in order to test the system and to refine it accordingly. The most extensive tests until now have been performed with two collections.

Where the Apennine begins is a website devoted to the peculiarities of a mountainous region in northern Italy, known as the Quattro Province. Information provided in it has naturalistic as well as cultural components, including landforms, dialects, villages, local history, traditional music and dances. It is thus a good example of an interdisciplinary domain. The website includes a bibliography on the region, which is indexed by ILC. The scheme is used here in its 'free classification' version: that is, each phenomenon class is combined with others by simply listing them separated by blank spaces, much like with tags in folksonomies (Gnoli 2010). This means that, while display in the search interface is simpler, the full expressive power of facets is not utilized. However, this simple application is already enough to show that phenomena can be a good unit, not less effective than other ones, for grouping and combining concepts, browsing them and retrieving them. This application also makes use of ILC special classes for locally-preferred concepts (deictics, represented as capital letters: Gnoli 2011).

The second relevant application is for the *BioAcoustics Reference Database* (*BARD*). This is an online bibliography of several thousands of research documents in the domain of bioacoustics, with special reference to vocal communication among whales and the impact of human-produced noises on them. It mostly includes papers, but also books and technical reports, dealing with this interdisciplinary domain across physics, biology, ethology, ocean management, technology, and sometimes even military science. Many BARD records are classified with freely-faceted ILC notation, and corresponding faceted captions are automatically synthesized and displayed (Gnoli et al. 2010). The records include such complex subjects as *t8ve49t0nm(9qvtn60v25c)* 'governments, administering conservation, by civil law, in relation to: populations, of whales, tainted by technologies, in oceanic zones,' corresponding to a highly interdisciplinary report entitled *Guidelines on the applications of the environment protection and biodiversity conservation act to interactions between offshore operations and larger cetaceans!*[5]

It is interesting to see how, by freely-faceted classification, any phenomenon can be given the role of the base theme of a document by expressing it at the beginning of faceted notation. In the document above, conservation law is the focus: hence it will be primarily grouped together with other documents on conservation laws (expressed as a facet of governments), although being also related to whales, oceans and so on. The document is retrievable by a search for these latter phenomena.

---

[5] A further example from this database was discussed in Chap. 2.

In other cases, the notation for whales, or for oceans, can be promoted to the leading position, making the item part of the documents focusing on them.

Another ILC feature that proves especially useful for BARD is the facet for methods of study: indeed, methods like remote sensing, underwater microphones, or statistical processing are often a relevant component in bioacoustics papers. Users can thus identify papers on the same phenomena studied by different methods, or on the same method applied to different phenomena, just as was recommended by the León Manifesto.

A Comparison Test

H.-Peter Ohly rightly suggested at a conference that classification by phenomena should be evaluated against a traditional disciplinary classification by some comparison test. Although no significant quantitative data are available yet, some insights can be drawn from a first set of books on nature conservation at the University of Pavia Science and Technology Library. These documents, already classified by DDC in the national online catalog SBN, were also classified by ILC, so that the resulting arrangements and indexes by the two systems could be compared. Land conservation is another domain where documents often manifest an interdisciplinary character, connecting geological, botanical and zoological components of natural areas with ecology, law, public administration, and economics including both production and tourism.

Indeed, DDC classes assigned to these documents in the national catalog belonged to various disciplinary classes such as social sciences (economy of natural resources, law, and management of environment-related social problems), natural sciences (ecology, botany), applied sciences (health, engineering, and forestry), the arts (landscape architecture), and geography. ILC classes, on the other hand, mainly belonged to phenomena at the levels of land (territories, aquifers), organisms (plants), populations and ecosystems, government institutions, and technologies (land management, industries). Classes of both systems were thus scattered, although their resulting sequence was quite different since they were based on different principles for main class order: intellectual capacities for DDC, and integrative levels for ILC. In some cases, potentially useful groupings proved possible in ILC ('plants') though not in DDC ('ecology of plants' is separated from 'botany').

The main difference was that DDC forced the indexers to choose one class while hiding others, as it prescribes that only one theme of the document be expressed: either a document is on economics of natural resources, or it is on ecology, while the links between the two disciplines are only committed to cross references in the classification schedules. On the other hand, in ILC the base phenomenon could easily be connected with other phenomena by means of free facets, giving compound concepts like 'ecosystems, as object of land management, by some law.'

Table 4.3 Facet categories in ILC

Notation	Facet
0	As for [perspective]
1	At [time]
2	In [place]
3	Through [process]
4	Made of [element]
5	With [organ]
6	From [origin]
7	To [destination]
8	Like [pattern]
9	Of [kind]

The nature of these relationships, expressed by the facet digits, can also prove useful for specialized searches. Table 4.3 lists the main facet categories in ILC.

These categories can combine into more specialized facets, e.g. *03* expresses process in perspective, that is method, as seen in the examples above.

Notation length can be an issue in classification, especially for shelving purposes (see Chap. 3). Although expressing a greater number of connected concepts, ILC classmarks proved to be of length comparable to DDC ones: indeed, each concept has on average a shorter notation, as being selected from arrays of 26 letters instead of 10 digits. On the other hand, DDC classmarks can be praised for their visual plainness, being formed only by a sequence of digits.

It has to be acknowledged that forcing the indexer to choose a single class is not necessarily a limitation of any disciplinary classification: indeed, another disciplinary system like UDC does allow for combinations between main classes separating them by a colon. In an online search, both UDC and ILC would then allow, in contrast to DDC, the user to retrieve particular themes connected to the one given priority. What remains different is that disciplinary schemes connect disciplines, like geography, botany or economics, rather than connecting phenomena, like territories, plants or management activities: they cannot avoid, when combining concepts, to carry disciplinary implications with them, although their meaning may represent the document content inaccurately (a plant is a plant in any context, but is not always an object of botanical study).

Furthermore, in some cases the DDC lists a very specific concept only under a given discipline, thus forcing the classificationist to choose that concept even if the actual document focus is on a combined concept that is not part of the same discipline; a phenomenon-based system, instead, can express both, and at the same time give priority to the one taken as the base theme in the document ('governments, managing conservation' as opposed to 'conservation, managed by governments' for a book on citizens participation in the management of nature parks, which was classed with DDC under 'economics of natural resources'). Also, a guide to trade laws and legal protection of animal and plant species, going under DDC class 'international law: protection and endorsement of natural resources,' was collocated by ILC into 'economies, administrated by the United Nations, of organisms, through trade,' thus reflecting priority of the economic facet in the actual book.

Another difference is that, while disciplinary classification tends to group documents into box-like classes having a certain scope, phenomenon-based classification tends to point to precise concepts, because its notation is built as a combination of individual concepts, much as happens with a thesaurus. In many cases the result is not very different, as even disciplines can be subdivided into deep hierarchies with longer numbers, and the deepest specifications are often labeled by phenomenon terms, as was observed above while discussing the class of bats within zoology. This is what happens in such cases as DDC class *363.73* 'social welfare and security: environmental problems and services: pollution,' assigned to a book which in ILC was classified as 'ecosystems, polluted by something, as related to organisms.' In some cases, however, box-like disciplinary classes cause a partial loss of meaning: a book on spontaneous flowers in Lombardy natural reserves, going under DDC class *581.9452* 'botany, Lombardy,' could be indexed by ILC classmark *mpw5w29ed* 'angiospermae, with flowers, in Lombardy,' thus keeping track of the focus on flowers as a relevant organ of those plants. Another book on rural society and buildings in a country municipality, filed under 'history of the Como province' in DDC, could be indexed more precisely in ILC as 'villages, in the Lambro basin, in the eighteenth to nineteenth century,' thus making the specific concept of villages as artifacts free from the disciplinary context of history, and, at the same time, giving the identity of the place in question as a physical-geographical territory (i.e., 'Lambro basin'), which maintains its identity over time, and so distinguishing it from its contemporary political administration (i.e., 'Como province'), which has changed over time.

The Basic Concepts Classification

The Basic Concepts Classification (Szostak 2013a) adheres to most of the organizing principles of the ILC outlined above. It also organizes its main classes around integrative levels (though as in ILC there are several main classes at the highest level of social interaction). It allows the free combination of any terms in the classification. Disciplines are themselves classified within the classification of phenomena, as in ILC, and thus can again be designated as necessary in describing any work. As with ILC, allowing the free combination of terms allows very precise classification of works utilizing modest schedules.

Though the BCC is grounded in the literature on facet analysis, it recognizes facets structurally rather than through the use of explicit facet indicators. Its macrostructure is based on three fundamental categories. The most extensive schedule lists classes of phenomena (there are some 20 main classes at present, each designated by a capital letter, usually the first letter of the class name: *C* is Culture). These classes are then subdivided (first by another capital letter, so that *CV* denotes values, then by numbers, then by lower case letters). Subdivision proceeds logically in terms of generic ('type of') or sometimes partitive ('part of') relationships. As noted in previous chapters this practice is facilitated by the synthetic approach: enumerative classifications often deviate from logical hierarchy in order to find a place for compound subjects. The second type of schedule classifies type of relationship. Non-causal relationships are designated with a variety of non-alphabetic and non-numeric symbols (-, <, ~, ^, and so on). Causal relationships are indicated by the use of arrows (which signal the direction of influence). Some 100 relationships are organized into four broad classes, and about a dozen subclasses in total (each relationship is designated by lower-case italicized pairs of letters). These hundred can be combined with each other, and/or with phenomena or properties (see below) or non-causal relationships, to generate hundreds of more precise relationships (persuasion—*rsrt*—combines control—*rs*—and talking: *rt*). The classification of relationships was developed in Szostak (2012a, b). The third type of schedule is the classification of adverbial/adjectival properties (these are designated by the letter *Q* for Qualities, and are subdivided in the same manner as phenomena).

The BCC website (Szostak 2013a) discusses how each of the facets recognized in both the Bliss Classification and the ILC are captured and clearly designated by the free combination of phenomena, relationships, and/or properties. Most obviously, the agent (cause), product (outcome), and patient (intermediate variable) in a causal relationship are clear in a classification of the form A(influences)B(influences)C.

The BCC is motivated by the recognition that the vast majority of scholarly research, and most non-scholarly works as well, focus on discussing how one or more phenomena influence one or more others. The best and easiest way to classify such works is a synthetic approach of the form (phenomenon) (type of influence) (phenomenon) (see Szostak 2012c). Note that this sort of approach was advocated by the Classification Research Group (see above). A minority of works discuss the internal composition or behavior of a single phenomenon. These are best captured through recourse to classifications of both phenomena and properties, or to the use of such relationships as 'contained in' or 'composed of.' This simple approach not only facilitates the work of both classificationist and classifier (because small schedules can in combination generate precise designations) but also the user, for they can search by combinations of simple terms.

The BCC instantiates a web-of-relations approach to classification as urged in Olson (2007). A user that starts with an interest in cats, can follow their curiosity to (cats) (compared to) (dogs), and on to (dogs) (bite) (mail carriers). Only a synthetic approach that allows the free combination of any phenomena, relationship and/or property allows users to so easily follow their curiosity from one subject to a related subject. And by facilitating this sort of movement through the web of information we greatly facilitate what is variously called 'undiscovered public knowledge,' 'literature-based discovery,' or 'serendipity:' the connection of related ideas from disparate literatures that generate a new insight (see Chap. 1).

The León Manifesto suggested that works should be classified not just in terms of phenomena and relationships, but also in terms of the theory and method applied in a work. As noted in previous chapters it is also beneficial to classify with respect to various elements of authorial perspective. The BCC, like the ILC, captures methods and theory types within its schedules, and aspires to capture various elements of perspective as well.

The most detailed application of the BCC has been in a translation exercise in which DDC classes *300* to *345* [and later all classes in ICONCLASS] were translated into BCC. This exercise (see Szostak 2013b) was summarized in Szostak (2011). It was straightforward to translate each DDC entry. The result in each case was a notation of quite manageable length. And the translation quite often served to clarify quite vague DDC terminology (see Chap. 5). If a system such as BCC were adopted as a complement to DDC, and such translation became automatic, then concepts added in future would be clarified at the outset. Moreover, it should be stressed that such a translation exercise undervalues the BCC, relative to an exercise that would code various works directly in BCC. The DDC tries to designate works according to brief class titles whereas the BCC designates works as combinations of terms. This, quite simply, gives a much more precise description of the contents of a work.

Like the ILC, the BCC is a work in progress. Yet the broad outlines of the classification are fully developed. The DDC translation exercise indicates that the classification can cope nicely with classifying social science material. Szostak (2014a) shows how the classification can cope better than existing classifications with the demands of the humanities. The natural sciences are a challenge for any classification because of the vast numbers of species and chemical compounds that must be classified. Much clarification of the classification of species can be anticipated from biologists over the next few years, due to advances in genetic analysis, and the BCC can take advantage of these developments.

Key Points

There are historical reasons for the dominance today of discipline-based classification systems. Yet there is a long tradition in the field of knowledge organization of advocating and exploring phenomena-based classifications. It is difficult to switch from one historical path to another, but hardly impossible. The rise of both interdisciplinarity and digitization facilitate and encourage such a transformation. The Integrative Levels Classification and Basic Concepts Classification have both been developed in response to these influences. They have each been developed and tested to an extent that establishes the broad feasibility of such a classification.

References

Augsburg T, Henry S (eds) (2009) The politics of interdisciplinary studies. McFarland Press, Jefferson, NC

Austin DW (1969) Prospects for a new general classification. J Librarianship 1(3):149–169

Austin DW (1984) PRECIS, a manual of concept analysis and subject indexing, 2nd edn. British Library, London

Bawden D (2008) Smoother pebbles and the shoulders of giants; the developing foundations of information science. J Inform Sci 34(4):415–426

Beghtol C (2004) Exploring new approaches to the organization of knowledge: James Duff Brown. Libr Trends 52(4):702–718

Bonner R (1982) Community information classification research project: user oriented empirical methods of classification construction. In: Dahlberg I (ed) Universal classification: proceedings of the 4th international study conference on classification research. Indeks, Frankfurt, pp 227–234

Broughton V (2004) Essential classification. Schulman, London

Brown JD (1906) Subject classification. The London Supply, London

Classification Research Group (1969) Classification and information control. Library Association, London

Classification Research Group (1973) Bulletin n. 10. J Doc 29:51–71, 56

Classification Research Group (1978) Bulletin n. 11. J Doc 34(1):21–50, 25

Dahlberg (1974) Grundlagen universaler wissensordnung. Probleme und möglichkeiten eines universalen klassifikationssystems des wissens. Pullach bei München: Verlag Dokumentation

Dahlberg I (1978) Ontical structures and universal classification. SRELS, Bangalore, India

Dahlherg I (2009) Concepts and terms: ISKO's major challenge. Knowl Org 36(2/3):169–177

De Grolier E (1962) A study of general categories applicable to classification and coding in documentation. UNESCO, Paris

Gnoli C (2005) BC2 classes for phenomena: an application of the theory of integrative levels. Bliss Classif Bull 47:17–21

Gnoli C (2006) The meaning of facets in non-disciplinary classification. In: Budin G, Swertz C, Mitgutsch K (eds) Knowledge Organization for a global learning society: proceedings of the 9th ISKO conference. Ergon, Würzburg, pp 11–18

Gnoli C (2010) Themes and citation order in free classification. IASLIC Bull 55(1):13–19

Gnoli C (2011) Animals belonging to the emperor: enabling viewpoint warrant in classification. In: Landry P, Bultrini L, O'Neill ET, Roe SK (eds) Subject access: preparing for the future. De Gruyter, Berlin, pp 91–100

Gnoli C, Hong M (2006) Freely faceted classification for Web-based information retrieval. New Rev Hyperm Multimedia 12(1):63–81

Gnoli C, Merli G, Pavan G, Bernuzzi E, Priano M (2010) Freely faceted classification for a Web-based bibliographic archive: the BioAcoustic Reference Database. In: Sieglerschmidt J, Ohly H-P (eds) Wissensspeicher in digitalen Räumen: Nachhaltigkeit, Verfügbarkeit, semantische Interoperabilität: Proceedings der 11. Tagung der Deutschen Sektion der Internationalen Gesellschaft für Wissenorganisation, Konstan [Knowledge storage in digital space: persistence, availability, semantic interoperability]. Ergon, Würzburg, pp 124–134

Gnoli C, Pullmann T, Cousson P, Merli G, Szostak R (2011) Representing the structural elements of a freely faceted classification. In: Slavic A, Civallero E (eds) Classification and ontology: formal approaches and access to knowledge: proceedings of the International UDC Seminar, The Hague. Ergon Verlag, Würzburg, pp 193–206

Golub K, Lykke M, Tudhope D (2014) Enhancing social tagging with automated keywords from the Dewey Decimal classification. J Doc 70(5):801–828

Hartel J (2003) The serious leisure frontier in library and information science: Hobby domains. Knowl Org 30(3/4):228–238

Hjørland B, Nissen Pedersen K (2005) A substantive theory of classification for information retrieval. J Doc 61(5):582–595

Integrative Levels Classification (ILC) (2004) ISKO Italia. www.iskoi.org/ilc/

Kaiser JO (1911) Systematic indexing. Pitman, London

Klein JT (1990) Interdisciplinarity: history, theory and practice. The Wayne State University Press, Detroit

Knapp JA (2012) Plugging the 'whole': librarians as interdisciplinary facilitators. Libr Rev 61 (3):199–214

McIlwaine IC (2007) The universal decimal classification: a guide to its use, Revised ed. UDC Consortium, The Hague

Olson H (2007) How we construct subjects: a feminist analysis. Library Trends 56(2):509–541

Otlet P (1896) Rules for developing the decimal classification. Office international de bibliographie, Bruxelles, Translated in W. Boyd Rayward (1990) International organization and dissemination of knowledge: selected essays of Paul Otlet. Elsevier, Amsterdam. pp 63–70

Perrault JM (1969) Towards a theory for UDC. Bingley, London

Repko AF (2012) Interdisciplinary research: process and theory, 2nd edn. Sage, Thousand Oaks

Satija MP (1979) Extension of two-phased subjects in the Colon Classification. Herald Libr Sci 18 (4):344–348

Scheele M (1977) Ordnung und Wortschatz des Wissens, v. 1: Das Ordnungssystem, Universal Faceted Classification. Schlitz, Guntrum

Scheele M (1983) Automatic indexing of titles and keywords on the basis of a model for an overall thesaurus of knowledge. Int Classif 10:135–137

Shpackov AA (1992) The nature and boundaries of information science(s). J Am Soc Inform Sci Technol 43(10):679

Slavic A (2007) On the nature and typology of documentary classifications and their use in a networked environment. El profesional de la información 16(6):580–589

Szostak R (2011) Complex concepts into basic concepts. J Am Soc Inform Soc Technol 62 (11):2247–2265

Szostak R (2012a) Classifying relationships. Knowl Org 39(3):165–178

Szostak R (2012b) Toward a classification of relationships. Knowl Org 39(2):83–94

Szostak R (2012c). Classification in terms of basic concepts. Advances in Classification Research 2012, proceedings of the ASIST SIG/CR Workshop, October 26, 2012, Baltimore, MD, USA. http://journals.lib.washington.edu/index.php/acro/article/view/14234

Szostak R (2013a) Basic concepts classification. https://sites.google.com/a/ualberta.ca/rick-szostak/research/basic-concepts-classification-web-version-2013

Szostak R (2013b) Translation table: DDC [Dewey Decimal Classification] to basic concepts classification. http://www.economics.ualberta.ca/en/FacultyandStaff/~/media/economics/FacultyAndStaff/Szostak/Szostak-Dewey-Conversion-Table.pdf

Szostak R (2014) Classifying the humanities. Knowl Org 41(4):263–275

Szostak R, Gnoli C (2008) Classifying by phenomena, theories, and methods: examples with focused social science theories. In: Arsenault C, Tennis J (eds) Culture and identity in knowledge organization, proceedings of the 10th international ISKO conference, Montréal. Ergon, Würzburg, pp 205–211

Vickery BC (2008) The structure of subject classifications for document retrieval. http://www.iskoi.org/ilc/vickery.php

Weinberg BH (1988) Why indexing fails the researcher. Indexer 16(1):3–6, http://people.unt.edu/~skh0001/wein1.htm

Weingart P (2010) A short history of knowledge formations. In: Frodeman R, Klein JT, Mitcham C (eds) The Oxford handbook of interdisciplinarity. Oxford University Press, New York, pp 3–14

Chapter 5
The Feasibility of Developing Such Knowledge Organization Systems

Existing classification systems such as the Library of Congress (LCC) or Dewey Decimal (DDC) benefit from over a century of refinement. It is thus no simple task to develop a novel classification that might supersede (or simply complement) these. Knapp (2012) is one scholar who applauds the sort of classification being urged in this book, but worries about the feasibility of developing an entirely new classification. Yet the argument of this chapter is that it is indeed possible to do so. We will first make some general remarks regarding feasibility, and then proceed to a discussion of each of the elements of a new system that were proposed in the preceding chapters.

The Digital Revolution and the Historical Moment

The digital revolution creates a unique opportunity for the development of a new system for it highlights the limitations of classifications developed for card catalogs (Dean 2003). Moreover the proliferation of new databases with unique classifications increases the desirability of a classification that could be general in application. There is even a direct connection with interdisciplinarity: online access increases the likelihood of citation of works in other fields on a topic, articles by lesser-known authors, articles in less prestigious journals, and older articles—but only at the cost of increasing information overload (Wu et al. 2012).

While the digital revolution exposes certain weaknesses of existing systems, it at the same time creates opportunities for the new. In particular, digitization means that it is easier to classify documents along multiple dimensions. In an age of card catalogues, it was expensive to classify a work in more than one or two ways through such procedures as chain indexing (Coates 1988), for each entry point required a new card to be typed and placed in the catalogue. For example the freely faceted PRECIS system (Austin 1984) proved very demanding in terms of production work and costs. Today, the cost of adding another entry point is much smaller.

© Springer International Publishing Switzerland 2016
R. Szostak et al., *Interdisciplinary Knowledge Organization*,
DOI 10.1007/978-3-319-30148-8_5

Thus, even if we were not facing the rising importance of interdisciplinarity, it would make sense at this historical moment to explore the possibility that a system designed for the digital age might be preferable to systems designed for card catalogues. And in particular it makes sense to ask whether we should provide much more information about particular works than is done at present. As the trend toward the assignment of more kinds of metadata (data about documents, such as title, author, subject, and so on) attests, the digitization of KOSs encourages the indexing of documents along a wider range of dimensions. We will not reiterate this point in what follows but rather will presume that in the present age it makes sense to provide more information as long as this can easily be provided in a useful format. We can thus focus on questions of classification rather than cost.

Classifying Comprehensively with Respect to Phenomena

The main objection to the feasibility of a comprehensive classification of phenomena is that the meaning of concepts differs too much across fields. It is thus felt that a comprehensive classification would lead to confusion, for scholars from different fields would attach quite different meanings to the terms employed.

A variety of theoretical arguments can be made in support of the feasibility of a comprehensive classification. These are summarized in Table 5.1.

Questions of feasibility cannot be decided on theoretical grounds alone. It is necessary to develop at least some significant portions of such a classification in order to fully establish feasibility. There are two contemporary classifications that do precisely that:

- The Integrative Levels Classification (ILC 2004).
- The Basic Concepts Classification (BCC) (Szostak 2013a).

Each of these classifications (which differ primarily in how they employ facet analysis, and how far they proceed in the decomposition of complex concepts) builds upon the efforts of the Classification Research Group (CRG, especially Douglas Foskett and Derek Austin) to develop general classifications of phenomena. As with the earlier works of the CRG (and indeed all classifications to at least some extent), these classifications are hierarchical. A manageable set of main classes of phenomena is identified, and these are unpacked or disaggregated into multiple degrees of constituent phenomena. In both cases, phenomena can usually be well defined, either in terms of their internal essence or their function. [Gnoli and Poli (2004) argue that functional definitions only make sense for phenomena of a level of complexity equal to or beyond biological organisms; for atomic particles and chemical elements definition in terms of essence are superior.] It can thus be expected that a comprehensive classification of phenomena will not be invalidated by time: most phenomena included will retain their

Table 5.1 Theoretical justifications of comprehensive phenomenon-based classification

Ambiguity differs only by degree between general and discipline-specific classifications, though that difference of degree is likely quite significant. The degree of ambiguity lessens within groups that regularly interact (though it does not disappear). Yet it is equally clear that conversations across groups speaking different primary dialects are possible (or international tourism would be impossible).
The classification structure itself contributes to making clear the meaning of a concept and the terms expressing it, by showing for each class its hierarchical and associative relationships with related classes, as well as by providing scope notes. This is true both in a classification by disciplines and in one by phenomena: in the latter case, concepts will take more general and neutral meanings, depending on their 'unique definition' within the classification rather than their contexts of use. This will make them reusable in a variety of domains.
The degree of ambiguity generally increases with the complexity of a term. 'Dog' lends itself to a greater degree of shared understanding across fields (or indeed people) than does 'globalization.' If, as was suggested in Chap. 3, works about globalization were classified in terms of how particular economic, political, or cultural developments affected other particular economic, political or cultural elements (and also in terms of the ethical and ideological perspective pursued), the degree of ambiguity is thus much less than if they are just classified in terms of 'globalization.' We return to this line of argument in Chap. 9.
Interdisciplinary scholars recommend a strategy of 'redefinition' to confront the problems that arise when a term has different meanings across disciplines (or other groups). The term is provided with a specific meaning that will make sense to scholars from all disciplines (see Repko 2012). This strategy is employed successfully in several chapters in Repko et al. (2012). Van der Lecq (2012), for example, notes that different fields studying the emergence of language in humans employ the terms 'evolution' and 'communication' in slightly different ways; redefinition alleviates much (though not all) of the conflict with respect to identifying the causes of this important development. To be sure, the strategy is employed narrowly to allow interdisciplinary investigation of a particular problem. But its success certainly at least opens the door to a broader effort at 'redefinition.'
Psychologists suspect that there are universals in how human beings think and perhaps in how they organize their conceptual maps (especially evolutionary psychologists; Barkow et al. 1992). Neelameghan argued at length in the 1970s that it should be possible to develop subject representations grounded in these universals (Iyer 1995, 184). Evolutionary psychologists would suggest that such universals are more likely with respect to activities that humans undertook during the millennia humanity operated as hunter-gatherers. If so, general classifications will face greater difficulties in some realms than others. Yet it seems likely that any innate human classification system will be organized around phenomena rather than disciplines: 'If . . . the patron asks for a book on birds, he expects that a section in the library contains all bird books. . . . To the extent that they do not (e.g. bird books are spread out into many different places), the system is awkward and irrational from the patron's perspective, regardless of its logical consistency from the librarian's' (Donovan 1991, 26). The conceptual atomism approach advocated by some philosophers of concepts indicates that diverse people should share broadly similar understandings of concepts signifying the things (and relationships) that we regularly perceive in the world around us (Szostak 2011).

meaning. While neither classification has yet been subjected to detailed user testing (a matter we will return to in the concluding chapter), both projects have proceeded far enough to establish feasibility in several respects. This empirical evidence is summarized in Table 5.2.

Table 5.2 Empirical evidence of the feasibility of a comprehensive phenomenon-based classification

Lengthy schedules of phenomena have been developed for each (with ILC having focused relatively more attention on natural science and BCC on human science). Readers are urged to peruse the schedules and contemplate whether most/all of the entries would be understood similarly across fields (or could be provided with a definition that would facilitate this).
Hundreds of records in special bibliographies as different as local culture (Gnoli 2010) and bioacoustics (Gnoli et al. 2008) have been carefully classified by ILC and can be searched by it through online interfaces.
The entries in the Dewey Decimal Classification (DDC) from 300 to 340 [and also all of ICONCLASS] have been translated into terms of the BCC (Szostak 2011; 2013b). Arguably, the BCC translation provides a less ambiguous classification than the DDC original. And this is the standard that a new classification needs to meet: not that it can provide a complete absence of ambiguity but that it can achieve at least the same degree of ambiguity as existing systems of document classification. Most DDC entries can be translated into 'very basic' concepts for which the degree of ambiguity is minimal. All DDC entries can be translated into concepts that are 'somewhat basic' in the sense that the degree of ambiguity, at least potentially, might be considered acceptable from the point of view of information science. They are certainly much 'more basic' than the complex terms translated. Recall that the translation of DDC entries often served to clarify the meaning of DDC entries themselves. Such clarification would be even greater if new DDC entries were made with translation to/from basic concepts in mind. The translation thus has the potential to enhance cross-disciplinary communication while also enhancing within-discipline communication.
Szostak (2003) established that *the arguments of* hundreds of works from across the human sciences could be classified in terms of a simple but general classification of phenomena. Indeed this was possible employing a much less sophisticated classification than the present BCC.

The Feasibility of Classifying Relationships

As we have seen, interdisciplinary research usually involves the study of relationships among phenomena studied in different disciplines. Yet it is not only interdisciplinary researchers who would benefit from increased classificatory attention to relationships. Indeed, most scholarly research studies not just one phenomenon but the influence that one or more phenomena exert on others. A scholar interested in how, say, economic productivity is influenced by the level of trust in a society will wish to consult works investigating that causal link but not every work on trust or economic productivity. This outcome can be achieved by using linked notation between phenomena to indicate the main causal link(s) pursued in a work. This focus on links would further enhance the utility of document classifications to researchers. Note in this regard that discipline-based classifications would face difficulty in capturing interdisciplinary causal links. The different terminology used for each phenomenon involved would multiply the number of ways in which the same link might be classified. But once we successfully develop a comprehensive classification of phenomena it should be straightforward to allow these to be linked to express causal or other relationships.

The information science community has displayed a renewed interest in classifying relationships in recent years (see Green 2008). Khoo and Na (2006) predict that relationships will become increasingly important in the field. Notably, they argue that research in information retrieval has proceeded about as far as it can without addressing relationships. They appreciate that there is a great deal of experimental evidence that relationships are 'real' and that there are cross-cultural similarities in perception.[1] Moreover, relationships are of critical importance to human memory. These observations bode well for the feasibility (and desirability) of developing a comprehensive classification of relationships.[2]

The next question is how detailed should we be in classifying relationships? Much that is useful can be achieved by simply indicating that A affects B (or is associated with B, and so on). But if we hope to capture the relationships referred to across diverse fields, a much more detailed classification is surely called for. Is it feasible to develop a more detailed classification of relationships? Szostak (2012a, b) has produced such a classification, which is now incorporated into the Basic Concepts Classification (see above; Szostak 2013a). Most of the attention is devoted to causal relationships—organized into a handful of categories (three types each of physical, biological, and intentional causation, plus a general class)—but a schedule of non-causal relationships is also developed (not, or, by, of, for, of type, in, about, compared to, associated with, from the perspective of, collection of, and a handful of mathematical relators). ILC facets, by which any phenomena can be linked, are based on the set of ten fundamental categories introduced in Chap. 4 (kind, pattern, destination, origin, organ, element, process, place, time, perspective) and their subtypes; in principle, indefinitely specific subtypes can be created through categories combination (Gnoli 2008). While care must be taken in evaluating any novel classification—and we will return to questions of evaluation in Chap. 10—a few characteristics of these two relationship-oriented classifications are worthy of note, as summarized in Table 5.3.

It is useful in Table 5.4 to provide some examples of the compound relators employed in BCC. These examples highlight how a synthetic approach can generate thousands of precise relationship terms from less than 100 basic relationship terms (many more examples are provided in Szostak 2013b).

As noted above, the classification developed in Szostak (2012a) devotes the bulk of its attention to causal relationships, but does include a set of non-causal relationships. This accords with the arguments made in Chap. 3 regarding the particular importance of causal relationships. Previous efforts to classify relationships as surveyed by Perrault (1994) had not placed the same emphasis on causal relationships. Moreover those classifications were generally deductive exercises not grounded in an inductive evaluation of the needs of researchers. This fact, plus the inertia associated with noun-focused classification systems that largely

---

[1] López-Huertas (2013) has studied cross-cultural understandings more generally, and found that there are shared understandings of some terms but not others.

[2] Khoo and Na (2006) proceed to discuss different sorts of semantic relationship (such as conjunction versus disjunction) and note that there is no scholarly consensus on a classification of these. But we have not identified that sort of distinction in our inventory of classificatory needs.

Table 5.3 Characteristics of the classification of relationships

The schedules are of very manageable length.
They are logically organized into a very manageable number of classes, each containing a handful of entries.
The distinctions among classes are transparent.
Yet these schedules and the compounds that can be generated from them capture all of the terms uncovered in a very broad inductive search for relators, as well as those implicated in previous deductive efforts to develop such a classification.
Thus all such terms can potentially be represented notationally within a mere handful of notational spaces.
Inspection of the schedules indicates that classes in the schedules would generally be interpreted in a very similar manner across disciplines and cultures (see Szostak 2011). Indeed, there may be less ambiguity associated in general with 'action' words.
This classification of relationships thus potentially allows for the first time searches by 'type of relationship' across an entire general classification.

eschewed synthetic notations, could explain why none of these previous efforts were incorporated into a larger classification. The renewed interest in relationships within the field of information science suggests that the time has come for the development and utilization of a classification of relationships that is grounded in an understanding of user needs. This will benefit all users but interdisciplinary scholars in particular.

Classifying with Respect to Theory Applied

Theories present great challenges for classification. One problem is that there is a potentially infinite number of theories, for new theories are invented every day in the scholarly enterprise. On its own this is a challenge often faced in classification, and one that can be dealt with by a hospitable (that is, expandable) classification with room for new classes.

More importantly, and as noted previously, there is considerable terminological confusion in the area of theory: the same theory name encompasses quite different types of theory, while quite similar theories go by different names (especially across disciplines). Even advocates of a particular theory quarrel about what the essence of their theory is (see, for example, Turner 2000). A classification grounded *only* in the names used by authors to describe their theories would thus generate the same sorts of confusion that the classification of subject matter in terms of disciplinary categories does. Nor is the only problem one of cross-disciplinary communication, for theories evolve through time (much more than do definitions of phenomena, though these if not carefully defined could evolve too), and thus an author using a theory today could have quite different ideas from an author using the same theory a decade before. While a classification in terms of the theoretical terms used by authors would be an important improvement over no classification by

Table 5.4 Examples of compound relators

Type of compound	Examples
Causal relator with causal relator	'Persuade' combines 'control' and 'talk'
	'Imagine' combines 'think' and 'desire'
	'Agree' combines 'decide' and 'cooperate'
	'Monitor' combines 'observe' and 'evaluate'
Causal relator with non-causal relators	'Herd' is (move) (collection of) (animals or people)
	'Attach' is (cause) (to be connected)
	'Search' is (look) (for)
Causal relator with indicators of internal changes (such as grow, decline, and maintain stability)	'Enhance' is (cause) (growth)
	'Stabilize' is (cause) (stable).
	'Include' is either (cause to be) (combined) or (cause to be) (contained in) [note that the ambiguity in the verb 'include' is thus addressed]
Causal relator with adverbial properties	'Suffer' is (experience) (bad)
	'Conspire' is (cooperate) (secretly)
	Dozens of combinations of 'cause' are possible such as (cause) (decorated) or (cause) (clean)
Causal relator with phenomena	'Possess' is (control) (by) (ownership)
	'Flying' is (moving) (by) (airplane)
	Again many combinations with 'cause' are possible such as (cause) (injury)
Complex causal chains	'Campaign' is (attempt) ((control) (by) (talking)) (associated with) (election)
	'Zoning' is (local government) (controls) (economic output) (associated with) (land)
	'Evict' is (move) (someone) (from) (home or office)

theory whatsoever, it would thus be insufficient in important respects. The researcher wondering if a particular theoretical argument has been applied to a particular set of phenomena will receive limited guidance if the literature is classified only with respect to the names of theories.

This terminological problem might be approached inductively, in order to identify what meanings are attached by different communities to different theory names. Recall, though, that inductive methods are generally applied only within particular scholarly communities. Happily, a deductive approach is available. A variety of theory types can be identified along several key dimensions: who is the active agent(s) in the theory, what do they do, why do they do it, what sort of process through time is envisaged, and how generalizable is the theory? This five-dimensional typology of theory types was developed through recourse to one of the simplest classificatory devices: asking the 5 W questions, who, what, where, when, and why. These in the context of theory yield more precise questions, and in each

Table 5.5 Dimensions of theory types

Questions	Possible answers
Who is the agent?	There are two immediate distinctions here: non-intentional (including volcanoes or institutions) versus intentional agency (of beings that can act on purpose), each of which can take the form of individual, group, or relationship agency.
What does the agent do?	There are three broad answers: passive reaction, active action, changes in attitude.
Why does the agent do this?	With non-intentional agents, action can only be understood in terms of their inherent nature. With intentional agents, scholars can explore the five distinct types of decision-making: rational, intuitive, process oriented (which emphasizes how one behaves rather than what one achieves, and encompasses various virtues or values that one might pursue), rule-based (where one follows certain guidelines such as the Golden Rule), and tradition-based. For groups and relationships, scholars can also ask how individual preferences are aggregated.
Where does the causal process occur? *(How generalizable is the theory?)*	There is a continuum from nomothetic (highly generalizable), through somewhat generalizable, to idiographic (situation- or causal-link-specific) theory.
When does the causal process occur?	Though inspired by the temporal question 'when?', the possibilities refer ontologically to directions of change. There are five broad time-paths that a causal process might follow: return to the original equilibrium, cyclical oscillation, movement to a new equilibrium, change in a particular direction, or stochastic/uncertain.

case a mere handful of possible answers (see Table 5.5; Szostak 2004). Note that this set of dimensions, though logically derived, is expandable should other useful dimensions be identified.

We noted in Chap. 1 that a major driver of interdisciplinary research is the desire to tackle complex challenges. Since complex social problems involve multiple types of agency, decision-making, and so on, the typology suggests that any one theory will give incomplete guidance. Familiarity with the typology would guide analysts to recognize the limitations of a particular theory for a particular question, and to identify other theories with compensating strengths. The use of the typology is thus consistent with postmodern concerns that multiple perspectives be heard. Yet whereas postmodernists are often skeptical of the ability of different communities—either scholarly communities or societal groupings—to converse with each other, the typology indicates that it is quite feasible to understand the strengths and weaknesses of different theories and at least strive toward some consensus on how important different theoretical arguments are for particular questions.

Individual theories can be placed within the typology, and thus works can be classified simultaneously by theory and by theory type. Researchers can then search by theory name or by a particular type of theory. The typology has been applied to the set of social 'grand' theories identified in Turner (2000) in Szostak (2004), and also to a random set of more narrowly focused theories in Szostak and Gnoli (2008). That paper surveyed a handful of research areas in social science, and showed that the theories encountered in each can be reliably classified in terms of theory types. That paper also provided ILC notation for each theory type. [The various theory types have since been incorporated into the BCC as well.] In both cases it proved straightforward to classify particular uses of a theory in terms of theory types.

The analysis of Marxian theory in Szostak and Gnoli (2008) highlights how classifying works in terms of theory type will clarify the theoretical approach taken in a work much better than simply referring to a theory name such as Marxian theory. Marxian theory at times stresses technological determinism, and other times stresses the importance of class struggle. The first is a form of non-intentional individual causation, while the latter reflects intentional group agency. The first invokes passive reaction to technological innovations. The second argument also at times assumed inevitability but at other times Marx (and especially later Marxists) stressed active action. References to class consciousness bring groups and attitudes to the fore, but assumptions of historical inevitability counteract this tendency. Inevitability implies movement to a new (socialist) equilibrium; some Marxian theories accept instead the importance of historical contingency and thus imply a stochastic process. Contingent approaches open space for intentional individual or relationship agency. As for generalizability, though Marxian theory is often perceived as universal in orientation Marx himself at least once suggested that his historical process applied only to Europe.

The approach of classifying by theory type solves immediately the problem of different theories operating under the same name. It would be hoped that users would be informed in scope notes that a particular theory name is associated with quite different theory types. The user should also be guided to quite similar theories operating under different theory names. The user might even specify an interest in alternative theories that are similar in certain respects: same type of agency or action or dynamic process.

As noted above, theories evolve through time. And theorists disagree about what a particular theory entails. As a result many theories sprawl across multiple theory types. While this fact complicates the life of the classifier—they must look beyond theory name—it has enormous advantages for the researcher who wishes to only read, say, 'Marxian theory of a particular type.'

One difficulty encountered by Szostak and Gnoli (2008) deserves mention. In some cases, authors are vague about the theory type that they are applying. But this challenge also presents an opportunity for information science to encourage an improvement in scholarly practice. Theory classification should thus act as a tool, and at the same time as a stimulus, for a clearer description and definition of theories. Authors could be encouraged to classify their own theories in terms of theory types (and perhaps comparisons with other existing theories). Classification by authors could then be overseen by classifiers to ensure that works are placed in suitable places in classification schemes. In the meantime the classifier can simply omit theory dimensions for which the author provides no clear guidance.

Classifying with Respect to Method Applied

Classifying with respect to method applied is much easier than classifying with respect to theory applied. Broadly speaking, methods can be grouped into only a dozen general classes (see Szostak 2004, 101–2). These are summarized in Table 5.6. Some would treat 'evaluation' of programs as distinct, though this can be seen as a combination of some of these methods. Similar arguments can be made with respect to demography, case study, feminism, and perhaps also hermeneutics.

These methods generally are called by the same name in different disciplines. They can be disaggregated into a manageable set of more specific tools and techniques. These tools and techniques also are often (though not always) referred to by similar terminology in different disciplines: for example the terminology of econometrics is widely employed when statistical analysis is pursued in other disciplines. More generally, 'econometrics' involves an overlapping set of techniques from those employed in 'biometrics' or 'psychometrics.' While there is certainly value in using 'econometrics' as a subject heading (for, say, textbooks on the subject) it will also be valuable wherever possible to classify a work on a particular technique by that technique so that scholars in any field can find it readily.

It should be stressed that the classification of a document in terms of method applied will be independent of its classification in terms of phenomena studied (which will determine its shelf placement) and theory applied. Each of these three distinct elements can be incorporated by means of notation within a single, analytico-synthetic classmark. Researchers using electronic catalogues will be able then to search by combinations of theory, method, and phenomena.

Scholars often employ multiple methods. Indeed there is an extensive literature on how and why to employ multiple methods in a particular research project. This may even occur within a discipline, as when quantitative and qualitative methods are combined in sociology. This literature overlaps in many ways with the literature on how to perform interdisciplinary research (Szostak 2015a). We should thus strive to identify multiple methods employed in a work, and perhaps also in some way to indicate the use of a multiple-method approach. As with works that engage

Table 5.6 The dozen scholarly methods

Classification itself	Experiments
Interviews	Surveys
Observation	Statistical analysis
Mathematical modeling	Textual analysis
Mapmaking (conceptual and representational)	Hermeneutics/semiotics (the study of symbols)

many relationships, it could prove necessary at times to eschew classification of a work by a method that is only superficially addressed.

Of course, many works do not involve (at least explicitly) the application of any theory or method. In such cases, these works will not be classified along those dimensions. First experiences with indexing bibliographies by ILC indicate that dimensions occur with different frequencies in different domains: in a natural science domain like bioacoustics, method is expressed far more frequently than theory (Gnoli et al. 2008), while the opposite seems to happen in the human sciences.

Classifying Authorial Perspective

In some ways, and at least along some dimensions, perspective is the easiest element from the point of view of the classificationist. We create a new dimension along which works or ideas can be classified (along with phenomenon, carrier, and so on; Gnoli 2012a). We call this dimension 'perspective.' The theories and methods addressed above might be subsumed within this broader category of perspective. Several other arrays are possible. It should be stressed that key elements of authorial perspective do not necessarily reflect disciplinary boundaries (though all elements of disciplinary perspective as outlined in Chap. 1 are subsumed). Some elements of perspective may indeed serve to facilitate cross-group communication more than cross-discipline communication. Szostak (2014) had argued that the best way to facilitate respect for social diversity is a comprehensive classification that coded works in terms of authorial perspective; it would then be easy for members of any group to find works from other groups or from their own as they wished. All of the elements of perspective might be considered by users in evaluating the relevance of a work. These elements are summarized in Table 5.7.

To be sure, it is not a trivial task to flesh out each of these arrays. Yet it should prove feasible to do so along at least some arrays. Notably, all of these elements should already be classified within the classification of phenomena. All that is needed here is an indicator of 'perspective applied' (this is 0 in ILC). Still other arrays might be imagined. Some that have been suggested in the literature include: local viewpoint (Beghtol 1998), epoch of knowledge (Tennis 2002), and application to human activity (Vickery 2008).[3]

While the task for the classificationist is straightforward, the task for the classifier may be more challenging, for authors are rarely explicit regarding perspective. This task could be alleviated if authors self-declared their perspective at the time of publication. Note in this regard that Greenberg et al. (2006) found that

---

[3] Condorcet had said that systems of classification that imposed a uniform view of nature were a great obstacle to science. He proposed a faceted approach that would include objects of study, methods, perspectives, uses of the knowledge, and ways of knowing (Glushko 2013, 299).

Table 5.7 The elements of authorial perspective

Element	Possible approach to classification
Discipline itself (and interdisciplinarity)	For this we need to classify all disciplines. Since disciplines are themselves phenomena (Gnoli 2005),[a] this would occur naturally if all phenomena can be freely combined. New interdisciplines could potentially be captured by combining existing disciplines, though we would want to allow the possibility of a new interdiscipline that drew upon multiple existing disciplines.
Theories applied	See above.
Methods applied	See above.
Epistemological outlook	A classification of approaches to epistemology (such as in existing domain analyses of philosophy) could be applied (see Hjørland 2005). Or we could pursue the epistemological dimensions identified in Looney et al (2014) in their efforts to facilitate interdisciplinary communication (see Szostak 2015b).
Ethical outlook	The five main ethical approaches are consequentialism, value-based, rule-based, tradition, and intuition (see Szostak 2005). These reflect in turn the five ways that humans can make any decision, which were listed above when discussing theory types.
Aesthetic attitudes	It could be that we need nothing more here than to link to various properties: (values) (beautiful).
Ideological outlook	There are several commonly recognized ideologies, which can be loosely associated with different types of ethical analysis: Conservative valuing tradition; Conservative valuing individual rights (often styled 'Classical Liberal'); Liberal stressing consequences; Socialist stressing communal values; and so on.
Rhetorical strategy	Feinberg (2011) suggests possible entries such as logical argument (manipulation of evidence), ethos (incorporation of audience beliefs and values to establish trust), and genre adaptation (adjustment of formal elements).[b] Her tripartite division parallels that often drawn by rhetoricians. Clavier and Paganelli (2012) argue that we should classify works by stance: criticism, agreement, consensus, and so on. Rhetoricians have identified over a hundred rhetorical strategies, but many of these—such as alliteration—apply to phrases rather than texts (though these may still be important for some works, such as poetry). There may be about a dozen that are commonly employed at the level of texts.

[a]We should strive, though, for a logical categorization of disciplines. Vickery (2008) sagely observed that general documentary classifications are organised into main classes that are often called "disciplines", perhaps because we think of them as the knowledge domains studied in an academic setting. But such classes as Mining and Education are, in the first instance, not domains studied but activities pursued, by the mining industry and by teachers. Only secondarily do they become objects of academic study. Vickery found it helpful to replace the idea of disciplines with that of "fields of human activity", activities in which people engage practically and are then led to study and write about (Gnoli 2012b)

[b]Her purpose is to argue for an explicit authorial voice in classifications, but her argument can perhaps be used for classifying works by authorial voice

authors could do a good job of reporting Dublin Core metadata, often better than metadata professionals. Even without self-declaration, discipline will usually be easy to identify (by, say, institutional affiliation). And the other elements will be as well for those works that self-consciously pursue a particular ethical, epistemological, or ideological outlook. The challenge will be greatest for works that are not self-conscious in their perspective. Some arrays will be of greater importance for some works than others, and thus author or classifier can focus only on those arrays that seem of particular importance to a particular work (see Szostak 2015b).

A Hybrid KOS?

In Chap. 3, we suggested that a KOS suited to interdisciplinarity could likely not be achieved with minor tweaks to existing discipline-based KOSs. We did hold out some hope that some sort of hybrid classification might prove feasible. Our analysis in this chapter has supported the feasibility of a phenomenon-based KOS. It is appropriate to revisit here also the possibility of a hybrid classification.

As noted above, Szostak (2011, 2013b) showed how class numbers *300* through *339.9* in DDC could be translated into the terminology of the BCC. A similar exercise could undoubtedly be performed for ILC. It is thus quite possible that a new system containing the elements described above could emerge as a complement to rather than a substitute for existing classification systems. In a hybrid system, users could be allowed to search for documents (or ideas) using either system. If class numbers in one system translate automatically into another, we gain increased retrieval without incurring additional costs in classification. While subject analysis by phenomena as performed by human classifiers would likely produce different, more refined classmarks, such an automatic procedure would provide at least a first, cheap approximation.

But of course not all class numbers translate flawlessly. Happily, Szostak did find it straightforward to translate the vast majority of DDC entries. In many cases, the DDC heading itself was a combination of two or three basic concepts [Yet within DDC it is not generally straightforward to search by the concepts within such compounds.]. As an example, DDC *302.35* 'Social interaction in complex groups' can be translated as (Interpersonal relationships) (in) (groups) [It is noteworthy here that the subdivisions in DDC refer to (formal) organizations rather than (informal) groups. The schedules of BCC list types of both groups and organizations (Szostak 2013a). In this case as many others, translating into basic concepts serves to clarify DDC terminology.] In all cases, a manageable handful (often one or two) of basic concepts was all that was required, and thus these could potentially be represented notationally in a quite limited notational space.

When it was not obvious how to translate a DDC entry, this was usually the result of ambiguity in DDC terminology. Take *332.41* 'Value of money.' Such an entry appears at first glance to be an obvious compound of simpler terms. Yet in fact this vague term seems in the context of the *332* hierarchy to mean 'inflation/

deflation;' and thus is best captured by a more precise (increase/decrease) (price level). Philosophical considerations of economic value are captured elsewhere in DDC and would be translated by linking ethical analysis to economic elements. This example provides further evidence that translation into basic concepts can serve to clarify the meaning of terms in existing classifications. And if such translation became standard practice then terms added in future would be clarified at the outset.

It should be stressed that the purpose of this section was merely to establish the feasibility of a hybrid system. It is not at all the authors' intent to suggest that this is the preferred option. It may well be best to focus future classificatory efforts on a stand-alone phenomenon-based classification that is truly comprehensive. This is an empirical question that can only be answered after user testing of completed systems. But it should be stressed that in a hybrid system users would necessarily have better access than at present, for they could always search as at present but also in terms of the synthetic approach we have recommended. Once users became familiar with the comprehensive, phenomenon-based classification they might rarely, if ever, wish to search in terms of the traditional, discipline-based ones.

Comprehensive Thesaurus

A comprehensive phenomenon-based classification would be most useful if accompanied by a comprehensive thesaurus providing preferred captions, synonyms and related terms for each class. Such an integration of a classification and a thesaurus has been described as a 'classaurus' by G. Bhattacharyya (Gnoli et al. 2011). Indeed, the existence of such a thesaurus would not only be useful to the interdisciplinarian but might banish any fears that the disciplinarian would have trouble navigating the new system.

It is useful to reflect here on the nature of the relationship between thesauri and classification systems. 'There are obvious advantages of a conceptually well-structured classification when generating a thesaurus, since the clear identification of relationships allows some degree of mechanical handling of the process...' (Broughton 2010, 275). Though Broughton's emphasis was on hierarchical relationships, her insight has broader application: development of the sort of classification urged above would facilitate the development of a comprehensive thesaurus.

Chan and O'Neill (2010, 18–9) recognize that thesauri and subject heading lists overlap in purpose. Thesauri are usually more strictly hierarchical because each entry is a single concept. Notably, thesauri are often multilingual because it is easier to translate simple terms. It would seem then that a classification that allowed simple terms to be combined would bridge the gap between subject headings and thesauri, and by extension disciplines and languages.

López-Huertas and Torres Ramírez (2007) note that many existing domain-specific thesauri are organized around general rather than domain-specific classes. This can be problematic in that scholars in a particular domain might be far more interested in some general classes than others (see Chap. 6). But just as we have advocated a combination of general and domain-specific approaches to classification, we could urge the same for thesauri. A domain-specific thesaurus could employ concepts from a general classification or thesaurus while organizing these in a way that reflected the dominant interests of the domain. It would contribute to and be consistent with a comprehensive thesaurus.

More generally, the arguments in favor of only domain-specific thesauri are broadly similar to arguments for domain-specific classifications, and rest on the assumption that conceptual ambiguity is too great for a general thesaurus to be feasible. If ambiguity can be overcome in classification, then this should prove also be the case with regard to thesauri. And recall that the act of classification reduces ambiguity. This will inevitably reduce the barriers to a general thesaurus. And success there would further reduce ambiguity.

The success of WordNet deserves mention. This website aspires to identify a variety of thesaurus-like relationships (especially but not exclusively hierarchical and equivalence relationships) across all words in the English language. It is widely consulted, and efforts are now underway to duplicate this effort in and across other languages.

We could also make note of the scale and scope of thesauri in the medical field. The NCI Metathesaurus, sponsored by the National Cancer Institute in the United States, has over 2 million terms in its controlled vocabulary (and over 4 million entry terms) and describes over 22 million relationships between different cancers, therapies, and other phenomena. Its goal is to standardize terminology across cancer research in particular but biomedical research more generally.

In Chap. 2 we also discussed the value of being more specific regarding the different types of Related Term (RT) identified in a thesaurus. Since guidelines for thesauri already identify the sorts of relationships that are to be captured in a RT reference, and indicate that these specific types of RT can be indicated when applied, it is presumably issues of cost that prevent these from being indicated in practice. The developer of the thesaurus will presumably have a good idea of the type of RT in question when they identify an RT. A greater appreciation of the benefits—especially in a digital age—of specifying particular RT relationships, should encourage this practice. Several distinctions could usefully be drawn:

- Causal relationships of various types. ISO2788 distinguishes operation/process, agent/instrument, cause/effect, cause/affected, and thing/counter-agent.
- Other types of relationship. The UMLS thesaurus, used in the medical field distinguishes physically related to, spatially, temporally, functionally [a type of causation], and conceptually.
- Properties. ISO2788 distinguishes concept/property, concept/origin, action/property, and unit of measurement. Discipline/object could be considered a very specific type of property.

Other more specific types of related terms could likely be added. And improvements are also possible in other thesaural practices. With respect to hierarchical relationships, it is important to distinguish 'type of' (some would also distinguish 'instance of') from 'part of.' With respect to equivalence relationships, it would be helpful to distinguish the degree of equivalence.

Ontologies

It is clearly possible to develop upper-level (that is, comprehensive in coverage) ontologies. Several of these already exist (see Masolo et al. n.d.). The main challenge at present is to achieve any degree of consensus regarding these. It is also not clear that these ontologies actually serve the needs of the Semantic Web. Indeed Hart and Dolbear (2013) suggest that research on the Semantic Web has turned away from the exploration of ontologies.

The classifications of both phenomena and relationships provided for above could be useful in the development of upper level ontologies. These characteristically are each comprised both of things and relationships (and properties; Masolo et al. n.d., 43; Almeida et al. 2010). While precise definitions have not been attempted of each entry in the schedules of either BCC or ILC, this could be done. And then precise definitions of the much larger set of compound terms would follow. Relationships between classes in terms of integrative levels—that is, existential dependence between concepts—are a feature of phenomenon-based classifications still hardly considered in ontologies, where they could bring significant improvements.[4]

The classification urged in this book might thus serve as a stepping stone to an ontology. That ontology would inherit the various advantages of the classifications itself, while enhancing the ability of computers to navigate the classification. In later chapters it will be worthwhile to look at exactly what is required of an ontology for the Semantic Web and see to what extent this sort of classification is appropriate.

Key Points

The coincidental rise of digitization and interdisciplinarity in recent years makes it both desirable and feasible to develop a comprehensive and multi-dimensional classification. Works (and ideas) can be classified in terms of phenomena and relationships, theories and methods applied, and various other elements of authorial (including disciplinary) perspective. Numerous detailed practices for achieving

---

[4] The General Formal Ontology developed by Heinrich Herre and others considers levels of reality as one structuring principle, under influence of continental philosophy. Dependence between levels as a promising additional feature in ontologies has been discussed in a formal meeting between one of the authors (Gnoli) and ontologists at the University of Trento (Fumagalli, Maltese, Farazi and others).

each of these types of classification were outlined in this chapter. Such a classification system could either complement or substitute for existing systems. It in turn could be complemented by a comprehensive thesaurus and perhaps ontology.

References

Almeida MB, Souza RR, Fonseca F (2010) Semantics in the Semantic Web: a critical evaluation. Knowl Org 38(3):187–203

Austin DW (1984) PRECIS, a manual of concept analysis and subject indexing, 2nd edn. British Library, London

Barkow J, Cosmides L, Tooby J (eds) (1992) The adapted mind: evolutionary psychology and the generation of culture. Oxford University Press, New York

Beghtol C (1998) Knowledge domains: multidisciplinarity and bibliographic classification systems. Knowl Org 25(1/2):1–12

Broughton V (2010) Concepts and terms in the faceted classification: the case of UDC. Knowl Org 37(4):270–279

Chan L, O'Neill E (2010) FAST: faceted application of subject terminology: principles and application. Libraries Unlimited, Englewood, CO

Clavier V, Paganelli C (2012) Including authorial stance in the indexing of scientific documents. Knowl Org 39(4):292–299

Coates EJ (1988) Subject catalogues: headings and structure, 2nd edn. Library Association, London

Dean RJ (2003) FAST: development of simplified headings for metadata. http://www.oclc.org/research/projects/fast/international_auth200302.doc

Donovan JM (1991) Patron expectations about collocation: measuring the difference between the psychologically real and the really real. Catalog Classif Q 13(2S):23–43

Feinberg M (2011) How information systems communicate as documents: the concept of authorial voice. J Doc 67(6):1015–1037

Glushko RJ (ed) (2013) The discipline of organizing. MIT Press, Cambridge, MA

Gnoli C (2005) BC2 classes for phenomena: an application of the theory of integrative levels. Bliss Classif Bull 47:17–21

Gnoli C (2008) Categories and facets in integrative levels. Axiomathes 18(2):177–192

Gnoli C (2010) Themes and citation order in free classification. IASLIC Bull 55(1):13–19, http://arizona.openrepository.com/arizona/handle/10150/111813

Gnoli C (2012a) Metadata about what? Distinguishing between ontic, epistemic, and documental dimensions in Knowledge Organization. Knowl Org 39(4):268–275

Gnoli C (2012b) Vickery's late ideas on classification by phenomena and activities. In: Gilchrist A, Vernau J (eds) Facets of Knowledge Organization: proceedings of the ISKO UK second biennial conference. Emerald-Aslib, Bingley, pp 11–24

Gnoli C, Poli R (2004) Levels of reality and levels of representation. Knowl Org 31(3):151–160

Gnoli C, Merli G, Pavan G, Bernuzzi E, Priano M (2008) Freely faceted classification for a Web-based bibliographic archive: the BioAcoustic Reference Database. Repositories of knowledge in digital spaces: proceedings of the Eleventh German ISKO conference, Konstanz. Ergon, Würzburg

Gnoli C, Pullmann T, Cousson P, Merli G, Szostak R (2011) Representing the structural elements of a freely faceted classification. In: Slavic A, Civallero E (eds) Classification and ontology: formal approaches and access to knowledge: proceedings of the International UDC Seminar, The Hague. Ergon Verlag, Würzburg, pp 193–206

Green R (2008) Relationships in knowledge organization. Knowl Org 35(2/3):150–159

Greenberg J, Pattuelli MC, Parsia B, Robertson WD (2006) Author-generated Dublin Core metadata for web resources: a baseline study in an organization. J Digit Inform 2(20)

Hart G, Dolbear C (2013) Linked data: a geographic perspective. CRC, Boca Raton, FL

Hjørland B (2005) Empiricism, rationalism and positivism in library and information science. J Doc 61(1):130–155

Integrative Levels Classification (ILC) (2004) ISKO Italia. www.iskoi.org/ilc/

Iyer H (1995) Classificatory structures: concepts, relations and representation. Indeks Verlag, Frankfurt/Main

Khoo C, Na J-C (2006) Semantic relations in Information Science. Annu Rev Inform Sci Technol 40:157–228

Knapp JA (2012) Plugging the 'whole': librarians as interdisciplinary facilitators. Libr Rev 61 (3):199–214

Looney C, Donovan S, O'Rourke M, Crowley S, Eigenbrode SD, Rotschy L, Bosque-Perez NA, Wulfhorst JD (2014) Using Toolbox workshops to enhance cross-disciplinary communication. In: O'Rourke M, Crowley S, Eigenbrode SD, Wulfhorst JD (eds) Enhancing communication and collaboration in interdisciplinary research. Sage, Thousand Oaks, pp 220–243

López-Huertas MJ (2013) Transcultural categorization in contextualized domains. Inform Res 18 (3), http://InformationR.net/ir/18-3/colis/paperC16.html

López-Huertas MJ, Torres Ramírez I (2007) Gender terminology and indexing systems: the case of woman's body. Libri 57:34–44

Masolo C, Borgo S, Gangemi A, Guarino N, Oltramari A (n.d.) Ontology Library. Laboratory for Applied Ontology - ISTC-CNR. http://wonderweb.semanticweb.org/deliverables/documents/D18.pdf

Perrault JM (1994) Categories and relators: a new schema. Knowl Org 21(4):189–198

Repko AF (2012) Interdisciplinary research: process and theory, 2nd edn. Sage, Thousand Oaks

Repko AF, Newell WH, Szostak R (eds) (2012) Case studies in interdisciplinary research. Sage, Thousand Oaks

Szostak R (2003) A schema for unifying human science: interdisciplinary perspectives on culture. Susquehanna University Press, Selinsgrove, PA

Szostak R (2004) Classifying science: phenomena, data, theory, method, practice. Springer, Dordrecht

Szostak R (2005) Unifying ethics. University Press of America, Lanham, MD

Szostak R (2011) Complex concepts into basic concepts. J Am Soc Inform Soc Technol 62 (11):2247–2265

Szostak R (2012a) Classifying relationships. Knowl Org 39(3):165–178

Szostak R (2012b) Toward a classification of relationships. Knowl Org 39(2):83–94

Szostak R (2013a). Basic concepts classification. https://sites.google.com/a/ualberta.ca/rick-szostak/research/basic-concepts-classification-web-version-2013

Szostak R (2013b) Translation table: DDC [Dewey Decimal Classification] to basic concepts classification. http://www.economics.ualberta.ca/en/FacultyandStaff/~/media/economics/FacultyAndStaff/Szostak/Szostak-Dewey-Conversion-Table.pdf

Szostak R (2014) Classifying for social diversity. Knowl Org 41(2):160–170

Szostak R (2015a) Interdisciplinary and transdisciplinary multi-method and mixed methods research. In: Hesse-Biber S, Johnson RB (eds) The Oxford handbook of mixed and multi-method research. Oxford University Press, Oxford, pp 128–143

Szostak R (2015b) Classifying authorial perspective. Knowl Org 42(7):499–507

Szostak R, Gnoli C (2008) Classifying by phenomena, theories, and methods: examples with focused social science theories. In: Arsenault C, Tennis J (eds) Culture and identity in knowledge organization, Proceedings of the 10th international ISKO conference, Montréal. Ergon, Würzburg, pp 205–211

Tennis J (2002) Subject ontogeny: subject access through time and the dimensionality of classification. In: López-Huertas MJ (ed) Challenges in knowledge representation and organization for the 21st century. Integration of knowledge across boundaries. Proceedings of 7th International ISKO Conference, Granada. Ergon, Würzburg, pp 54–59

Turner B (2000) Introduction: a new agenda for social theory? In: Turner B (ed) The new Blackwell companion to social theory. Blackwell, Oxford, pp 1–16

Van der Lecq R (2012) Why we talk: an interdisciplinary approach to the evolutionary origin of language. In: Repko A, Newell WH, Szostak R (eds) Case studies in interdisciplinary research. Sage, Thousand Oaks, pp 191–224

Vickery BC (2008) The structure of subject classifications for document retrieval. http://www.iskoi.org/ilc/vickery.php

Wu L-L, Huang M-H, Chen C-Y (2012) Citation patterns of the pre-web and web-prevalent environments: the moderating effects of domain knowledge. J Am Soc Inform Soc Technol 63(11):2182–2194

Chapter 6
Domain Oriented Interdisciplinarity

We have often in preceding chapters stressed the complementarity of domain analysis with the sort of comprehensive classification advocated in this book. A classification such as we have proposed will work for scholars from different domains only if the terminology of those domains has been accurately translated into the terminology employed within the comprehensive classification.

This chapter explores domain analysis. It will focus on the domain analysis of interdisciplines (fields that span multiple disciplines). This focus allows us to accomplish two goals simultaneously. We can describe techniques of domain analysis (in a particularly challenging environment), and discuss how these can support our classificatory project. We can also see how poorly interdisciplines are treated within conventional classifications, and thus enhance our understanding of the information challenges faced by interdisciplinary researchers. This project illustrates how the sort of KOS urged in this book can lead to a classification that is both more fair and effective.

We begin by discussing some challenges in classifying interdisciplines. We then explore strategies for domain analysis. We later review some of the key findings of domain analyses of interdisciplines. This allows us to draw conclusions regarding the possibility of applying domain analyses toward the development of comprehensive phenomenon-based KOSs.

Challenges in Classifying Interdisciplines

Bibliographic classifications are always challenged when new topics emerge. As we have noted elsewhere, one advantage of a synthetic approach to classification is that new topics can often be handled by new combinations of existing classes. New topics emerge both within and between disciplines. The latter are particularly challenging to discipline-based classifications because it will not be obvious where to place the new interdisciplinary field of inquiry.

© Springer International Publishing Switzerland 2016
R. Szostak et al., *Interdisciplinary Knowledge Organization*,
DOI 10.1007/978-3-319-30148-8_6

Table 6.1 Characteristics of interdisciplines

Terminology is not consensual and is thus unstable.
Terminology is created rapidly, and the meaning of a particular term (for example, gender studies itself) changes often. This is especially the case when the interdiscipline is of recent creation. Researchers often refer to 'Terminology of alluvium.'
Conceptual limits are not always well defined. That is, the scope of particular terms is unclear.
There are confusing epistemological borders, since many key terms are borrowed from other disciplines.
There is generally a lack of taxonomies or prior scientific classifications.
There is no definition of conceptual dynamics. That is, the behavior of terms within the interdiscipline cannot easily be predicted in the absence of a deep study of terminology.
There are unknown interactions among the fields that constitute the interdiscipline. Researchers need to specify the sort of relationships that exist between broad subject areas within the interdiscipline, and the relative weight of these subject areas.
There is a lack of theoretical models to address interdisciplinary spaces (López-Huertas et al. 2004).

When addressing an interdiscipline, it is generally necessary to immerse oneself in the literature before one can establish the key subjects that are addressed by the interdiscipline. While some subjects can be deduced from the title of the interdiscipline (gender studies can be expected to investigate gender) other foci of interest can only be identified inductively. This problem can arise within disciplines as well: Szostak (2014) discusses how the explanatory focus of art history has shifted over time, with serious implications for efforts to classify works in the field. But this challenge is inherent in the very nature of interdisciplines.

The first step in studying an interdiscipline thus involves identifying the broad subject areas that are generally addressed within the field. That is, we need to know the field's subject dynamics. We can then address issues of subclasses and terminology. Specialists in interdisciplines often find that their terminology is poorly represented in general classification schemes. Nor do they find such schemes to be organized in a way that captures the essence of their field.

We can see already that there will be challenges in performing a domain analysis of an interdiscipline. We summarize in Table 6.1 several key characteristics of interdisciplines that must be addressed in domain analysis.

Due to these peculiarities, some aspects of the process of building KOSs for interdisciplines are of special importance, among them: the identification of the interdiscipline's internal subject dynamics, the management of the problems that the interdiscipline's terminology may cause, the naming of the chosen categories of concepts according to the field's demands, and the possible connection of the interdiscipline's knowledge with general systems. These will each be addressed in the next sections.

Domain Analysis of Interdisciplines

As noted above, the first step in the domain analysis of an interdiscipline must involve identifying the major subject areas addressed and how these relate to each other.

It is these relationships among subject areas which represent the essence of the interdiscipline. It is important to capture the dynamics of the field at a point in time but also allow scope for the field to evolve and engage different subjects and relationships. This is one way in which placing the domain within a broader classification can be helpful: it facilitates the classification of works in the field that take on novel topics.

How to proceed? There are a few strategies for domain analysis that have achieved considerable success (see Hjørland 2002). We survey some of these here.[1]

The Bibliometric Approach

The bibliometric technique is an approach that can be used for knowledge organization in any field (Hjørland 2002) but it is of special interest when used for interdisciplinary knowledge organization. The bibliometric technique has been applied for a variety of purposes in the study of interdisciplines: to evaluate research within an interdiscipline (Jacob 2008), establish the degree of interdisciplinarity (Porter and Rafols 2009; Rafols and Meyer 2010), or establish the subject composition of an interdiscipline. It is this last application that concerns us here.

Citation analysis is the most familiar bibliometric approach, but multivariate analysis and neural networks are also pursued. Importantly, citation analysis allows the identification of the key relationships among subjects that are pursued in a field without the necessity of carefully reading documents. The researcher instead traces what sort of works are cited by authors investigating a particular subject. Domain analysis has tended to rely instead on careful analysis of texts.

An example of using multidimensional scaling to identify the subject structure of Biotechnology is in Hinze (1996). Another contribution using multivariate analysis to determine the conceptual structure of Biotechnology and Applied Microbiology (with categories taken from the Journal Citation Records) is that of Moya and López-Huertas (2000). Some other studies related to the structural discovery of interdisciplinary fields can be seen in Schwechheimer and Winterhager (2001), López-Huertas and Jiménez (2004) and in Glenisson et al. (2005). Tomov and Mutafov (1996) have studied interdisciplinary relations in order to know the structure of a given interdiscipline.

---

[1] We focus on those types of domain analysis with the greatest implications for classification. We do not, for example, discuss network analysis here because the purpose of network analysis is to identify the connections among researchers.

The Terminological Approach

The linguistic model has been widely used to study domains and build tools for indexing and information retrieval. This approach involves carefully analyzing the terminology employed and internal dynamics of a particular field. It has become increasingly common in the development of KOSs with the contemporary emphasis on domain analysis. It is difficult to identify the terminology that is truly representative of an interdiscipline, especially when it is an emerging domain, but this knowledge is essential if we wish to know the thematic composition of the interdiscipline.

Terms Coming from Mixed Sources

Recent attempts have been made to identify the subject composition of interdisciplines by studying their terminology. Kobashi et al. (2001) used this approach to study the field of information science. These authors have collected terminology from different sources in order to identify the terms that represent the information science field. Each term was provided with a definition. After submitting this terminology to an in-depth study, they could unveil the problems that this terminology posed and its dynamics (see below). This methodology allowed them to identify the knowledge structure of information science, concluding that the fields comprising information science are Logic, Administration, Linguistics, Computer Science, Sociology, Communications, Cognitive Sciences and Librarianship. This approach can also shed light on the levels of description (the depth of the hierarchies) that is required for each general category.

Terms Coming from the Indexing of Primary Sources

This approach in fact uses three of the methods indicated by Hjørland (2002) to perform domain analysis: The study of documents, the indexing of documents and the study of the terminology found in them. In this instance, the case study was gender studies in documents published in Uruguay (López-Huertas et al. 2004; López-Huertas 2006a, b, c, 2009). It is noteworthy that almost all documents on this topic could be identified and processed. For this reason, this study was excellent for our purposes: We could learn about the epistemological dynamics of this field, identify the dynamics of the terminology used in the domain, discover the different discourses implicated in the interdiscipline, and identify the problems of terminology transfer that might exist in the domain and the expressive ability of the interdisciplinary space to generate or not a language exclusively unique and representative of it.

A total of 600 documents were analyzed (monographs, articles, proceedings and research and sociopolitical reports). Indexing these documents yielded the identification of 460 descriptors. This terminology was analyzed to identify the specialties involved in gender studies. It was thus possible to name these specialties and to know the weight or importance that each played in the interdiscipline.

The set of terminology analyzed shows the existence of two major types of concepts. A first group represented the terms created by the interdiscipline of gender studies itself, and a second group involved concepts shared with other disciplines. Those terms pertaining to the first group represented 32 % of the total and they display little ambiguity. They represent the core of gender studies.

The terminology belonging to the second group is the largest, representing 68 % of the total. It has been incorporated into the field as a result of the interaction of gender studies with various disciplines and specialties. Such concepts may not always have the same meaning in gender studies as in other fields. In particular, we might worry that studying something (say, hygiene) from a gender perspective imparts a different meaning than studying it from a different perspective. The synthetic approach urged throughout this book should alleviate this challenge, for we can distinguish (gender) (affects) (hygiene) from other analyses of hygiene, while potentially having similar understandings of 'hygiene' itself. But we will want to explore the specific meanings attached to a concept such as 'hygiene' across fields.

According to the previous study of the terminology, a proposal for the subject composition of gender studies can be given. The impact of each area is indicated by the number of terms found for each area. The results have shown that Rights/Law, Politics, Customs, Family/Society and Health are clearly significant for the inter-disciplinary map of gender studies. Other subjects such as Psychology, Culture, Administration, Body/Image, and other topics (Demography, Religion and Groups) were less important in the thematic settings of gender studies. Figure 6.1 represents the detailed subject map for gender studies that, in turn, has been grouped into five general thematic areas:

- *Social environment* (28 %), backed by 157 terms, which includes in order of importance: Politics, Family, Rights, Law, Education, Society, Costumes, Culture, Sports and Demography
- *Gender* (28 %), backed by 145 terms, which represents the core terminology
- *Health/Hygiene* (26 %), backed by 132 terms, which includes Health, Sexuality, and Body/Image
- *Economic environment* (16 %), backed by 83 terms, including Employment, Economy and Business
- *Others* with only nine terms which includes Groups, Psychology and Religion

There is no doubt that this thematic composition and especially the weight of different subjects in the interdiscipline may vary, because gender studies is a topic greatly influenced by the socio-cultural context (López-Huertas 2008). For instance, if we consider the Cuban context some changes are noted. Though the same concepts tend to be used, there is a great difference in their relative importance compared to Uruguay.

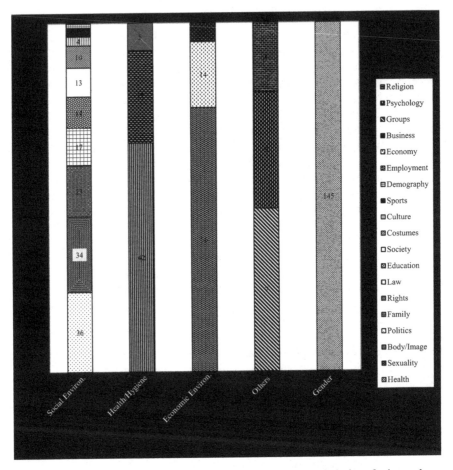

Fig. 6.1 Thematic weighted composition of gender studies from the indexing of primary documents. *Source*: López-Huertas 2008

The most important theme in Cuba was that of *Health/Hygiene*, representing 44 % of the total. Within this theme, *sexuality* was stressed, and backed by 135 terms, compared to the Uruguayan context where *sexuality* was only backed by 17 terms. This is followed by the *social environment* group (42 %), in which *Groups* is quite numerous and *Violence/Abuse* has more visibility compared to the Uruguayan context. The *Gender* core terminology followed (11 %) and then the *Economic and Political environment* representing only 2 % of the total. We also have results from Spain and some differences can also be detected there: The *Social environment* specialty is much more important than in the other geographical areas studied (46 %), followed by *Health//Hygiene/Body*, where topics such as *Feelings and Attitudes* are common while these are virtually non-existent in the other geographical spaces studied. The category Body is also much more important for

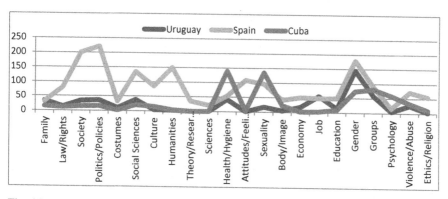

Fig. 6.2 Composition and quantification of gender studies topics in Uruguay, Spain and Cuba. *Source*: López-Huertas 2008

the Spanish area. Gender studies in Spain devotes considerable attention to the relationships that gender has with other disciplines (21 % of the selected terms). Other topics with much more impact on this interdiscipline compared to Uruguay and Cuba are *Society* and *Politics/Policies*. Figure 6.2 compares the composition and quantification of gender studies in Uruguay, Spain and Cuba.

In developing a KOS for gender studies, then, we would want to ensure hospitality, for the particular interdisciplinary linkages stressed may vary across authors, space, and time. As noted above, this is one advantage of placing the results of our domain analysis within the context of a comprehensive classification.

Analysis of Actual KOSs

Another way of knowing the composition of a given interdisciplinary domain is to study the actual KOSs on the topic (again see Hjørland 2002). Some results from this approach were obtained by López-Huertas et al. (2004). In this article several thesauri on gender studies were analyzed (IIAV 1998; Instituto de la Mujer 2002; Sebastiá i Salat 1988; Bruschini et al. 1998). The results of this study showed a lack of uniformity in the terminology provided by the thesauri (that is, there was a very low overlap of terms). This result indicated that there is little consensus regarding the terminology belonging to the domain. As a consequence, a high thematic dispersion or diversification was detected (34 different main classes were counted across the four thesauri). On top of that, the co-occurrence of classes or areas was very low in these thesauri: only eight areas (23.5 %) co-occurred at this first level in three thesauri (two hits): Communication/Media, Culture, Law, Economy, Education, Philosophy, Government/Politics/Public Policy, and Health which are not core terms within Gender Studies. On the other hand, 18 classes out of the total (34) are not shared. Table 6.2 shows the classes included in the four thesauri and their co-occurrences.

Table 6.2 Main classes and co-occurrences in the four thesauri

No.	Main classes	Brazil	Catalonian	European	Spanish	Hits
1	Communication—Media	X		X	X	2
2	Culture	X	X		X	2
3	Law	X		X	X	2
4	Economy	X		X	X	2
5	Education	X		X	X	2
6	Philosophy	X	X	X		2
7	Government/Politics/Policies	X		X	X	2
8	Health/Body	X		X	X	2
9	Arts/Shows	X		X		1
10	Sciences			X	X	1
11	Family			X	X	1
12	History and Social Change	X		X		1
13	Language	X		X		1
14	Literature	X		X		1
15	Religion/Visions of the World	X		X		1
16	Labour/Work	X			X	1
17	State Administration				X	0
18	Sociodemographic Environment				X	0
19	Anthropology			X		0
20	Social Welfare				X	0
21	Centers				X	0
22	Science and Technology	X				0
23	Life Sciences		X			0
24	Natural Sciences	X				0
25	Social Sciences		X			0
26	Documentation				X	0
27	Women Studies			X		0
28	General			X		0
29	Social exclusion				X	0
30	Leisure			X		0
31	Psychology			X		0
32	Social relations			X		0
33	Sexuality				X	0
34	Housing			X		0

Source: López-Huertas et al. 2004

Notably, topics that are indeed nuclear in the literature, according to expert opinions, are excluded (Family, Sexuality, etc.). In general, the main subjects go from broad areas (Health) to very specific topics (such as Social Exclusion). These last are too specific for a first level of subdivision. Differences were also observed in the classification of the same topic in the studied thesauri. For instance, the class 'Sexuality,' which is independent in the Spanish thesaurus, is included in the class 'Health/The Body' in the European thesaurus. In some cases, two autonomous classes in a thesaurus are partially or totally associated in another thesaurus: for example the classes 'Economy' and 'Work' are separate in the Spanish thesaurus, but together in the Brazilian one. These facts limit the internal visibility of each topic area and impede the estimation of the relative weight of each main class in the interdiscipline's subject set. From a qualitative point of view, the main classes of the four thesauri studied remind us of a general KOS with a broad spectrum of classes where the gender perspective is often hidden, rather than a domain-oriented KOS. We will explore below the question of whether we can have the advantages of a comprehensive KOS without losing the domain-specific recognition that these thesauri seem to lack.

Concept Mapping

Concept mapping, as the name suggests, involves the visual mapping of relationships among concepts. Advances in software mean that it is now very easy to create such maps. Concept maps take three main forms. In the hierarchical format, a main concept appears at the top, and subsidiary topics are organized below this. Such a topic map could be very useful in mapping the hierarchical relationships within a KOS (see Julien et al 2013). In the 'spider' format the key concept is placed in the middle and inter-relationships with and among various related concepts are mapped around this. Figure 2.1 produces a simple spider concept map of interdisciplinary knowledge organization itself. In the flow chart format, causal relationships among concepts are emphasized. Figure 2.2 is an example of such a flow chart.

Though concept maps can be used to visualize relationships within a domain, they can also be used to describe relationships across domains. McAlpine (2014) indeed describes the value of concept mapping to interdisciplinary inquiry, and provides examples. Repko (2012) and AIS (2013) also emphasize the value of mapping in the interdisciplinary research process.

Concept maps could prove invaluable in facilitating both disciplinary and interdisciplinary search. The correct visualization techniques make it much easier for users to appreciate how their initial search term is related to other possible search terms. Interdisciplinary researchers, who will want to follow their curiosity from a phenomenon or relationship studied in one discipline to a phenomenon or relationship studied in another, will particularly benefit from such techniques.

Some Conclusions Regarding the Internal Subject Composition of Interdisciplines

The first consideration is that each interdiscipline has its own subject composition, dynamics, and terminology, as is observed in any domain. However, interdisciplines have the added difficulty of lack of previous models, as is the case with the disciplinary specialties. Therefore, the terminological acquisition process, the structural recognition of the interdiscipline, and the assignment of categories is particularly complex. The methodology involved in the processes of representing and organizing interdisciplines is of particular importance, and more research effort should be devoted to its study.

Any of the methodologies discussed above are able to shed light on the internal subject composition of interdisciplines. However, it is best to use several methods at the same time. For instance, the bibliometric method provides information that cannot be obtained using only the terminological method and vice versa. On the other hand, if we only use the information stored in previous interdisciplinary KOSs to get to know the terms and structure of a given interdiscipline, we have seen in the case of gender studies above that the results will be a poor guide to the nature of the interdiscipline. Gender studies is likely the most-studied interdiscipline by information scientists, and it is clear from that case that studying only pre-existing KOSs will be unsatisfactory. Nevertheless studying these is a useful complement to pursuing other approaches.

We have already seen that there are differences of weight in the subject areas included in the gender studies domain that are likely caused by different cultural environments. In developing a KOS we generally provide a deeper description of areas that receive higher weights. The danger here is that a KOS developed for one geographical area will not provide enough detail for the subjects stressed in a different geographical area. One solution is to employ the maximum weights found in any geographical area. The resulting KOS will provide more detail than some geographical areas require for some subjects, but will treat all subjects in enough detail for all geographical areas. Such a strategy cannot, though, cope with the likelihood that scholars in future will certainly devote much greater attention to certain subjects that receive little attention today. This possibility might best be addressed by situating our domain analysis within a comprehensive classification.

Interdisciplinary Terminological Dynamics

Terminology is one of the main problems (maybe the most important one) faced when building interdisciplinary KOSs. The origin of an interdisciplinary field (and thus the combination of specialties involved) makes it difficult to identify its terminology and the dynamics to which this terminology is exposed. To what extent does a new interdiscipline develop unique terminology distinct from any discipline that it draws upon? A very new interdiscipline may not do so, but a mature discipline can be expected to develop its own unique concepts (or apply novel meanings to those it borrows). The degree to which new terminology is developed may also depend on the focus and nature of the interdiscipline.

Several questions arise around this issue: Where does the interdiscipline's terminology come from? Is it constituted by new concepts and their corresponding terms? Are there terms coming from other disciplines? If so, are they adapted to the interdiscipline or are they taken from outside specialties without adaptation? What is the proportion between the terms of new creation and the terms provided by other fields? The answers to these and other related questions are important and should be addressed prior to the construction of the KOS. They also give us an idea of the epistemological status and the nature of the interdiscipline.

We face a shortage of sources for interdisciplinary terminology since there are few specialized secondary (glossaries, dictionaries, etc.) and tertiary sources (KOSs), if any, devoted to interdisciplines. Considering this, the analysis of the publications issued by the interdiscipline seems to be the best source to collect terminology. Of course, the other sources mentioned (dictionaries, glossaries, KOSs, and so on) should also be considered if they exist.

Examining Information Science and Gender Studies

Some attempts have been made to study how to proceed with respect to two interdisciplines, information science and gender studies. Kobashi et al. (2001) studied the terminology that is representative of information science. They hoped not only to reveal the potential problems that this terminology might pose in the development of KOSs but also to determine the epistemological status of information science based on the terminology used by the domain. The terminological sources used were articles, dictionaries, encyclopedias and the specialized terminology of the ISO standards. This methodology allowed the authors to identify which terms were central and which peripheral. This distinction is necessary for understanding the terminological dynamics of interdisciplinary fields. It is also essential in order to organize interdisciplinary fields (López-Huertas et al. 2004). The authors identified four types of concept. First were 'notions of the area laid down over time' that indicate classic procedures of librarianship. This set presented stability and tended towards univocality. The second type, 'semi-elaborated notions of the area,' often have several meanings due to a diversity of opinions. The third type, 'notions from common empirical experience' are used frequently but do not have a distinctive meaning for information science, as in the case of 'book' or 'user.' Finally, 'confounded notions' are terms imported from other fields without going through a process of adaptation to the information science field (Kobashi et al. 2001, 83). The authors concluded that the central terms came to a large extent from the area of Information Science. The rest of the terms come from other areas and they often maintain the original meaning that they possessed in the disciplines of origin.

This last result is important for the project of this book. It indicates that many terms do indeed carry the same meaning across fields. If it is common for fields, when borrowing terminology from other fields, to interpret these in a very similar way, then the path to a comprehensive phenomenon-based classification becomes clear. Terms can be defined in the manner of their field of origin. Of course, we would need to study many more domains. And we can reasonably anticipate that some terms will come to carry quite different meanings in different fields over time. But the results from information science indicate that at least some terms sometimes will be understood in the same way across fields.

After this analysis, it is evident that terminology demands a great deal of attention. The problems described above can be expected to occur in many interdisciplines. So, when an interdisciplinary KOS is being built, special care must be taken to reduce the terminological ambiguity that exists for a large number of terms. If we do that for information science, we will be working on two main fronts: in favor of a unique terminology for information science that also will benefit the epistemological status of this field, as has been urged by several scholars (Hjørland 2002, López-Huertas 2008), and in favor of a more efficient end-user information retrieval (since terminological ambiguity negatively affects information retrieval).

The terminology representative of gender studies has also been studied in depth by several authors (López-Huertas et al. 2004; López-Huertas 2006a, b, c, 2009). The studied terminology came from different sources and this fact conditioned somewhat the results obtained. Two broad types of terminology were investigated: terminology coming from KOSs and terminology coming from indexing primary sources.

Regarding the first set (terms pulled from actual Gender Studies KOSs) three thesauri were analyzed: the European Women Thesaurus (IIAV 1998), the Women's Thesaurus, published by the Women Institute of Spain (Instituto de la Mujer 2002) and the Thesaurus d'Història Social de la Dona de Cataluña (Sebastiá i Salat 1988). The terms collected totalled 4057. These thesauri were compared to see the co-occurrences of terms in a core shared terminology. The results showed that only 18.2 % of the terms (considering descriptors and non-descriptors) were in each of the three thesauri. Even considering the effects that culture can have in the choice of terminology, this is a very low rate. For instance, the co-occurrences between the Spanish and the Catalonian thesauri was only 23 %, as can be seen in Table 6.3.

It was assumed that these percentages represented the core terminology for gender studies, with the rest of the concepts coming from other fields. It seems that a characteristic of interdisciplinary terminology is that the core terms represent a low percentage of the total of terms. However, though the interaction between gender studies and other disciplines did not generate new terminology, the gender perspective is implied and thus the imported terms come to be polysemic. We return to this issue below.

The core terminology used in Gender thesauri seems to be unstable and dispersed. That is, there is not much agreement about which are the terms that represent the interdiscipline. This characteristic is also responsible for the high number of main classes found in thesauri (that is, subject dispersion). It also speaks to the degree of maturity and the epistemological status of this field. It appears that the field of gender studies is still being constructed. As noted above, hospitality is an important criterion if change is anticipated. And one of the advantages of a comprehensive and synthetic classification is hospitality.

Table 6.3 Descriptors shared by pairs of thesauri

	Catalonian Thes.	% Catalonian	Spanish Thes.	% Spanish	European Thes.	% European
Catalonian Thes.	–	–	147/624	23.55	217/624	34.77
Spanish Thes.	147/799	18.39	–	–	226/799	28.28
European Thes.	217/1498	14.48	226/1498	15.08	–	–

Source: López-Huertas 2006b

The second set of gender studies terminology came from the indexing of primary documents (López-Huertas 2006b, c). As was said above, this source of terms is to our knowledge the best one due to the interdiscipline's peculiarities. After analyzing 600 documents, 537 terms were collected, of which 460 were descriptors, 48 identificators and 29 non-descriptors. A small proportion of these were well represented in documents, but most of the terms were not. There was an inverse relation between the number of descriptors and the frequency of appearance in documents. Out of 489 descriptors, 378 terms have only one citation. This fact also evidenced a terminological dispersion—and therefore a thematic dispersion—confirming the results of similar studies of gender terminology with other terminological resources, such as the Internet and thesauri (López-Huertas and Barité 2002; López-Huertas et al. 2004). That is, scholars of gender studies explore links with a wide variety of other domains.

A small proportion of the terminology is found to be generated from the interdisciplinary activity itself. That is, it does not come from any of the origin disciplines that interact within the domain. This terminology, rather, emerges to denominate objects and phenomena created by the interdisciplinary domain (feminisms, gender). Such terms represent 32 % of the total of 460 descriptors. The terms belonging to this group can be considered nuclear ones (the core terms), having a quite univocal behaviour; their pertinence to the interdisciplinary domain is beyond question. The rest of the terms (68 %) have been created by other disciplines. This group is formed by terminology which is a result of the aforementioned interaction among disciplines and specialties with the Gender perspective. Terms in this set show a twofold behaviour: (a) Terms that are adopted by the interdiscipline from other fields with the same form and apparently the same sense as they have in their original realm, and (b) a group of terms created by the interaction of the Gender perspective with other disciplines.

The first case (a) is represented by terms pulled from documents dealing with interactions between Gender Studies and other disciplines—labour, health, education, politics, economy, and so on. The titles of such documents often blend gender terminology and terminology from these other disciplines: *Women and Health, women salaries, women in politics,* and so on. In this way, the authors inform users that the contents are gender oriented. But capturing the nature of such works within traditional subject headings is difficult: categorizing a work about 'women and social security' under 'women' and 'social security' hardly indicates the unique nature of the work (though in this case a user familiar with Boolean searches might still find it). A synthetic approach will work as long as the term borrowed from another field ('social security') is employed as it would be in that field.

In structuring a domain-specific KOS, important questions arise regarding where (and indeed if) to place terms such as 'social security.' Such concepts may only be used in a minority of works, but may be essential to those works. Excluding such concepts limits our ability to capture the essence of works that focus upon them. Including them means that the bulk of concepts in a domain KOS are non-core concepts borrowed from elsewhere (68 % in the case of gender studies). And as noted above we can expect that scholars in any interdiscipline will investigate further links with other fields in future. Placing domain-specific terminology within a comprehensive classification provides one possible solution to this conundrum.

The second case (b) represents a small set of terms that has been created either to express new concepts (wage-earning job, under-representation in politics, vertical discrimination, glass ceiling, housewife salary, and so on) or terms representing concepts that already existed yet that gain importance because of the gender perspective (domestic violence, sexual harassment, violence against women, etc.). This set evidences the influence of gender studies in other disciplines to the point of creating new concepts or stressing the importance of others. It is sensible to consider this set as part of the core terminology in gender studies. It is noteworthy that the essence of these terms can generally be captured readily (and perhaps only) through a synthetic approach. ['Glass ceiling' can perhaps be captured as (barriers) (to promoting) (women)].

Some Conclusions Regarding Interdisciplinary Terminology

As has been seen above, interdisciplinary terms present greater challenges than those of disciplines. We must be aware of these challenges when creating KOSs. Though each interdiscipline has its own dynamics, it can be said that there are some common characteristics that condition the problems that we face in most cases. The most important one is the semantic ambiguity that terms coming from disciplines outside the interdiscipline may incorporate. We have argued that a synthetic approach can be critical in coping with this challenge. A related question involves whether and how to include concepts borrowed from other fields in a domain-specific KOS. We have noted above that this challenge can be at least alleviated by placing domain analysis within the context of a comprehensive classification.

Which terms can be said to belong to a particular interdiscipline? The core terms are not problematic, but the set of terms representing an interaction between the interdiscipline and other fields present greater challenges. As we have seen above this second type of term tends to be much more common than the first. The first question that must be asked is whether each term carries the same meaning as in the field of origin. Care must be taken not to assume this result. A term such as 'abortion' may seem straightforward but can carry a quite different connotation in gender studies than in medicine. If a KOS fails to address this difference in meaning, it will be characterized by ambiguity in terminology. A synthetic treatment may allow us to distinguish the two. Success in clarifying terminology will also serve to strengthen the epistemological base of the interdiscipline. But the synthetic approach then raises a challenge as to how we might clearly demarcate the terminology of a particular interdiscipline within a comprehensive classification. We might essay to indicate in some manner the terms that are most often used within a particular interdiscipline (see below).

Naming the Categories for Interdisciplinary KOSs

Concepts represent a given field and differentiate it from others. However, a KOS does not just identify terminology but places these within some organizing structure. People engaged in any field expect this to happen. When talking about interdisciplines, this expectation gains even more importance and is more demanding because of the way in which interdisciplines are constituted. There is a tendency to use categories that do not express the domain that they refer to. On the contrary, they could also be used to represent and organize any field. This is exactly what happens in the gender studies thesauri. Sexual mutilations (ablation of the clitoris) are considered a 'custom,' which does not signify their importance within gender studies. Indeed, treating sexual mutilation as a custom is problematic in general.

Gender studies scholars, in particular those who study homosexuality, are demanding terms and categories that better represent this domain. They worry that knowledge dilutes or disappears under general or neutral tags. Importantly they do not wish to see gender-related health problems treated in a general system as a medical phenomenon when studied by a medical researcher but as a gender phenomenon when studied from a gender studies perspective, and so on. Nor, though, do they wish to be unable to distinguish the two perspectives. If we classify these two perspectives separately, we limit the likelihood of interaction. The strategy urged in other chapters involves one comprehensive classification, where differences in perspective are captured often by the synthetic structure of subject headings, but also by classifying works in terms of the theory, method, and authorial perspective applied. As noted above, we might also wish to consider providing visual maps of (especially interdisciplinary) fields that would highlight the main relationships between phenomena (and perhaps also less frequent ones) that are studied in the field. Such maps in a sense allow us to identify a domain-specific KOS within a comprehensive KOS.

Gender Studies and the Internet

It is useful to address briefly here how the general classificatory systems in use on the contemporary Internet treat one of the interdisciplines addressed above: gender studies. Such an exercise serves to illustrate in practice the sort of classificatory challenges discussed in previous sections. It simultaneously illustrates the potential value of a logical comprehensive classification grounded in phenomena as advocated in this book.

A study by López-Huertas and Barité (2002) analyzed and compared the directories of eight search engines for different cultural areas (Google, Yahoo, Yahoo-Spain, Cadé Brasil, Uruguay Total, Directorio Argentino, 123 India and Ananzi Surafrica). They studied the general structure of each search engine, looking for the location of gender-related topics in the structure, the degree of autonomy or subordination to other specialties, the identification of the strongest disciplinary associations, the direct or indirect access to the topic in the sites, and the concentration or diffusion of gender-related subjects. Gender-related topics had low visibility in these structures and there was a lack of consistency in gender classification. Gender was often subordinated to different topics such as Society, Social Sciences, Family, Sexology and Health. However, Culture, Arts and Humanities, People, Psychology and Psychology and Sports were also used as generics for Gender. Only Cadé Brasil allowed direct access to Gender. Regarding the study of the terminology used, it was found that only international search engines (Google, Yahoo and Yahoo Spain) had a significant representation of the topic. Local search engines have a very poor representation of Gender. To sum up, gender knowledge is dispersed in different general categories in the directories; each directory uses different categories to classify gender, and the terminology chosen to represent gender vary in the studied directories. A similar situation can be found in general classification systems, most of them based on disciplinary knowledge. A disciplinary grounding causes the dispersion of the terminology employed in any interdiscipline. The deleterious effect that general classifications have upon interdisciplines has been noticed by several scholars who have suggested several ways of adapting general KOSs to interdisciplinary knowledge (López-Huertas 2007). This book has sought to outline an approach to general classification that would encourage and support, rather than obstruct, interdisciplinary endeavors.

It is clear that actual general systems do not address the problem faced by interdisciplinary knowledge. So, on one hand there is a need for KOSs to use terminology and categorization that are significant for interdisciplinary scholarship. On the other hand, there also exists the need to incorporate interdisciplines into general classification systems so that this kind of knowledge can be properly classified. As has been argued elsewhere in the book, the classical tension between general and specialized KOSs is best addressed not by choosing one over the other but by integrating the two approaches.

Possibilities of Connecting Interdisciplinary Knowledge to Comprehensive KOSs

Domain analysis has generally been pursued with the goal of developing domain-specific KOSs (and has often been guided by a belief that only such classifications were feasible). Care must thus be taken in drawing conclusions regarding the possibility of employing domain analysis with the goal of developing a comprehensive classification. Yet some key findings above indicate that this is indeed possible. Most importantly, it appears that fields often borrow terms from other fields without changing their meaning. When the meaning is changed, this often appears to reflect a change in perspective: 'hygiene' comes to mean 'hygiene as affected by gender.' In such cases the use of a synthetic approach should allow clarity in terminology across fields.

Terms borrowed from other disciplines represent the vast majority of concepts employed in an interdiscipline. Including these in a domain-specific KOS necessarily obscures the importance of the core terminology of the interdiscipline. Placing the interdiscipline within a general classification, and allowing synthetic links between any terms, provides a more accurate portrayal of the nature of any interdiscipline.

Each interdiscipline also has a core set of terms that it tends to develop internally. Notably, these are generally a small percentage of the total. These can generally be placed within one or a few classes: the core terms in gender studies are either subclasses of gender or synthetic constructs of these. If other fields borrow these terms without altering their meaning (at least in a way that a synthetic approach cannot handle in a very straightforward manner), then the path to a comprehensive classification is clear. We employ these terms as they are defined in the field of origin.

How many concepts carry subtle but important differences in meaning—beyond those resulting from differences in perspective alone—across fields? How difficult in practice is it to clarify these differences in meaning through synthetic qualification? Such empirical questions have rarely been investigated. Our analysis in other chapters suggests that the answers may well be 'a very small proportion,' and 'not very hard at all.' Comparative domain analysis (using similar strategies to the cross-cultural domain analyses explored above) could provide more precise answers. Further research across fields and with an eye toward a general classification is clearly called for (We return to questions of recommended empirical analysis in the concluding chapter).

It is also worth noting that there is a considerable degree of ambiguity within domain-specific KOSs. It is far from straightforward to identify core terminology: different KOSs stress different core concepts. It would be a mistake, then, to compare the degree of clarity that can be achieved in a comprehensive classification with an exaggerated sense of the clarity that is achieved within a domain-specific KOS.

Moreover the domain analysis of gender studies highlighted the likelihood of change: the field has not yet consolidated its terminology. In an academy characterized by the continual fragmentation and hybridization of fields (Dogan and Pahre 1990), this will be a common characteristic of fields. And thus hospitality becomes a critical desideratum of any KOS. A comprehensive and synthetic classification is inevitably more hospitable than a domain-specific classification grounded in the terminology employed at a particular point in time.

We should also appreciate that domain analysis is not easy. Multiple methods should be employed. Each is time-consuming. Only a small number of domains have been seriously engaged by information scientists performing domain analysis (Smiraglia 2012). If some/most/all of the terms borrowed by one domain from another could be treated expeditiously through reference to a general classification, domain analysis would be facilitated.

KOSs require structure as well as terminology. Even if we capture a field's concepts within a general KOS, the field could still feel under-represented if their concepts are always situated at lower levels within hierarchies that appear to privilege other fields. The solution here may well lie simply in an insistence on logical hierarchy. If all subclasses represent logical divisions ('type of,' 'example of,' or 'part of') of superior classes, then all fields must be treated fairly. If we stress in our classification a synthetic approach where terms from multiple (fairly flat) hierarchies are regularly linked, then fairness across fields is even more firmly entrenched. It still may be desirable to be able to somehow map the set of interactions emphasized within a domain and thus visually identify domain-specific KOSs within the broader KOS.

Key Points

Though domain analysis has not in the past been harnessed to the task of generating a comprehensive phenomenon-based classification, it seems feasible to do so. Comparisons should be made across domains (as they have been made within domains but across cultures). We can and should identify the degree of differences in definition across domains and then establish how difficult it is to cope with these. The goal would be a general classification that respects the terminology employed in each domain.

Domain analysis suggests that structure is also important. A stress on a synthetic approach, plus an insistence on logical hierarchy, should generate a structure that treats all domains fairly. It may be both possible and desirable to then identify particular domains within this broader structure.

We should appreciate that domain analysis is difficult. Several methods, each challenging, should be pursued in tandem. Given the overlap in terminology across fields, the development of a comprehensive classification should facilitate domain analysis.

References

Association for Interdisciplinary Studies (AIS) (2013) About interdisciplinarity. http://www.oakland.edu/ais/

Bruschini C, Ardaillon D, Unbehaum S (1998) Tesauro para Estudos de Gênero e sobre Mulheres. Fundación Carlos Chagas, Sao Paulo

Dogan M, Pahre R (1990) Creative marginality: innovation at the intersection of social sciences. Westview, Boulder, CO

Glenisson P, Glänzel W, Persson O (2005) Combining full-text analysis and bibliometric indicators. A pilot study. Scientometrics 63(1):163–180

Hinze S (1996) Mapping of RandD structures in transdisciplinary areas: new biotechnology in Food Science. Scientometrics 37(2):313–335

Hjørland B (2002) Domain analysis in information science. Eleven approaches—traditional as well as innovative. J Doc 58(4):422–462

International Information Centre and Archives for the Women's Movement (IIAV) (1998) European Women's thesaurus. IIAV, Amsterdam

Instituto de la Mujer (España). Centro de Documentación (2002). Tesauro "Mujer". Madrid, Instituto de la Mujer, 1999. 6ª ed. Rev. 2002. http://www.mtas.es/mujer/t2002.doc

Jacob S (2008) Cross-disciplinarization. A new talisman for evaluation? Am J Eval 29(2):175–194

Julien C-A, Tirilly P, Dinneen J, Guastavino C (2013) Reducing subject tree browsing complexity. J Am Soc Inform Sci Technol 64:2201–2223

Kobashi NY, Smit JW, Talamo MGM (2001) A função da terminologia na construção do objeto da Ciência da Informação. DataGramaZero–Revista de Ciência da Informação 2(2)

López-Huertas MJ (2006a) Análisis del dominio interdisciplinar para la representación y organización del conocimiento. Conferencia invitada en Memória, Informaçao e Organização do Conhecimento: Cruzando as fronteiras da identidade. UNIRIO-IBICT, Río de Janeiro, pp 209–236

López-Huertas MJ (2006b) Thematic map of interdisciplinary domains based on their terminological representation. The gender studies. In: Budin G, Swertz C, Mitgutsch K (eds) Knowledge Organization for a Global Learning Society. Proceedings of the ninth international ISKO conference, Vienna. Ergon, Würzburg, pp 331–338

López-Huertas MJ (2006c) Aproximación a un modelo para la construcción de mapas temáticos en dominios interdisciplinares. First international conference on multidisciplinary information sciences and technologies, InSciT2006, Cáceres. Instituto Abierto del Conocimiento, Badajoz. pp 548–552

López-Huertas MJ (2007) Comment on the León Manifesto. www.iskoi.org/ilc/leon.php

López-Huertas MJ (2008) Cultural impact on knowledge representation and organization in a subject domain. In: Arsenault C, Tennis J (eds) Culture and identity in Knowledge Organization, Proceedings of the 10th international ISKO conference, Montréal. Ergon, Würzburg

López-Huertas MJ (2009) La terminología como método para representar y organizar dominios multidimensionales. 1er Simposio sobre Organización del Conocimiento: Bibliotecología y Terminología. UNAM, México

López-Huertas MJ, Barité M (2002) Knowledge representation and organization of Gender Studies on the Internet: towards integration. In: López-Huertas MJ (ed) Challenges in knowledge representation and organization for the 21st century. Integration of knowledge across boundaries. Proceedings of 7th international ISKO conference, Granada. Ergon, Würzburg

López-Huertas MJ, Jiménez Contreras E (2004) Spanish research in Knowledge Organization (1992–2001). Knowl Org 31(3):136–150

López-Huertas MJ, Barité M, Torres I (2004) Terminological representation of specialized areas in conceptual structures: the case of Gender Studies. In: McIlwaine IC (ed) Proceedings of the 8th international ISKO conference. Ergon Verlag, Würzburg, pp 263–268

McAlpine S (2014) Concept mapping model, academic disciplines, and interdisciplinarity. Crossing Border Int J Interdiscipl Stud 2(1):7–12

Moya F, López-Huertas MJ (2000) An automatic model for updating the conceptual structure of a scientific discipline. In: Beghtol C, Howarth L, Williamson N (eds) Dynamism and stability in knowledge organization. Proceedings of the sixth international ISKO conference. Ergon Verlag, Würzburg, pp 55–63

Porter AL, Rafols I (2009) Is science becoming more interdisciplinary? Measuring and mapping six research fields over time. Scientometrics 81(3):719–745

Rafols I, Meyer M (2010) Diversity and network coherence as indicators of interdisciplinarity: case study of bio-nanoscience. Scientometrics 82:263–287

Repko AF (2012) Interdisciplinary research: process and theory, 2nd edn. Sage, Thousand Oaks

Schwechheimer H, Winterhager M (2001) Mapping interdisciplinary research fronts in neuroscience: a bibliometric view to retrograde amnesia. Scientometrics 51(1):311–318

Sebastiá i Salat M (1988) Thesaurus d'història social de la Dona. Generalitat de Catalunya, Barcelona

Smiraglia RP (2012) Epistemology of domain analysis. In: Smiraglia RP, Lee H (eds) Cultural frames of knowledge. Ergon Verlag, Würzburg, pp 111–124

Szostak R (2014) Classifying the humanities. Knowl Org 41(4):263–275

Tomov DT, Mutafov HG (1996) Comparative indicators of interdisciplinarity in modern science. Scientometrics 37(2):267–278

Chapter 7
How to Develop a KOS to Serve Interdisciplinarity

This chapter begins with several strategies for developing the sort of general classification urged in preceding chapters. It first discusses strategies for reducing ambiguity. It then addresses how to structure a phenomenon-based KOS. Integrative levels, dependence relationships, and general systems theory are explored. The chapter then looks in some detail at the practical classification of phenomena and relationships.[1]

How to Cope with Ambiguity

How can the problem of ambiguity best be coped with in a comprehensive classification? Table 7.1 summarizes the strategies that have been suggested in previous chapters.

We can draw on the field of semiotics for justification of the pursuit of such strategies. That field stresses that the words used to signify the things in the world never perfectly capture what they signify. There is thus inevitable ambiguity in human communication. The semiotician should aid in the process of interpretation (e.g. Barthes 2000). That is, while ambiguity is inevitable, we should pursue strategies to lessen the degree of ambiguity.

Wesolek (2012) worries that different disciplines may wish to break a complex concept into different basic concepts: a sociologist may disagree with an economist as to whether a loan shark is a 'financial institution.' But this is a strength of the approach recommended above rather than a weakness, for it illustrates how breaking complex concepts into more basic concepts allows us to precisely identify the

---

[1] More detailed advice on how to develop such a classification can be found on the websites of the Integrative Levels Classification (see Integrative Levels Classification 2004) and the Basic Concepts Classification (see Szostak 2013). These are described in more detail in Chap. 4.

© Springer International Publishing Switzerland 2016
R. Szostak et al., *Interdisciplinary Knowledge Organization*,
DOI 10.1007/978-3-319-30148-8_7

Table 7.1 Strategies for reducing ambiguity in a comprehensive classification

Break complex concepts into simpler 'basic' concepts that are subject to less ambiguity.
Place these simple concepts within clear hierarchies that are strictly organized according to logical rules. Such a logical classification will clearly indicate what a particular concept is and is not.[a]
Allow these simpler concepts to be freely linked with each other. This clarifies terminology by placing terms in 'sentences.'
Develop a comprehensive thesaurus to further clarify the relationship among concepts (and perhaps in time an ontology to provide logical definitions of each concept). Such a thesaurus could include entry points from domain-specific classifications and thesauri.

[a]In their textbook on critical thinking, Groarke and Tindale (2004, 95) identify 'Classification of the constituent parts of a term' as the first of three key strategies, along with 'Identification of a term's essential qualities,' and 'Stipulation of a particular narrow meaning at the outset of a particular argument.' Our other strategies seek a narrow essential definition

sources of misunderstanding. Both a sociologist and economist could understand a scope note discussing whether loan sharks were to be included in the class of financial institutions. Wesolek also worries that Szostak's attempt to define 'food' precisely in terms of physiological function fails to address usage such as 'food for thought.' But surely any classification (and thesaurus) has to distinguish metaphorical uses of a word.

By linking phenomena and relationships (and properties; see below), we can mimic to some extent the sentence structure employed in texts. It is well appreciated in the field of communication studies that sentences are less ambiguous than individual terms, for the sentence provides context for the terms it contains; communication theory emphasizes 'thought units' that may or not be sentences but contain multiple terms (Keyton and Beck 2010). There has also been some recent recognition of the value of sentence structure within knowledge organization. Fricke (2012) applies logical analysis to the field of knowledge organization, applauds a synthetic approach to classification, and recommends that we transcend Boolean searching in order to be able to clearly distinguish 'large library school' from 'large school library.' Such a goal can only be achieved by structuring synthetic subject headings. Blair (2006, 347–8) also argues that the best path to reducing terminological ambiguity is to place terms in sentences; this is why internet search engines provide search results within the context of sentences. The approach recommended in this book allows search by sentence.

We should note a critical relationship between the second and third strategies on the list in Table 7.1. The pursuit of a synthetic approach to classification greatly facilitates the pursuit of logical hierarchy. The synthetic approach means that we need not pretend that compounds of two classes are actually subclasses of one of these. Mazzocchi et al. (2007) discuss abuses of hierarchy at length. 'Recycling,' for example is clearly not a type of garbage but something that we do to garbage. The examples that Mazzocchi et al. provide could each be addressed through a synthetic approach. And thus we can focus our hierarchies on real subclasses.

Do the strategies in Table 7.1 reduce ambiguity 'enough' that diverse users will have similar enough understandings of the meanings of the terms employed in a comprehensive classification for the purpose of navigating that classification easily? This is, critically, an empirical question, and one that can only be evaluated after all ambiguity-reducing stratagems have been implemented. We will in Chap. 8 review some of the theoretical arguments that have been made with respect to the issue of ambiguity (since the question of ambiguity is of central importance to our project), but it deserves to be stressed here that empirical issues cannot be decided theoretically. Theoreticians may posit that there is 'too much' ambiguity or not, but these hypotheses must then be evaluated empirically. We will address strategies for empirical analysis in Chap. 10.

It should be stressed that information science need not entirely eliminate ambiguity. As long as different individuals have broadly similar understandings of the terms employed they will be able to navigate the same knowledge organization system. Philosophers have been troubled for millennia by their collective inability to provide very precise definitions of words such as 'freedom' or 'justice.' This has not prevented information scientists from guiding users to works about freedom or justice. Quite simply, knowledge organization can accept a greater degree of ambiguity than has troubled philosophers. And naturally philosophers have devoted most of their attention to the most troubling concepts. The likelihood that most concepts are in fact less ambiguous than 'freedom' or 'justice' has in fact been borne out in efforts to develop the ILC and BCC. It would be a serious error in judgment to leap from the recognition that philosophers are troubled by the existence of ambiguity to a conclusion that a comprehensive classification is infeasible.

It should also be stressed that ambiguity does not disappear within disciplines or cultural groups. To be sure, the degree of ambiguity increases when one crosses group boundaries. But we should be careful of assuming that it increases immensely in the absence of detailed empirical research. Again efforts to develop the ILC and BCC indicate that the degree of ambiguity is manageable if appropriate strategies are pursued.

Our emphasis on empirical analysis reflects an important point: differences of opinion regarding the feasibility of a comprehensive phenomenon-based KOS reflect differences of degree rather than of kind: nobody doubts that there is ubiquitous ambiguity in the world or that this is a challenge for KOSs. The question is how much ambiguity there is and how much particular classificatory projects can cope with (Szostak and Gnoli 2014). Figure 7.1 illustrates this key fact: the extremes along both continua are clearly ridiculous. We can only empirically establish our position along either continuum, and particularly whether the degree of ambiguity that exists (after we have pursued all ambiguity-reducing strategies) is greater or less than the amount of ambiguity that a particular classificatory project can withstand.

The degree to which ambiguity can be lessened by classification is hidden from us by the simple fact that most library users do not understand how library catalogs are organized (in part because these systems are not very logically organized; see

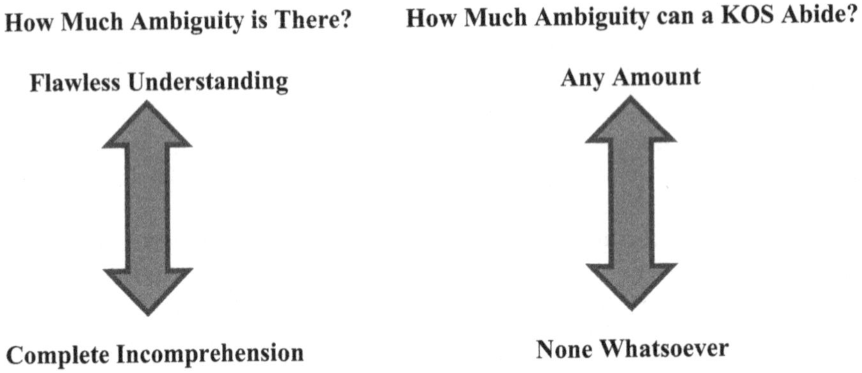

How Much Ambiguity is There?   How Much Ambiguity can a KOS Abide?

Flawless Understanding   Any Amount

Complete Incomprehension   None Whatsoever

Fig. 7.1 The continua of terminological ambiguity

Julien et al. 2013). If library users understood the logic behind some comprehensive classification, they would find the terminology used in that classification much less ambiguous. Nor do users need to master the entire classification: As long as a computer can be programmed with the logical structure of an entire classification, it can take a user from any search item to a visual outline of how the user's interests are reflected within the organization of knowledge (DeRidder 2007).

We should note in closing that these strategies for reducing ambiguity have uses far beyond KOSs. Interdisciplinary scholars have difficulty not just in finding relevant resources but in communicating across disciplinary boundaries. Szostak (2014) outlines how the simple act of breaking complex concepts into basic concepts facilitates interdisciplinary communication. Importantly, he appreciates that interdisciplinary conversation, like KOSs, can withstand a certain amount of ambiguity. He further notes the advantages of being able to refer to a logical hierarchical classification in clarifying the nature of a phenomenon. A comprehensive thesaurus would likewise be useful for clarifying terminology and suggesting alternatives.

Phenomena as KOS Units

As it is our thesis that discipline-based systems are an obstacle to interdisciplinarity, we should not rely on disciplines as the basic principle to build new systems. Disciplines will still be dealt with in the new KOSs, but not as the primary structuring principle as has been the case in traditional bibliographic classifications.

The logical alternative to grounding a KOS in disciplines is to take as the basic unit for the organization of knowledge the objects of study themselves.[2] In the

---

[2] A third option would be to start from kinds of documents, like school handbooks or academic articles or documentary films, that is from the dimension of *carriers*; but clearly this would lead us

Knowledge Organization literature (e.g., Mills and Broughton 1977; Beghtol 1998) the studied objects are usually referred to as the *phenomena*. This term has the advantage of being very general, as it encompasses not only 'things'—what most usually comes to mind as the typical objects of knowledge, such as metals, lakes, trees, people, villages, hammers, or paintings—but also properties, processes, or events—like greenness, size, growth, friendship, rituals, or conferences [we will find it useful to distinguish properties from 'things' below]. Anything perceived and known by humans, either directly or by means of tools like microscopes or statistical calculations, is a phenomenon.

The word originally comes from a Greek verb meaning 'to appear.' Indeed, what we perceive and can thus incorporate into knowledge is always mediated by our senses. From the metaphysical viewpoint, 'things in themselves' cannot be perceived directly by humans: they are only known through phenomena. This does not necessarily imply that human knowledge is fundamentally limited: indeed, in time we are able to relate phenomena to each other, to test hypotheses and to develop increasingly sophisticated theories, so that our knowledge of phenomena becomes more precise. For example, a phenomenon like air was seen by ancient thinkers as a primary substance (together with fire, earth, and water), but it then came to be understood to be composed of more basic substances, nitrogen and oxygen: while the phenomenon is still there, it is now better placed within the system of knowledge.

In sum, phenomena, as they are currently known in the evolving corpus of knowledge, can be taken as the primary unit for a KOS supporting interdisciplinary research. What does this imply for the structure of such a KOS? Clearly, in order to arrange existing phenomena within a KOS we need to identify some structuring principles of an ontological nature. That is, the structure of the KOS should reflect directly the kinds of entities that exist. In contrast, epistemological principles, referring to ways of knowing, play a major role in disciplinary systems. For example, the Baconian tri-partition stating that disciplines can be divided into the products of human reason, of human creativity, and of human memory was inherited by the Dewey Decimal Classification (Gnoli 2006a; Dousa 2010). Epistemological principles can still be relevant to interdisciplinary systems: in particular they are necessary to organize theories and methods (Szostak 2004; see below), as recommended by the Léon Manifesto; or to account for different 'levels of knowing' that have evolved during the history of human knowledge (Kleineberg 2013). Nevertheless, the primary principles of an interdisciplinary system should be ontological. We consider next some good candidates.

---

even farther from an interdisciplinary approach. It is nevertheless valuable to classify documents in terms of this dimension, and facilitate searches that might illuminate how different types of carrier operate in different fields.

Principles for Helpful Sequence

Ranganathan (1967) identified eight general principles for arranging subjects in 'helpful sequences' in any classification context:

- later-in-time
- later-in-evolution
- spatial contiguity
- quantitative measure
- increasing complexity
- canonical sequence
- literary warrant
- alphabetical order

The principles are listed in order. Each of these principles should prevail on the succeeding ones in case of conflict: smaller entities may precede larger ones, but if a larger one has appeared earlier than a smaller one the time principle will then prevail over the measure principle.

Application clearly varies according to the domain context: spatial contiguity will thus be relevant for mountains or planets rather than for emotions. However, Ranganathan does not provide any further analysis of the relationships between the different principles, nor any theoretical rationale for them.

The three last principles clearly concern more pragmatic aspects of document management, and as such they are marginal to our search for ontological principles. On the other hand, the five other principles can be applied to both disciplinary systems (like Ranganathan's Colon Classification) and phenomenon-based systems. Indeed, phenomena can well be ordered according to their time of existence, evolutionary origin, spatial location, size, or complexity.

These properties of phenomena are often correlated: phenomena that have appeared later in evolution were also absent in early times, and are often more complex than their precursors. This suggests that it is possible to identify some more general principle, which provides a sort of synthesis of other principles. Admittedly, one has to be careful in adopting generalizations that may fail to fit the variety of actual phenomena dealt with in human knowledge: while Ranganathan's principles came from his practical experience with arranging subjects, further abstractions will have to be tested against the actual work of knowledge organization. However, generalizations may also offer powerful tools for systematizing knowledge.

Levels of Reality

The theory of integrative levels claims that the natural world is organized in a series of levels of increasing complexity: from physical particles and molecules, through biological structures, to the most sophisticated products of human thought. Each level cannot exist without the lower ones (e.g. there are no organisms not formed with atoms), but at the same time it has additional emergent properties not found at the lower levels (e.g. organisms can be said to be alive or dead, while atoms cannot). This view goes beyond the traditional opposition between reductionism—which argues that everything should be understood at the lowest levels of organization—and vitalism—which alternatively celebrates only the higher levels of organization—both of which have important limitations.

It is perhaps not surprising that these levels have proven attractive for the organization of knowledge. Philosophers of science attempting to systematize known phenomena have often found that these phenomena can be arranged quite easily in a series of classes of increasing organization. Each class is then based on the previous ones, but at the same time shows novel properties of its own. Organisms are made of chemical elements, but still the laws of chemistry are not enough to account for cell differentiation in embryos or sexual reproduction.

In the Middle Ages, this series of grades was described as the *scala naturae*: that is a ladder with phenomena of 'higher' nature laying at each next step: inanimate beings, then plants, animals, moral beings like men, and spiritual beings like saints and angels, with God on the top. Such a description also gave the ladder a connotation of value: the higher a phenomenon lays the more noble it is in the metaphysical ranking of the world. Book collections such as the library of Kremsmünster Abbey in Austria even mimic this model of knowledge, as books on 'higher' subjects are kept on higher floors.

Modern science takes a more neutral approach to phenomena, giving equal dignity to the study of atoms and molecules as to that of economic or technological systems. Reductionist thinkers like Jaegwon Kim even believe that the study of physical phenomena is the only fundamental one, as all other levels are derived from them (Kim 2006). Other philosophers, especially in the Continental tradition, instead emphasize that at each new level phenomena of the previous levels are now integrated into an organic whole, which is something ontologically very different from a simple collection of lower-level phenomena. For this reason they have been also described as *integrative levels* (e.g. Needham 1943, Feibleman 1954).

Similar pictures have been drafted by many philosophers since the second half of the nineteenth century, including Auguste Comte, Herbert Spencer, André-Marie Ampère, Friedrich Engels, Pierre Teilhard de Chardin, Samuel Alexander, Conwy Lloyd Morgan, C.D. Broad, Nicolai Hartmann, Roy Wood Sellars, Roberto Poli (see Blitz 1992 for an account of the English-speaking tradition). Some philosophers use different languages to describe similar ideas, such as Herman Dooyeweerd's (1997) 15 *aspects* that permeate all life with complementary meanings (numeric, spatial, kinematic, physical, biotic, sensitive, analytic, formative, lingual, social, economic, aesthetic, juridical, ethical, and pistic). That the idea appears in different forms and within several philosophical traditions is a hint of its general relevance.

Though the details are still debated there is considerable consensus regarding the actual levels that would deserve treatment in a classification system. Generally speaking, most lists of levels include such classes of phenomena as subatomic particles, atoms, molecules, cells, organisms, ecosystems, minds, societies, political institutions, artifacts, and intellectual products. [These are sometimes described in terms of the fields that study these phenomena—physics, chemistry, biology, and so on—rather than the phenomena themselves, but note that physics in particular operates at multiple levels.] This series is clearly a useful reference to which a sequence of main classes in a KOS can refer, as most users can grasp the rationale behind it. Indeed, it has been applied to bibliographic classification in more or less explicit ways by important authors in the field, including E.C. Richardson, J.D. Brown, H.E. Bliss, S.R. Ranganathan, B.C. Vickery, D.J. Foskett, and I. Dahlberg (Gnoli 2006a).[3]

The Classification Research Group, and especially D.J. Foskett (1961, 1978) took a keen interest in integrative levels. After much discussion, they adopted the version articulated by Feibleman. Although Spiteri (1995) doubts that the CRG was successful in implementing integrative levels in their classifications, at its most basic level this is fairly straightforward: one assigns main classes to sub-atomic particles, atoms, molecules, and so on. One challenge comes with the social sciences (as well as professional programs) which might be considered to analyze different aspects of the same level of social interaction. But even then the idea of levels provides a useful starting point, and at least serves to distinguish the psychological examination of individuals from the study of society. Both the ILC and BCC have been organized around integrative levels. Table 7.2 shows the main classes in ILC.

Emergence and Existential Dependence

A notion often associated with levels of reality is that of *emergence*, the transition from a lower level of phenomena to a higher one. Some distinguish between *weak emergences*, which are quite well understood by contemporary science, like those between atoms and molecules or between individuals and societies, and *strong emergences*, which look quite mysterious. *Strong emergences*, like the appearance of life from molecules or even more the appearance of conscious minds from the brain, are among the greatest philosophical (and scientific) challenges of all times.

---

[3] A detailed bibliography on levels theories and their application to knowledge organization, edited by Claudio Gnoli and Hong Mei, is available at www.iskoi.org/ilc/ref.php.

Table 7.2 The main classes in ILC

Class notation	Class title	Class notation	Class title
a	Forms	n	Populations
b	Spacetime	o	Instincts
c	Energy	p	Consciousness
d	Particles	q	Signs
e	Atoms	r	Languages
f	Molecules	s	Civil society
g	Bodies	t	Governments
h	Celestial objects	u	Economies
i	Weather	v	Technologies
j	Land	w	Artifacts
k	Genes	x	Art
l	Bacteria	y	Knowledge
m	Organisms	z	Religion

Indeed Hartmann (1943, 1952), an important source for recent authors in knowledge organization, claims that there are actually two kinds of levels: *layers*, that are connected by a material relationship of 'overforming' such as that between atoms and molecules, and *strata*, that are connected by the stronger relationship of 'building-above' like those between organisms and minds or between individual minds and collective spirit (culture) (Poli 2001). Both of these types of relationship are cases of existential dependence: the phenomena at the higher level could not exist without the prior existence of those at the lower level (dependences other than existential also exist: for example, being a husband depends on a wife, although without the wife the individual who was the husband does not cease to exist: see Lowe 2005).

Hartmann's works only focus on the properties of entities belonging to the different levels, without discussing whether these ontological levels are there since the beginning, or they have originated each from the others at some time. Still, many find that such a pattern fits well an evolutionary framework, in which the emergence of new levels has occurred at some points in the history of the universe, despite the fact that in many cases we ignore the details of how this has happened.

A promising direction for investigation comes from the observation that the major strata, like matter, life, mind, society and culture, usually include some form of memory (genes, neural memory, spoken language, published documents, and so on). Such memories can be seen as systems capable of *modeling* the forms of other phenomena using new material elements: documents can record any other phenomena, language can discuss anything, minds can perceive and imagine anything, and even genes can be seen as a 'model' of the external environment that the organism has to fit in order to survive. Thus, while dependence between layers is material, dependence between strata may be formal.

In any case, knowledge organization does not need to solve all of the philosophical debates concerning emergence and levels. What it needs is only some principles general enough to arrange phenomena into consistent systems. The notion of levels of reality does provide such general principles, as well as the general relationship of existential dependence (Gnoli et al. 2007; Gnoli 2013), of both the material and the representational varieties. Dependence can thus be coupled with the classical relationships that have been used for centuries in hierarchical classifications and taxonomies, genus/species and whole/part. The complex of these relationships is able to provide the skeleton of general KOSs capable of managing quite a rich variety of concepts (Gnoli 2010).

It should be stressed that it is both feasible and common to study how phenomena at one level influence phenomena at another. The field of biochemistry studies how chemical processes influence biological functions. Environmental studies as a field devotes much of its attention to how human activities affect chemical and biological (and sometimes physical) processes. We should thus employ integrative levels as a strategy for organizing main classes in a KOS, but allow also in some fashion for interactions among these main classes. The latter has, of course, been one of our primary concerns in this book.

General Systems Theory

Another way of looking at classes of phenomena irrespective of the details of their particular domain is general systems theory. This was initiated by biologist Ludwig von Bertalanffy (1968), economist Kenneth Boulding (1956) and others, who were interested in considering the properties and behavior of a wide variety of phenomena in term of abstract principles, so that these could be treated in mathematical models. The first applications of general systems theory included cybernetics and engineering. However, the theory also has a wider relevance to philosophy of science and, as a consequence, to knowledge organization (Foskett 1972, 1974).

In general systems theory, phenomena are seen as systems composed of parts, and their behavior is described by abstract laws in terms of relationships between the parts as well as with the external context. Philosophers like Mario Bunge (1979) emphasize that any system has a triadic nature: its constituting elements, its structure, and its external environment. Hofkirchner (2012) describes these as a micro-structure, a meso-structure, and a macro-structure. The generality of such a model suits well the needs of knowledge organization. Indeed, the categories provided by systems theory can be applied to most classes of phenomena, irrespective of their particular nature.

Note that the notion of system is in a way orthogonal to that of level: at each level in the series of main classes, a local analysis can be performed by looking at the phenomena of the level as systems: atoms are systems of electrons and protons, organisms are systems of cells, economies are systems of producers and consumers, and so on. In the tradition of knowledge organization, sets of attributes of each main class have often been represented as facets.

Facet Analysis

Unlike theories of levels, of emergence, and of systems, the theory of facets has been developed mainly within the field of information science. The facets of a given domain of knowledge are standard ways to analyze and represent its subjects: in gardening they can be plants, organs, operations, seasons, climates, tools; in ethnography they can be peoples, rituals, regions, methods of enquiry; and so on (Vickery 1960). Facet theory was first articulated by Ranganathan in the 1930s (see Ranganathan 1967). It inspired the Colon Classification and the work of the Classification Research Group in Britain. Many enumerative classifications that already existed have adopted elements of facet analysis, notably the UDC and the Bliss Classification.

The facets of any given domain can usually be reduced to a general set of *fundamental categories*. Different authors have generated differing lists of fundamental categories, but mostly these follow a common pattern including the objects of study, their parts, their constituent materials, their properties, processes they undergo, actions performed on them, agents of such actions, means used for them, spatial location, time period, and so on. These, when occurring in a subject, should be expressed in a standard citation order, so that the most relevant information is at the beginning of a subject string or classmark, and consistency is kept throughout the system.

While *facet* is a special term within information science, other terms such as *roles* or *links* are used in different systems to manage basically the same functionalities (Gardin 1973). The theory also has parallels in general linguistics in the notion of deep cases, as well as in philosophy in that of general categories (Gnoli 2008a). Again, very general principles are the most suitable to be used for the structure of general KOSs.

In their prototypical implementations by Ranganathan and the Classification Research Group, facets have been applied to disciplinary classes. However, it has been shown that the same faceted syntax can also be applied to classes of phenomena (Gnoli 2006b). In this case, the fundamental categories need to be identified as categories of phenomena themselves, such as kind, pattern, destination, origin, part, element, process, place, time, and form (Gnoli 2008b). Some of these could serve as the syntactical device to represent relationships identified by the theories considered above: parts of systems can be expressed by part facets, material dependence by element facets, and representational dependence by pattern facets.

Some Guidelines for Classifying Phenomena

Extant classifications generally focus on classifying phenomena, albeit within disciplinary categories. The main innovation of the approach recommended in this book is to develop a comprehensive classification of phenomena. Strategies for reducing ambiguity in such an enterprise were addressed above.

Phenomena are disaggregated in our recommended classification usually by 'type of,' but occasionally also/instead by 'parts of.'[4] It is almost always clear which is the appropriate operative principle. Subdivision in terms of 'elements of' is much more common in natural science, but occurs in human science in areas such as technology, science, health and population. Logical disaggregation of classes—grounded in an ontological understanding of the world—is naturally supplemented by an inductive 'literary warrant' approach—itself informed by an epistemological appreciation of the academy—that ensures that all topics are represented.

Notation is often eschewed in classification of digital materials but is still of critical importance for bibliographic classification. The UDC is criticized for unwieldy synthetic notations. Much of the problem stems from very long notation for simple subjects (because UDC builds upon DDC7), though UDC may also sometimes put more detail in the call number than is required (Foskett 1996, 186). The general solution is to have very short notations for simple subjects. This can be accomplished if there are shallow hierarchies within a manageable number of main classes. This is achieved within both ILC and BCC. It should be stressed that notationally compact synthesis is difficult to achieve within an enumerative classification, for the classes to be synthesized will often have lengthy notations themselves. Synthesis is more feasible in a classification designed from the outset with the intention of facilitating synthesis of simple terminology across all domains.[5] The ILC and BCC are both designed such that phenomena, relationships, and properties can be linked synthetically.

An Example: Economic Phenomena

Let us take the study of the economy as a starting point. There are two major kinds of economic phenomena (which can be thought of as facets). The first are the components of economic output (the types of expenditure, such as investment and consumption; the types of income, such as wages and profits; and finally the output of particular goods and services). The second are types of economic institution

---

[4] This does not mean that all parts are identified hierarchically. Molecules, for example, are not treated as parts of organisms, but are rather classified in their own right. Only parts that are tied to a particular class—such as the administrative units of a particular state—are treated hierarchically.

[5] There are still challenges. Gnoli et al. (2011) discusses several practical problems in providing notation within a freely faceted classification.

(financial, trade, labor, and so on). [There are three other subdivisions: economic ideology, income distribution, and economic fluctuations; these do not lend themselves to the same degree of subdivision.] This logical structure can claim an ontological basis: output must either be used for consumption today or invested to enhance consumption tomorrow; the several types of institution can be defined in terms of their function or purpose. Yet in its details it also reflects epistemology: as we have seen 'investment' is defined in a particular way by economists. Yet the very place of investment in the classification reinforces this meaning: it involves the devotion of real output to increases in the capital stock (and thus can be distinguished from paper transactions which just reallocate funds among people without any effect on the size of the capital stock). This logical structure, then, simultaneously reflects an ontological understanding of the world, applies terminology in a way that all economists can readily appreciate, and yet is amenable to understanding by non-economists. Whereas it is often thought that these goals are in conflict, this logical structure arguably performs each of these functions better than existing classifications in which related phenomena like consumption and investment are often dispersed. The Library of Congress Classification (LCC) separates the study of economic growth from the study of fluctuations; economists increasingly appreciate that these are related. At the same time, distinct phenomena are commingled: the institutions of property are treated by LCC in the same subclass as income from property; likewise capital is treated together with the institution of capitalism.

A synthetic approach to classification avoids many additional problems in the LCC treatment of the economy. At present, LCC needlessly mixes philosophical and economic treatments of such phenomena as price. It would be useful to appreciate that entries such as 'value' reflect a philosophical evaluation of economic behaviors. Likewise, utility is a psychological evaluation of economic output. Most subdivisions under management would be better characterized by synthetic notation (management of economic phenomena in many cases but also non-economic phenomena such as technology or gender relations.)

A Note on Properties

We have said little about 'properties' in this book. Yet as was noted above the synthetic approach recommended in this book allows us not just to combine things[6] and relationships, but to qualify these through synthesis with a set of adjectival/adverbial properties. Such properties are often included within subject headings in enumerative classifications, but not in a systematic manner. By pursuing a synthetic approach we facilitate search by property. An interdisciplinary researcher might be interested in what things (or relationships) are treated as 'beautiful' or 'authentic' or

---

[6] We utilize the terms 'things' or 'entities' here, as 'phenomena' are often defined to include 'properties.'

Table 7.3 Elements of a classification of properties

Selected main classes	Selected subclasses
Aesthetic	Beautiful, intense, and decorated
Behavioral	Intensely, elegant, and anonymous
Comparative	Superior, complementary and more
Evaluative	Successful, safe, and enjoyable
Functional	Necessary, sufficient, and strategic
Informational	Secret, fictional, and symbolic
Natural	Dry, bright, and acidic
Physical	Hard, smooth, and fuzzy
Perceptual	Clear, mysterious, and balanced
Relational	Full, united, and orderly
Time-related	Fast, historic, and delayed

'mysterious.' We thus follow Metcalfe, who had distinguished between 'specification' (types of a thing), which should be handled by the creation of a hierarchy of subject headings, and 'qualification' (everything else: process, aspect, form), which should be addressed through linked notation (in Foskett 1996, 127). The UDC, it should be noted, has also taken steps to develop auxiliary tables of properties that could be combined with the entities in its schedules (Broughton 2010).

We describe elsewhere how a mix of deduction and induction has been employed in the development of classifications of things and relators. The approach taken to classifying properties has leaned more heavily on induction: properties encountered in the literature were placed in the classification in categories of affinity and these categories were then expanded through reflection: once 'hot' was recognized as a property it made sense to allow for 'cold.'

At present the classification of properties [class Q] within the BCC groups some 200 distinct properties into two dozen categories. We can summarize some of these in Table 7.3.

It should be noted that the notation for properties is very compact: beautiful is $QA1$; fictional is $QI5$; and fuzzy is $QP8$. Notational space is saved by allowing the opposite of a property to be indicated by underlining: superior is $QC1$, while inferior is $\underline{QC1}$. The classification is also hospitable: there is room to add more properties if additional properties are found to be important.

Classifying Relationships

The stress on synthetic notation above encourages us to classify the relationships that exist among phenomena. Since this is a more novel enterprise than the classification of phenomena, it merits a somewhat more detailed discussion. We focus for the most part on justifying the extensive use of compounding, but close with several pieces of practical advice.

Though there are far fewer verbs than nouns in any language—and therefore it is reasonable to aspire to a much more compact classification of relations than of things—there are still thousands of verbs in the English language (Khoo 1995). As Khoo found, these can for the most part be grouped into classes of verbs with very similar meanings. This finding indicates that it is reasonable to seek a classification of relationships that need not contains thousands of main entries.

We have encouraged linking any two concepts above. This strategy turns out to be very useful with respect to verbs. Many verbs are compounds of two simpler verbs, while others are compounds of a verb with an adverb or phenomenon (see Szostak 2012a, or Table 5.4 in this book, for examples). And thus Szostak (2012a) could argue that *all* verbs could be captured through recourse to compounding fewer than a hundred verbs with each other or with entries in a comprehensive classification of things and properties (see Table 5.4 for examples).

Farradane (1967) attempted to develop preliminary classifications of 'entities,' 'activities,' 'abstracts,' and 'properties,' and argued that these four together comprise the essence of what needs to be classified.[7] The first and last of these classes comprise for the most part the noun-like things and adjective-like descriptors that account for the vast bulk of entries in existing classifications. The 'abstract' class is more troublesome. It includes non-causal relators associated with time and space (above, below, before, after). It also includes symbols (letters, numbers, words, sentences, etc.), which would generally be treated in the same way as 'entities.' Yet it also includes two subclasses of physical abstracts (rays, energy, heat, light) and behavioral abstracts (love, hate, pain) that—while they are in some ways 'entities'—are best conceived as relationships: [They might be conceived as self-activities, where a self-activity is defined by Farradane as a relationship between a thing and itself.] A heated B, C loves D, E feels pain.

Farradane's 'activity' class (supplemented by the physical and behavioral abstract subclasses) provides some idea of how to begin classifying causal relationships. He distinguishes physical activities (moving) from living activities (breathing), physical abstracts (increasing, using) and mental abstracts (counting, reasoning). Within each subclass, he identifies simple activities and complex activities. He also appreciates that complex activities may draw on simpler activities from more than one subclass: singing combines the physiological and mental.

Three of Farradane's main classes bear some similarity to three of Aristotle's four types of causation: Aristotle's efficient cause encompassed physical actions, his final cause dealt with the purpose intended by an intentional agent, and his formal cause analyzed the internal structure of a causal agent and thus would include physiological behaviors. Aristotle's material cause (the material of an object causes its existence) might best be captured by the whole/part subdivision within a hierarchical classification of things.

Farradane does not develop this classification in enough detail for it to be applied. His appreciation that complex activities are combinations of simpler activities supports our stress on synthesizing concepts above. A couple of other key lessons can be drawn:

---

[7] We ignore here Farradane's more abstract discussion of appurtenance, concurrence, and so on.

- It makes sense to identify key subclasses of causal relationships. Among these will be physical activities, physiological/biological activities, and mental activities. In all three cases both relationships and self-activity can be identified.
- Casual empiricism suggests that some activities (moving) will appear much more often than others (breathing) in a general classification. It might prove desirable to provide simple notation for a small number of often-used relationships, and more complex notation for a larger set of more rare relationships. Such a practice should also facilitate the use of combined notation for some complex relationships, if it is the more commonly used relationships that are most often combined.

Fellbaum (2002) provides further justification both for compounding and for identifying distinct classes of verbs. She argues that we should think of verb subclasses as primarily expressing 'manner': running and flying involve moving in a particular manner. Fellbaum also appreciates that verb subclasses might express differences in function (criticized versus advised as subsets of talking) or result (win versus lose as subsets of playing). She does not seem to have appreciated the possibility of whole/part subclasses (basting and rolling are subsets of cooking) [but Szostak 2012a, b found that these are rarely necessary.]. Fellbaum's emphasis on manner is important, for Fellbaum found that subordinate verbs often do not behave in the same way as their super-ordinate verb. In other words, they are not true subordinates. And thus they fail our desideratum of wanting clear logical rules for hierarchy. This indicates that we should be open to the possibility of using compounding rather than hierarchy. Fellbaum's suggestion that subordinate verbs often express manner further justifies this approach. Fellbaum found that different types of manner mattered for different types of verb: speed and type of transport for 'move' verbs, force for 'hit' verbs, type of fight for 'fight' verbs, purpose and means for 'communication.' She also found that direction of movement is generally far more important than manner. This too can best be captured by compounding a verb with some indicator of direction or location.

Fellbaum implicitly provides several other arguments for the use of compounds. She notes that exercise has a similar relationship to move verbs as pet has to animal nouns: it expresses function (running for exercise). Punish has few subordinate terms, but is associated with types of hitting, prison etc. Wave, nod, and shrug are movements of particular body parts but are more importantly gestures. Finally there is a set of result verbs including open, shut, melt, break, destroy, and clean. Fellbaum says they can have subordinates too (slam, bang). But again these seem more like compounds than subordinates.

If a classification will rely on post-coordinated synthetic terms (that is, where the classifier is allowed to synthesize, rather than being prescribed a set of allowable combinations), then it is essential that there always be one obvious way to make a compound. The classifier should not face a choice between 'ruffle feathers' and 'cause feathers to be ruffled.' This obvious point has an important implication: that we would want the concept 'ruffle' to appear only once in the classification. Since classifications of things and properties have progressed farther than classifications of relators, a pragmatic principle follows: When a concept has applications as relator and/or thing and/or property, it should generally be classified as thing or property, and then the relator will generally be captured by the compound 'causes x.' Several further pragmatic strategies for classifying relators are captured in Table 7.4.

Classifying Theories, Methods, and Perspectives

Much practical advice on how to proceed here was provided of necessity when discussing feasibility in Chap. 5. Since theories, methods, and perspectives are themselves each phenomena, then the advice given above regarding phenomena in general applies also to them.

Method is the easiest to classify, for there are only about a dozen methods, and these—and the more precise techniques applied within each broad method—are often though not always known by similar terminology across disciplines. Theory presents a greater challenge, but this challenge (for the classificationist at least) can be met by classifying theory types along at least five dimensions. Authorial perspective can be classified along several arrays.

In all three cases, it would make the task of classifiers much easier if authors would self-declare the theories, methods, and perspectives that were employed in a particular work.

Key Points

This chapter identified several critical elements for the development of a novel classification:

- Break complex concepts into simpler 'basic' concepts that are subject to less ambiguity;
- Place these simple concepts within clear hierarchies that are strictly organized according to logical rules. Such a logical classification will clearly indicate what a particular concept is and is not;
- Allow these simpler concepts to be freely linked with each other;
- Employ integrative levels to establish a set of main classes;
- Ensure that the system has a place for all facets;

Several more detailed strategies were outlined as well.

Table 7.4 Strategies for classifying relationships

Relators can generally be listed in the past participle. It should be stressed, though, that they can generally be used as present participles as well: 'A causing B' is similar to 'A causes B' for most classificatory purposes. If distinctions needed to be made, this could be done through compounding with suitable temporal indicators.
The linking terms 'to' or 'to be' can generally be omitted: 'cause to lose' is 'cause lose' and 'cause to be free' is 'cause free.'
Since most causal relators have opposites (move/rest, cause/ do not cause), we can reduce the complexity of our classification of relators by allowing the opposite of each to be signified notationally.
Some relators also have inverses: imply is the inverse of infer. It should generally be both possible and desirable to represent inverse meanings in precisely the same way. Since A implied X to B has the same meaning as B inferred X from A, these should be represented by exactly the same notation.
Since many relators refer to doing something again (most/all of the 're-' verbs do so, but there are others), it is also useful to capture all such relators by 'do X' combined with notation for 'again'.
Both Farradane and Perrault (1994) emphasize a distinction between 'causing' and 'reacting'. This precise distinction was also stressed in a different context by Szostak (2003, 2004). Yet the classificationist need not make this distinction. The statement 'Cats react to stress by hiding' could be reworded as 'Stressed cats hide.' The act of hiding in the second is equivalent to the reaction of hiding in the first. Either way, reaction is clear in context. Likewise a general statement that 'A encourages B to influence C' makes it clear that the impact of B on C is at least in part a reaction to the impact of A on B. Should it prove desirable in some contexts to distinguish reaction from action, this could be done by adding a notation for 'reaction' to the notation for any type of action. That is, since reactions involve the same set of verbs as actions, it is not necessary to develop separate classifications of these.
Similar arguments can be made with respect to distinctions between 'intended versus unintended,' 'enabling versus causing,' and 'focused versus peripheral.'
Nor is it necessary to develop detailed classification of 'cases.' Grammarians seek to identify a set of cases or roles that a relationship might connect, such as agent, experience, instrument, object, or goal. Yet grammarians disagree on a precise list of such cases. [There is a loose connection here to the facets identified in different applications of facet theory.] Only if it were thought that the same relator took on quite different meanings depending on the cases it connected, and such differences were not clear in context, would we need to develop separate case-specific classifications.
Must we distinguish necessary and sufficient? We need at most here a notation that expresses the degree of causal influence posited within a certain work. We need not in general worry about this matter of degree in classifying. Note, though, that a word such as 'forced' means 'caused in a sufficient manner' while 'required' denotes 'caused in a necessary manner.' The classificationist may thus wish to indicate more specific instances of causation of a necessary or sufficient manner. Along with necessity and sufficiency, some indicator of probability of effect might be valuable: how often is a particular effect anticipated to occur? (Barriere 2002)
The same advice can be applied to issues of temporality. Does the causal relationship occur at one time or continuously? Does the relationship between cause and effect cycle? Synthesis with temporal indicators can be pursued as necessary.
A slightly different distinction does, however, merit attention. Barriere (2002) follows others in distinguishing causes that affect the very existence of a result from causes that merely affect some characteristic(s). In the first case, there are four possibilities: creation, destruction, maintenance, and prevention. All must be captured in a classification of relationships. In the second, change may occur in diverse ways, but the three most common are changes in size, duration, and length. Along dimensions such as these, the possibilities are increase, decrease, and maintain, while the more generic 'modify' can be used when the direction of change is unknown or does not exist. These sorts of causation obviously lend themselves to compounding.

References

Barriere C (2002) Hierarchical refinement and representation of the causal relation. Terminology 8(1):91–111

Barthes R (2000) Mythologies (Lavers A, Trans.) Hill and Wang, New York [Originally published 1957]

Beghtol C (1998) Knowledge domains: multidisciplinarity and bibliographic classification systems. Knowl Org 25(1/2):1–12

von Bertalanffy L (1968) General system theory: foundations, development, applications. Braziller, New York

Blair D (2006) Wittgenstein, language, and information: 'Back to the Rough Ground!'. Springer, Dordrecht

Blitz D (1992) Emergent evolution: qualitative novelty and the levels of reality. Kluwer, New York

Boulding K (1956) General systems theory: the skeleton of a science. Manage Sci 2(3):197–208

Broughton V (2010) Concepts and terms in the faceted classification: the case of UDC. Knowl Org 37(4):270–279

Bunge M (1979) A treatise on basic philosophy, vol 4, Ontology 2: a world of systems. Kluwer, Dordrecht

DeRidder JL (2007) The immediate prospects for the application of ontologies in digital libraries. Knowl Org 34(4):227–246

Dooyeweerd H (1997) A new critique of theoretical thought. Edwin Mellen, Lewiston, NY

Dousa TM (2010) The simple and the complex in E.C. Richardson's theory of classification: observations on an early KO model of the relationship between ontology and epistemology. In: Gnoli C, Mazzocchi F (eds) Paradigms and conceptual systems in knowledge organization: Proceedings of the Eleventh international ISKO conference, Rome, Italy. Ergon, Würzburg

Farradane J (1967) Concept organization for information retrieval. Inform Storage Ret 3:297–314

Feibleman JK (1954) Theory of integrative levels. Br J Philos Sci 5(17):59–66, Reprinted in Theory of subject analysis (1985) Chan et al LM (eds) Libraries Unlimited, Littleton. pp 136–142

Fellbaum CD (2002) On the semantics of troponymy. In: Green R, Bean CA, Myaeng SH (eds) The semantics of relationships. Kluwer, Dordrecht, pp 23–34

Foskett AC (1996) The subject approach to information, 5th edn. Library Association Publishing, London

Foskett DJ (1961) Classification and integrative levels. In: Foskett DJ, Palmer BI (eds) The Sayers memorial volume. Library Association, London

Foskett DJ (1972) Information and general systems theory. J Librarianship 4(3):205–209

Foskett DJ (1974) Information and systems philosophy. J Librarianship 6(2):126–130

Foskett DJ (1978) The theory of integrative levels and its relevance to the design of information systems. Aslib Proc 30(6):202–208

Frické M (2012) Logic and the organization of information. Springer, Berlin

Gardin J-C (1965) SYNTOL. Graduate School of Library Service, Rutgers, the State University, New Brunswick, NJ

Gnoli C (2006a) Phylogenetic classification. Knowl Org 33(3):138–152

Gnoli C (2006b) The meaning of facets in non-disciplinary classification. In: Budin G, Swertz C, Mitgutsch K (eds) Knowledge Organization for a global learning society: proceedings of the 9th ISKO conference. Ergon, Würzburg, pp 11–18

Gnoli C (2008a) Facets: a fruitful notion in many domains. Axiomathes 18(2)

Gnoli C (2008b) Categories and facets in integrative levels. Axiomathes 18(2):177–192

Gnoli C (2010) Levels, types, facets: three structural principles for KO. In: Gnoli C, Mazzocchi F (eds) Paradigms and conceptual systems in knowledge organization: proceedings of the eleventh international ISKO conference, Rome, Italy. Ergon, Würzburg, pp 129–137

Gnoli C (2013) Facets, levels, and semantic factoring. SRELS J Inform Manage 50(6):751–762

Gnoli C, Bosch M, Mazzocchi F (2007) A new relationship for multidisciplinary knowledge organization systems: dependance. In: Bravo BR, Diez LA (eds) Interdisciplinarity and transdisciplinarity in the Organization of Scientific Knowledge: Actas del VIII Congreso ISKO-Espana, Leon. University of Leon, Leon, pp 399–410

Gnoli C, Pullmann T, Cousson P, Merli G, Szostak R (2011) Representing the structural elements of a freely faceted classification. In: Slavic A, Civallero E (eds) Classification and ontology: formal approaches and access to knowledge: proceedings of the International UDC Seminar, The Hague. Ergon Verlag, Würzburg, pp 193–206

Groarke LA, Tindale CW (2004) Good reasoning matters: a constructive approach to critical thinking. Oxford University Press, Toronto

Hartmann N (ed) (1943) Systematische Philosophie. Kohlhammer, Stuttgart

Hartmann N (1952) New ways of ontology. Greenwood Press, Westport, CT

Hofkirchner W (2012) Emergent information: an outline unified theory of information framework. World Scientific, Singapore

Integrative Levels Classification (ILC) (2004) ISKO Italia. www.iskoi.org/ilc/

Julien C-A, Tirilly P, Dinneen J, Guastavino C (2013) Reducing subject tree browsing complexity. J Am Soc Inform Sci Technol 64:2201–2223

Keyton J, Beck SJ (2010) Perspective: examining communication as macrocognition. STS Hum Fact 52(2):335–339

Khoo C (1995) Automatic identification of causal relations in text and their use for improving precision in information retrieval. Ph.D. dissertation, Syracuse University

Kim J (2006) Being realistic about emergence. In: Clayton P, Davies PCW (eds) The re-emergence of emergence: the emergentist hypothesis from science to religion. Oxford University Press, Oxford, pp 189–202

Kleineberg M (2013) The blind men and the elephant: towards an organization of epistemic contexts. Knowl Org 40(5):340–362

Lowe EJ (2005) Ontological dependence. In: Stanford encyclopedia of philosophy. http://plato. stanford.edu

Mazzocchi F, Tiberi M, De Santis B, Plini P (2007) Relational semantics in thesauri: Some remarks at theoretical and practical levels. Knowl Org 34(4):197–214

Mills J, Broughton V (1977) Bliss classification. Introduction and auxiliary tables, 2nd edn. Butterworth, London

Needham J (1943) Integrative levels: a revaluation of the idea of progress. In: Time: the refreshing river: essays and addresses 1932–1942. Allen and Unwin, London, pp 233–272

Perrault JM (1994) Categories and relators: a new schema. Knowl Org 21(4):189–198

Poli R (2001) The basic problem of the theory of levels of reality. Axiomathes 12(3-4):261–283

Ranganathan SR (1967) Prolegomena to library classification, 3rd edn. SRELS, Bangalore

Spiteri LF (1995) The classification research group and the theory of integrative levels. Katharine Sharp Rev 1(Summer):1–6

Szostak R (2003) A schema for unifying human science: interdisciplinary perspectives on culture. Susquehanna University Press, Selinsgrove, PA

Szostak R (2004) Classifying science: phenomena, data, theory, method, practice. Springer, Dordrecht

Szostak R (2012a) Classifying relationships. Knowl Org 39(3):165–178

Szostak R (2012b) Toward a classification of relationships. Knowl Org 39(2):83–94

Szostak R (2013) Basic concepts classification. https://sites.google.com/a/ualberta.ca/rick-szostak/research/basic-concepts-classification-web-version-2013

Szostak R (2014) Communicating complex concepts. In: O'Rourke M, Crowley S, Eigenbrode SD, Wulfhorst JD (eds) Enhancing communication and collaboration in interdisciplinary research. Sage, Thousand Oaks, pp 34–55

Szostak R, Gnoli C (2014) Universality is inescapable. Paper presented at the ASIST Sig/CR Workshop, Seattle, November 2014. Advances in Classification Research 2014. Proceedings of the ASIST SIG/CR Workshop, 1 Nov 2014, Seattle. https://journals.lib.washington.edu/index. php/acro/article/view/14906

Vickery BC (1960) Faceted classification: a guide to the construction and use of special schemes. Aslib, London

Wesolek A (2012) Wittgensteinian support for domain analysis in classification. Libr Philos Pract 1 (1):1–10, http://digitalcommons.unl.edu/cgi/viewcontent.cgi?article=1933&context= libphilprac

Chapter 8
Benefits of a Comprehensive Phenomenon-Based Classification

With the broad outlines of a novel classification sketched in previous chapters, it is useful to note in this chapter that—while this approach to classification has its challenges—such a classification would have many advantages for classificationist, classifier, and user. We review first the advantages for scholarly users, and then for general users. We close the chapter with a brief discussion of the practical challenges of achieving adoption of the recommended approach to classification. It is argued that certain of the myriad advantages of the new approach should facilitate adoption.

Advantages for KO and for Interdisciplinary Users

We have in Chap. 5 addressed the feasibility of a comprehensive phenomenon-based classification. That chapter and Chap. 7 necessarily noted certain challenges associated with the endeavor, but argued that they were surmountable. Now that we have sketched what such a classification might look like in practice it is possible to note that it has a variety of advantages as well.

Most centrally, the proposed system more closely captures the unique characteristics of (especially scholarly) works. If most works address how some phenomena affect others, then both classificationist and classifier struggle unnecessarily at present to capture the nature of works under a particular heading. Both will find it far easier if they can freely link concepts and especially phenomena and relationships. Recourse to a standard classification of relationships would spare the classificationist from having to develop a new class for works that engaged a novel relationship among existing things: they could simply employ compound notation of existing things and relationships. If a classifier confronts a book discussing the effect of attitudes toward punctuality on employment patterns in country X, both their task and user retrieval are best served by the use of linked notation rather than for both to try to imagine a unique class heading. The same argument can be made

© Springer International Publishing Switzerland 2016
R. Szostak et al., *Interdisciplinary Knowledge Organization*,
DOI 10.1007/978-3-319-30148-8_8

with respect to works that explore the properties of a single phenomenon: compounding phenomena and properties will be both easier and better than inventing new classes for each possible combination.

To rephrase: we should move away from the idea inherited from the enumerative classifications developed in the nineteenth century that each work should be described by a notation that gives the impression but not the reality of a unique place in the classification. Many of the terms used within existing classifications are in fact compound terms (albeit expressed as if they were simple terms) that contain references to both things and relationships (Szostak 2011). Rather, classifications should begin from the idea that a work's uniqueness reflects the particular combination of phenomena and types of influence (and perhaps properties) that it addresses. An expressive notation, then, would strive to make these distinct elements clear, perhaps by using facet indicators, or spaces between elements, or a different notational base (letters versus numbers versus symbols) for the different elements.

As has been stressed in previous chapters, the classification will be a great boon to interdisciplinary researchers while also aiding disciplinary researchers. The same logic applies to any group: the proposed classification will encourage cross-group cooperation and understanding while also encouraging within-group conversation. The latter task will be enhanced if works are also classified in terms of authorial perspective (see Szostak 2014a).

In addition, such a classification solves many problems identified within existing approaches to classification. Coates (1988, 60), for example, stresses that we cannot, as Cutter had wished, rely exclusively on natural language for subject headings: these will often prove too ambiguous. But we have seen in Chap. 7 that various practices associated with our recommended approach serve to reduce the ambiguity associated with natural language terminology (Szostak 2015).[1] Later (1988, 174) when Coates reviews the shortcomings of existing classification schemes he stresses, 'makeshifts are resorted to in order to present an appearance of solving problems of subject interpolation.' In other words, logical hierarchies are deviated from (see also Mazzocchi et al 2007). Again, compound headings are the obvious solution (Cheti and Paradisi 2008 make a similar point).[2]

Coates on that same page also argues that ideally it should be much easier to add new entries to a classification. He notes that Ranganathan had hoped that at some point a classification would become self-sustaining: that new subclasses would be generated in a straightforward manner by new combinations of existing subclasses. New headings are regularly added to the Library of Congress Subject Headings (LCSH) (Leong 2010). Moreover, internet communities often create naïve

---

[1] Svenonius (2004) had argued that information scientists had to choose to either employ natural language ambiguously, or to provide formal precise terminology quite distinct from common usage. An approach that limits ambiguity potentially allows us to employ natural language precisely (Szostak 2015).

[2] The synthetic approach may also allow the out-performance of purely pre-coordinated or post-coordinated systems. See Szostak (2015).

classifications because they are working on new topics for which formal classifications do not exist. Only with the creation of a usable classification of relationships does it become possible to anticipate that complex new subjects can be readily rendered in terms of combinations of previously identified things and relationships.[3]

Notably, users will achieve better results whether they know precisely what they are looking for (for they can specify a precise causal relationship) or are performing an exploratory search (for they will find works across all disciplines that address a particular phenomenon or relationship in combination with any other thing or relationship). In the latter regard, a unified and comprehensive classification has great potential for enhancing literature based discovery: connections between existing but dispersed pieces of scholarly understanding that are of critical importance to the advance of scholarly understanding (Davies 1989). Coding works by relationship may prove especially valuable in this context.

The advantages noted above and some others discussed elsewhere in this book are summarized in Table 8.1.

Coping with Information Overload

While the focus of this book is on interdisciplinarity, we have mentioned from time to time that the sort of classification envisaged here would be useful for general users as well. It is worth noting in this regard that the world we live in is itself interdisciplinary in nature. We each in our daily lives face problems that are complex in nature. In our further roles as members of society and citizens, complexity is ever-present. The users of public libraries and online databases of various sorts are thus often pursuing complex queries that span disciplines (Marshall et al. 2009). Certainly few general users limit their searches to only one discipline. And thus classification systems that presume disciplinary mastery disserve the general user.

Present systems of classification contribute to the sense that the world is simply too complex to be coped with. A classification system that clearly provided one and only one place for any bit of information would contribute to a healthier sense that humanity can cope—albeit imperfectly—with the world's complexity. [As noted elsewhere such a classification would have to be transparent in structure so that users and/or computers could readily navigate it.] A classification system that reflected the efforts of scholars to understand the causal relationships among

---

[3] In recognition of the limitations of LCSH, especially in the digital age, a somewhat faceted application of LCSH, termed FAST (faceted application of subject terminology) has been developed which facilitates synthesis of common geographical, time-related, and other elements of LCSH. Notably the developers of FAST considered developing an entirely new system but decided instead to adapt LCSH in order to maintain its rich vocabulary (Dean 2003, Chan and O'Neill 2010).

Table 8.1 Advantages of a comprehensive phenomenon-based classification

It more closely captures the unique characteristics of (especially scholarly) works.
The synthetic approach accommodates novel works without the necessity of creating a new class.
Communication across and within disciplines and social groups is encouraged.
Both precise and exploratory searches are enhanced, and thus literature based discovery.
Terminological ambiguity is reduced.
Logical hierarchy can be pursued.
We are able to achieve very precise classifications of a work with limited and expressive notation.
Users can judge the relevance of a particular work in terms of the relationships it addresses and the theories, methods, and perspectives employed.
By distinguishing different sorts of relationship, we enable searches by verb-like terms as well.
While LCC provides specific instructions in multiple places for coding by time or place or people, the proposed system would have a common coding for such elements. This renders both classification and searching easier.
The classification can alert users to closely related linkages.
The use of linked notation serves to place works within multiple hierarchies (and of relations as well as things). It thus facilitates a web-of-relations among works.
It should be possible to translate all search or entry terms employed in other classifications into the terms employed in the classification. Note that in addition we create the possibility of (fairly) automatically coding for new works or for existing works that are at present poorly classified.
It is possible that different databases could adopt this new system (since phenomena and relationships are of general interest), and thus cross-database searching would be facilitated. We expand on this idea below.
The classification aids both scholar and general user in coping with information overload (see below).
The classification appears well suited to the digital age (see below).
We focus above on the practical benefits. Szostak (2015) used a typology of ethical considerations developed by Fox and Reece (2012) to argue that the sort of approach recommended here is also ethically sound: it serves the needs of those facing the most difficulty in information acquisition, it encourages porous borders between disciplines and across social groups, it respects user rights, and it does no wrong.

phenomena would send an important signal that we are gradually advancing our understanding link by link. It would at the same time enhance the ability of scholars to do precisely that by enhancing their ability to find relevant information (see Szostak 2015). As noted in Chap. 2, such a classification would also decrease the chances that information is simply forgotten—either forever or to be unnecessarily 'reinvented' later—simply because it was not classified in a manner that made it accessible to those interested in it. In sum, present systems of classification decrease both our sense of coping and our ability to cope with complexity (Szostak 2014b).

In other words, the sort of classification recommended in this book quite simply better captures both the nature of the world and of scholarly understandings of this. The world, we all know, is not neatly divided into disciplinary compartments. Organizing our resources around phenomena and relationships captures the way the world actually works: a host of phenomena influence each other in diverse ways.

Organizing our understandings around disciplines instead supports a sense among users that we are not really grappling very well with the world we inhabit in its manifest complexity. Our collective understandings of that world are best understood in terms of a (large but finite) set of causal links. The recommended classification thus communicates correctly the idea that some set of scholars somewhere has and is studying (almost?) every possible causal relationship. Our collective understanding is imperfect, and more imperfect along some causal links than others. But a classification should communicate to users that there is almost certainly some insight out there into any causal relationship that they might wish to investigate.[4]

Scholars often disagree. It can indeed seem that scholars always disagree. This encourages skeptical attitudes about the possibility of us collectively understanding the world around us well enough to alleviate pressing problems. A better classification system would identify many instances where disagreement was only apparent: scholars were actually talking about different causal relationships or defining the same term in quite different ways. In cases where disagreement was real, the approach recommended in this book would serve to identify precisely what was being disagreed about. This alone is highly significant: the scholarly enterprise can be seen as not a congeries of discordant insights but a coherent exercise with some areas of consensus and some well-defined areas of disagreement. If works are classified in terms of perspectives applied, including theories and methods, then we will often identify the sources of these conflicts (Szostak 2014b). We then set the stage for interdisciplinary strategies for alleviating conflicts (see Repko 2012, Bergmann et al 2012).

Importantly, a classification that actually captures the nature of the world and our understandings of it can serve educative purposes. Students can be exposed to the broad structures of the classification. They will learn both about the nature of the world and about how they can explore our understandings of that world. A further indirect benefit would be an enhanced educational role for school (and other) librarians (Szostak 2015).

Lambe (2011) worries that KOSs need to become more complex as science does, but then they will exceed our human capacity to comprehend. This is an understandable problem within traditional approaches to classification, where scientific evolution generates a bewildering proliferation of new fields. But in a classification grounded instead in phenomena, new scientific fields generally just involve the more intense scrutiny of relationships among phenomena already classified (occasionally, such as on the frontiers of nuclear physics, new phenomena are posited, but the accretion of these is slow). The user, importantly, need not understand the

---

[4] Though beyond the scope of this book, Szostak (2012) urged the pursuit of comprehensive survey articles along each causal link as a further strategy for coping with information overload. These might be updated annually. They would need to be jargon-free and might thus narrow the gap between scholarly and popular understanding, and support better public discourse around policy issues. An informed public could in turn suggest questions, point to shortcomings in scholarly analysis, and suggest possible ways forward.

entire scholarly enterprise (though the proposed classification would help them gain an appreciation of its broad contours) but rather need only know where to find what they are looking for. The accretion of knowledge is not a threat but a benefit within a phenomena-based approach to classification.

Users will often know that they want to find something like 'stop dogs from attacking mail delivery person,' and can readily access the relevant works if these are coded in terms of the relevant things (dogs) and relationships (attacking). The more adventurous or scholarly user may instead search across all instances of attacking (a task not facilitated within existing classifications) and find some previously unappreciated similarity or difference across the attacking behavior of different animals. Farradane (1967, 297) noted that 'The relations between concepts often appear to be absent, but if more than one word is used in indexing or in a search there is clearly an implicit relationship in the mind of the indexer or questioner, and other relations possible between the words would lead to false drops.' That is, failure to be explicit about relationships in a classification will often lead users astray. Green (2008) notes that even when relationships are captured in a classification the type of relationship is usually not specified; failed searches are thus common. She urges the specification of particular relationships.

One emerging area of research in information science is 'exploratory search' and in particular how to use visual aids in guiding users who are exploring possibilities. [Lambe (2011) appreciates that visual design, as well as better classification, can reduce information overload.] A user that starts with some curiosity about 'dogs' might be presented with a visual representation of the causal (or other) relationships which connect dogs with other phenomena. Causal links that have received the most attention might be emphasized, but the curious could readily follow links that have received less attention. Causal links to dogs could be distinguished by color from causal links from dogs. Other relationships, including hierarchical, could be represented in other colors or styles. Users could be shown where their search terms fall within relevant hierarchies, and then decide whether to search broader or narrower terms.[5] Such visual aids can be employed to great effect in conjunction with a classificatory approach that stresses phenomena and relationships. One problem faced by researchers in this area is that documents are often not coded in terms of all of the relationships they wish to display. The proposed classification would alleviate this problem as well.[6]

---

[5] The approach recommended in this book usually leads to relatively compact hierarchies. But in areas such as classifying species, complex multi-level hierarchy is unavoidable. The techniques for compacting hierarchy identified by Julien et al. (2013) might then be useful.

[6] Zhang (2014) explored how users might utilize the Medline database in order to find health information. Zhang's key recommendations for improvements are: a more natural interface to facilitate user questions, more effective hierarchies to facilitate query reformulation, focusing the search results page on accessing answers rather than documents, and providing multiple schemas to help users navigate. We have touched on all of these here: recall that the approach recommended in this book would classify documents (and thus facilitate search) in terms of the key insights that documents contain.

In sum, the proposed KOS would greatly facilitate the general user's search for information of various types. Importantly it would—both in reality and in appearance—support a sense that human understandings are coherent and that we are progressing in our understanding of the world. It thus enhances the educational role of libraries in general and school libraries in particular. Visual aids will work well with the proposed KOS and further enhance the ability of general users to comprehend their world.

Seizing Digital Opportunities

We noted in Chap. 5 that digitization creates an opportunity for the development of a new approach to classification. But digitization has sometimes also seemed a threat. The increasing use of full-text searching has caused many users to eschew subject searching entirely.[7] Library administrators have wondered if traditional subject catalogues will become obsolete (LaBarre 2007).[8] But full-text searching is not perfect. The terminological ambiguity that we have had much cause to discuss in this book ensures that users find much that they do not want and miss much that they do. Scholars of information retrieval appreciate that more structured searching may be advantageous (Wallach 2006). The sort of classification recommended in this book, which is more easily mastered (and taught) would encourage a much greater use of controlled vocabulary in searching.

Similar arguments can be made with regard to machine indexing of web-based materials. The sheer volume of digital material renders manual classification a challenge. But machine indexing is problematic. As our discussion of the Semantic Web below indicates, the sort of classification urged in this book may both encourage and facilitate manual classification of digital material.

One important development is that there are now a host of accessible digital databases: libraries, archives, museums, government agencies, and a variety of private and non-profit organizations have each placed enormous amounts of information online. Users often want to search across diverse resources.[9] They can use internet search engines but these face the problems of all types of free-text searching. There are also concerns about biases in the algorithms employed in

---

[7] Even here, Sandgrind (2010) makes an interesting observation: "The explosion of information made available by the Internet makes the role of parliamentary libraries and research services more, not less important, as busy parliamentarians need people to filter information for them and to do so in a timely, accurate, and politically neutral way." This point resonates far beyond parliamentary libraries. The Internet creates challenges as well as opportunities for users of all types. And the best antidote to information overload is information organization.

[8] LaBarre proposed user studies of scholars with an emphasis on how faceted classification might aid them.

[9] Lambe (2011) notes that it is increasingly important to provide access to 'behind-the-scenes' science. But this sort of science is generally not to be found in library databases but elsewhere.

internet search engines; among other things these sort results by the links to a website rather than the content of a website. Each resource inevitably organizes its material around some sort of classification system, but different resources employ different systems. It is thus exceedingly difficult to search across different resources.[10]

Indeed the challenge of searching across different resources and databases is quite analogous to the challenge of searching across different disciplines. We again face the difficulties inherent in different terminology and different perspectives. It thus makes sense to seek the solution in the same direction. Database managers recognize an advantage in facilitating search, and thus using a familiar classification. But we can hardly expect firms or NGOs, or even most archives and museums, to master the details of the Library of Congress Classification, or any other major classification used widely in the world.[11] A classification that was organized around phenomena and relationships might be much more attractive (Szostak 2016). A classification grounded in the nature of the world (ontology) rather than the nature of disciplines (epistemology) is much more supportive of the interoperability of databases (and also less subject to change over time) (Gnoli 2012).

Special attention should be paid here to the Semantic Web. The idea behind the Semantic Web is that computers should be able to explore and draw inferences across databases. But it is not hoped that they will do so through free-text searching. Rather each database needs to be purposelessly coded in a manner such that a computer would know what sort of information the database contained. Indeed the founders of the Semantic Web appreciated the advantages for search of having documents coded in terms of controlled vocabulary rather than relying on vague keywords. 'Instead of text, which cannot be processed by a computer without analysis by complex natural language processing algorithms, information is published on the Semantic Web in a structured format that provides a description of what that information is about' (Hart and Dolbear 2013, 29). Coding occurs in terms of RDF 'triples' of the form (phenomenon) (predicate or property) (phenomenon). Computers can only navigate seamlessly across databases if the terminology employed in RDF triples is identical across databases or can readily be translated.

Marcondes (2013) recognizes that the immediate purpose of the Semantic Web is to allow search engines to better identify what a website is communicating. This, though, is the means to a greater end: to 'assist the evolution of human knowledge.' He sees the Semantic Web as the purpose of formal ontology. He cites Gnoli on the need to classify in terms of phenomena rather than disciplines in order to facilitate

---

[10] Even an individual database may face controlled vocabulary challenges. Greenberg et al. (2011) discuss how they developed the HIVE vocabulary to allow translations across the multiple controlled vocabularies used by researchers wishing to deposit data into the Dryad data repository.

[11] Glushko (2013, 290) notes that the standard classification system for supermarkets has only 300 categories, whereas libraries may have over a million distinct records.

the Semantic Web. We would concur with Marcondes in a causal chain that extends from phenomenon-based classification through ontology and the Semantic Web to progress in human understanding.

The Semantic Web is developing slowly, but arguably surely. Some libraries have begun to experiment with RDF triples, and the new Resource Description and Access standard for descriptive cataloging encourages RDF coding (Glushko 2013, ch. 4, 224). Two inter-related sources of delay are network effects and ontologies. The value of the Semantic Web to any adopter depends on the number of other adopters *employing the same controlled vocabulary* (or at least controlled vocabularies linked by a translation device). O'Hara and Hall (2012) appreciate that the network is not yet big enough globally to make the benefits of participating exceed the costs. Not surprisingly, no consensus has been achieved on a particular controlled vocabulary to employ on the Semantic Web. The Semantic Web has come over time to rely on formal ontologies, but there are many of these, and they are each hard to master (Hart and Dolbear 2013 suggest that research has been moving away from this focus on ontology because of these and other problems).[12] The detailed assumptions at the heart of formal ontologies are not only difficult to appreciate but offend the open and democratic values on which the Semantic Web was based (O'Hara and Hall 2012). It would seem that an easier approach to providing controlled vocabulary and syntactic rules to the Semantic Web would be highly desirable, and perhaps essential to its success.

Scholars not only wish to navigate diverse databases but increasingly have web presences that they hope will communicate their insights to a broad audience. Interdisciplinary scholars in particular may find attractive the idea of opening their insights to the Semantic Web by coding these with RDF triples. But—given the challenges to interdisciplinary communication discussed elsewhere in the book—they will appreciate the value of a widely accepted controlled vocabulary so that their insights will be captured by the widest possible audience. Likewise interdisciplinarians will want to take advantage of the Semantic Web in order to search for relevant information and will again appreciate the value of thus searching as widely as possible.

While it would be folly at this moment in time to predict the precise form that the Semantic Web might take in future, there are several reasons to think that the sort of classification recommended in this book (supplemented by a comprehensive thesaurus) might be admirably suited to the needs of the Semantic Web. These are summarized in Table 8.2. These build upon and clarify the general advantages for digitization noted in Table 3.3.

Table 8.2 emphasized classification systems. If we wish to allow database managers some flexibility in terminology, but yet allow the potential for computer navigation inherent in the Semantic Web, then we will also need a detailed and comprehensive thesaurus. After all, one great value of thesauri is mapping

---

[12] A handy introduction to both RDF and the OWL ontologies is at LinkedDataTools.com.

Table 8.2 Suitability of the recommended classification for the Semantic Web

Most obviously, what the Semantic Web needs is classifications of entities (things), relationships, and properties. RDF triples utilize these three elements exclusively. Computers need to be able to recognize how the entities, relationships, and properties coded for one database relate to those coded in another database. So there needs to be controlled vocabulary and structured relations for these three elements.

We have discussed in earlier chapters how the recommended approach to classification might serve as a stepping stone to an ontology. It thus makes sense to see what other sorts of logical inferences are necessary in order for the Semantic Web to function (Hart and Dolbear 2013, for example, speak of how it may be useful to specify that a river generally flows into a lake or a sea, so that computers might draw connections between references to rivers and to lakes and seas), and add these to this sort of classification. This sort of 'build up' strategy might avoid unnecessary complexity in ontology construction. Some of the roles for ontology identified in the literature, such as establishing hierarchy and the nature and boundaries of classes, can be accomplished within a well-designed classification (and RDF allows scope notes), the definitional role of ontology can be accomplished to a considerable degree by logical classification, and the inferences or reasoning facilitated by ontology can arguably be accomplished with simple and flexible syntactic rules, without introducing the unnecessary complexity, confusion, and errors associated with the sort of formal ontologies applied to date (Szostak 2014c).[a]

Our approach generates very clear terminology. Upper level ontologies at present are often characterized by impenetrable jargon. 'There are, however, some drawbacks to using upper ontologies, not least because it can be very difficult for an expert in a particular domain such as GI to understand exactly which of the oddly termed classifications to assign to their concepts. Should a County be classed as a Physical Region or a Political Geographic Object? Is a flood an endurant or a perdurant? It depends on your point of view. These quandaries become even more apparent when confronted with terms like "Non-Agentive Social Object" or "Abstract."' (Hart and Dolbear 2013, 13–4). We can achieve exhaustive coverage without resorting to vagueness in terminology.

Though the Semantic Web literature appears to pay little heed to the undiscovered public knowledge literature, one could hope that the Semantic Web would indeed facilitate the latter. A further advantage of the 'build up' strategy is that we lessen the possibility of excluding some important relationships from consideration (what if some rivers just peter out in the desert or disappear underground?). One of the principles of the classification we have been recommending is that it should be possible to freely combine all terms. A similar sort of freedom should be pursued on the Semantic Web to the degree possible.

Critically, computers will face enormous difficulty if a particular phenomenon used in RDF triples might have several different meanings to accord with its place in several different disciplinary hierarchies. It will be much easier if each phenomenon has one unique place in a comprehensive classification.

Computer navigation is also aided by the use of strictly logical hierarchies. The sorts of abuse of hierarchy identified by Mazzocchi et al (2007) would require at the very least that each particular deviation from logical subdivision be redefined in a more logical way.

A classification of relationships that allowed simple verbs to be combined in order to generate more complex verbs (as in Szostak 2012) would allow computers to readily appreciate connections between these simple and complex verbs.

It is worth noting that the literature on the Semantic Web also engages with the distinction between comprehensive and domain analysis. It recognizes that the Semantic Web needs at the very least highly interoperable ontologies, but also worries about the uniqueness of each domain (Hart and Dolbear 2013). The complementary application of domain analysis and pursuit of comprehensive classification urged in this book (see Chap. 6) should thus be well suited to the Semantic Web.

(continued)

Table 8.2 (continued)

We will discuss in the next chapter how our recommended KO could provide greater coherence (in both appearance and reality) to the scholarly enterprise. The multidimensional map of scholarship thus envisaged could support a unified Semantic Web.

[a]SKOS is a first solution to representing thesauri and classifications in RDF. Being originally developed for thesauri, however, it does not allow representation of notation and its components typical of synthetic classifications. In particular, SKOS representation of ILC has been found to be problematic (Gnoli et al. 2011)

synonyms onto preferred terms (Shiri 2012, 16). We have discussed in preceding chapters how a comprehensive classification both calls for and supports a comprehensive thesaurus. And we have recommended that such a thesaurus include independent verbs, adjectives, and adverbs along with nouns and noun phrases; since RDF triples always include predicates or (adverbial or adjectival) properties, this approach will be critical if a thesaurus is to serve the Semantic Web.

We have also discussed the advantages of expanding the set of terminology through which thesauri indicate the relationships between terms. Shiri (2012, 26) celebrates how thesauri, with their rich semantic relations, can aid exploratory search. Tudhope et al. (2001) recognize that interoperability of thesauri rests on the simple set of relationships long employed, but that there has been with digitization increased calls for augmented set of relationships. A thesaurus with an expanded and precise set of relationships between terms would allow computers to draw much better inferences. Recognizing the costs involved, Tudhope et al. (2001) propose a measured augmentation. It should be noted that a thesaurus which clarified relationships of all sorts would serve some of the purposes of formal ontology.

This may be a moment in time—much like the late nineteenth century—when approaches to KOSs are developed for a particular environment but have long-lasting impacts. Work on the Semantic Web has been dominated by IT professionals but there appears to be an important role for input from experts on classification *at precisely this point in time* to ensure that the Semantic Web evolves in a manner that reflects our understanding of how best to classify. But we can only provide input by focusing on a format amenable to RDF triples.[13] And this means a classification that treats entities (things), relationships, and properties in a manner that facilitates their combination.

---

[13] We should in particular want the Semantic Web to be open to diversity of all sorts. The web-of-relations approach advocated by Olson (2007) in the interests of social diversity involves fortuitously precisely the components identified above as necessary for the Semantic Web (Szostak 2014a).

Overcoming Classificatory Inertia

'Libraries resist radical change, in part because the existing knowledge structures reinforce themselves' (Searing 1992, 24). We noted in Chaps. 4 and 5 that one important barrier to the development and (especially) use of a new classification system is the cost of switching from systems now in use. The Library of Congress (LCC) and Dewey Decimal Classifications (DDC) have not just over a century of development behind them, but also a paid staff to both oversee adjustments to the classification in order to capture new topics (or better reflect changes in social attitudes) and to classify new works in terms of the classification. Other classification systems generally struggle to maintain viability. How, then, can it be hoped that a new system can be accepted? A system that is not widely adopted cannot support the maintenance required to maintain viability, but adopters will be wary unless confident of viability. There are also network effects, especially online, such that the value of a classification increases as more databases adopt it.

The previous section has provided one powerful answer to this question: There are a host of databases whose managers are unwilling to master a complex system such as LCC or DDC or UDC. But there is immense pressure from users for the adoption of some sort of controlled vocabulary that can facilitate searches across databases. There is thus a potential market for a new classification, where it need not compete with LCC or DDC. As noted above, the cross-database communication challenge is similar in important ways to the cross-discipline communication challenge. Moreover, the sort of synthetic approach grounded in basic concepts urged in this book is at least potentially much easier for database managers to master.

The Semantic Web may be particularly important here. The desirability of a shared controlled vocabulary is widely appreciated but has proven an elusive goal. Any classification system found to serve the needs of the Semantic Web will then be adopted across a wide array of databases. But only a classification of entities, relationships, and properties can do so.

Special note should be made of archives, galleries, and museums. Researchers want to know what types of artifacts each possesses. Archives have tended to classify their documents primarily in terms of provenance. They would perhaps be encouraged to provide more information on the subjects addressed in these documents if this were facilitated by an easy-to-use classification. The same is true of museums and galleries. These increasingly have an online presence, but struggle to precisely identify the uniqueness of the objects they possess (Szostak 2016).

These markets outside of bibliographic classification may facilitate the adoption of a new classification. Its advantages for bibliographic classification itself may then be easier to realize. As noted in Chap. 5, one possibility here is that a new approach could be seen as complementary to existing systems. We should also note that a number of small public libraries in the United States have in recent years switched from DDC to BISAC, the classification employed in most bookstores. They have felt that their users are not comfortable with DDC (Martinez-Avila et al. 2014,

Martínez-Ávila and Kipp 2014). Such libraries might prove open to a classification that was easier for their users to understand. So also might journal publishers prove open to an easy-to-use system for subject classification of journal articles that would facilitate retrieval across disciplinary boundaries.

We live in a world of change, where changes in technology, politics, and economic performance constantly surprise (just decades ago, apartheid, the Soviet Union, and sluggish economic performance in China and India seemed solidly entrenched, to name but a few major transformations). We should thus not presume that—simply because they have been around for over a century—classification systems like LCC and DDC will continue to dominate the world of classification. Kodak dominated photography for a century but failed to adapt to digitization. LCC and DDC themselves struggle to adapt to changes in both technology and scholarly practice. It would be naïve to ignore the challenges in introducing a novel approach to classification, but likewise myopic to doubt that a classification with myriad advantages cannot achieve success.

It must also be emphasized that the hospitality associated with the synthetic approach—new research topics can generally be handled efficaciously through a novel combination of existing terminology—will significantly reduce the maintenance costs of the sort of classification advocated in this book. These lower costs, in conjunction with the many possible uses of the classification, should ensure that this novel approach can succeed in the real world.

Key Points

The classification outlined in previous chapters has myriad advantages for classificationist, classifier, and user. This chapter began by reviewing the advantages for (especially) interdisciplinary scholars, and then proceeded to discuss advantages for general users.

A classification designed to facilitate interdisciplinarity will also serve the challenges and opportunities of the digital age. It will facilitate searches across databases. And it is suitable in a variety of ways to the needs of the Semantic Web.

It may prove that such a classification is more readily marketed to serve these last needs than to facilitate interdisciplinarity within libraries. But there are also opportunities within bibliographic classification itself. The challenge is to gain a large enough user base to become sustainable.

References

Bergmann M, Jahn T, Knobloch T, Krohn W, Pohl C, Schramm E (2012) Methods for transdisciplinary research: a primer for practice. Campus, Berlin
Chan L, O'Neill E (2010) FAST: faceted application of subject terminology: principles and application. Libraries Unlimited, Englewood, CO

Cheti A, Paradisi F (2008) Facet analysis in the development of a general controlled vocabulary. Axiomathes 18(2):223–241

Coates EJ (1988) Subject catalogues: headings and structure, 2nd edn. Library Association, London

Davies R (1989) The creation of new knowledge by information retrieval and classification. J Doc 45(4):273–301

Dean RJ (2003) FAST: development of simplified headings for metadata. http://www.oclc.org/research/projects/fast/international_auth200302.doc

Farradane J (1967) Concept organization for information retrieval. Inform Storage Ret 3:297–314

Fox MJ, Reece A (2012) Which ethics? Whose morality?: An analysis of ethical standards for information organization. Knowl Org 39(5):377–383

Glushko RJ (ed) (2013) The discipline of organizing. MIT Press, Cambridge, MA

Gnoli C (2012) Metadata about what? Distinguishing between ontic, epistemic, and documental dimensions in Knowledge Organization. Knowl Org 39(4):268–275

Gnoli C, Pullmann T, Cousson P, Merli G, Szostak R (2011) Representing the structural elements of a freely faceted classification. In: Slavic A, Civallero E (eds) Classification and ontology: formal approaches and access to knowledge: proceedings of the international UDC seminar, The Hague. Ergon Verlag, Würzburg, pp 193–206

Green R (2008) Relationships in knowledge organization. Knowl Org 35(2/3):150–159

Greenberg J, Losee R, Pérez Agüera JR, Scherle R, White H, Willis C (2011) HIVE: helping interdisciplinary vocabulary engineering. Bull Am Soc Inform Sci Technol 37(4):23–26

Hart G, Dolbear C (2013) Linked data: a geographic perspective. CRC, Boca Raton, FL

Julien C-A, Tirilly P, Dinneen J, Guastavino C (2013) Reducing subject tree browsing complexity. J Am Soc Inform Sci Technol 64:2201–2223

LaBarre K (2007) Faceted navigation and browsing features in new OPACs: a more robust solution to problems of information seekers? Knowl Org 34(2):78–90

Lambe P (2011) KOS as enablers to the conduct of science. Paper presented at the ISKO-UK conference. http://www.iskouk.org/conf2011/papers/lambe.pdf

Leong JH (2010) The convergence of metadata and bibliographic control?: Trends and patterns in addressing the current issues and challenges of providing subject access. Knowl Org 37 (1):29–42

Marcondes CH (2013) Knowledge organization and representation in digital environments. Knowl Org 40(2):115–122

Marshall JG, Solomon P, Rathbun-Grubb S (2009) Introduction: workforce issues in Library and Information Science. Libr Trends 58(2):121–125

Martínez-Ávila D, Kipp MEI (2014) Implications of the adoption of BISAC for classifying library collections. Knowl Org 41(5):377–392

Martínez-Ávila D, San Segundo R, Olson HA (2014) The use of BISAC in libraries as new cases of reader-interest classifications. Catalog Classif Q 52(2):137–155

Mazzocchi F, Tiberi M, De Santis B, Plini P (2007) Relational semantics in thesauri: some remarks at theoretical and practical levels. Knowl Org 34(4):197–214

O'Hara K, Hall W (2012) Semantic Web. In: Bates M (ed) Understanding information retrieval systems. CRC, Boca Raton, FL, pp 325–344

Olson H (2007) How we construct subjects: a feminist analysis. Libr Trends 56(2):509–541

Repko AF (2012) Interdisciplinary research: process and theory, 2nd edn. Sage, Thousand Oaks

Sandgrind G (2010) Introduction: the purpose, present situation and future of the Parliamentary library. Libr Trends 58(4):413–417

Searing SE (1992) How libraries cope with interdisciplinarity: the case of women's studies. Issues Integr Stud 10:7–25

Shiri A (2012) Powering search: the role of thesauri in new information environments. ASIS&T Monograph series, Medford, NJ

Svenonius E (2004) The epistemological foundations of knowledge representations. Libr Trends 52(3):571–587

Szostak R (2011) Complex concepts into basic concepts. J Am Soc Inform Soc Technol 62 (11):2247–2265

Szostak R (2012) Classifying relationships. Knowl Org 39(3):165–178

Szostak R (2014a) Classifying for social diversity. Knowl Org 41(2):160–170

Szostak R (2014b) Skepticism and knowledge organization. In: Babik W (ed) Knowledge organization in the 21st century: between historical patterns and future prospects Proceedings of the 13th ISKO conference Krakow. Ergon, Würzburg

Szostak R (2014c) The basic concepts classification as a bottom-up strategy for the Semantic Web. Int J Knowl Content Dev Technol 4(1):39–51, www.ijkcdt.net

Szostak R (2015) A pluralistic approach to the philosophy of classification. Libr Trends 63 (3):591–614

Szostak R (2016) Synthetic classification of museum artifacts using basic concepts. Paper presented at the Museums and the Web conference, Los Angeles, Apr 2016

Tudhope D, Alani H, Jones C (2001) Augmenting thesaurus relationships: possibilities for retrieval. J Digit Inform 1(8), http://journals.tdl.org/jodi/index.php/jodi/article/view/181/160

Wallach H (2006) Topic modelling: Beyond 'bag of words.' Proceedings of 23rd international conference on machine learning, Pittsburgh

Zhang Y (2014) Searching for specific health-related information in MedlinePlus: behavioral patterns and user experience. J Assoc Inform Sci Technol 65(1):53–68

Chapter 9
Responding to Potential Theoretical Critiques

We have already in preceding chapters addressed some of the critiques that might be lodged against the project of a comprehensive classification grounded in phenomena rather than disciplines. The purpose of this chapter is to bring together in one place our responses to these critiques.

We should stress at the outset, though, that the question of whether our suggested approach is feasible is in the end an *empirical* question. It cannot be decided on theoretical grounds alone. This is most obvious in the case of arguments regarding terminological ambiguity. These are essentially arguments that there is too much difference in cross-group understandings of particular terms for a comprehensive phenomenon-based classification to be possible. Such arguments must be decided empirically (see Chap. 10, Szostak and Gnoli 2014). This is especially the case given that the theoretical arguments from philosophy and literary theory that are drawn upon rarely if ever engage the question of 'how much' ambiguity there is.

It is nevertheless useful to respond to theoretical critiques. In particular, such responses help clarify the precise classification strategies most likely to succeed.

Concepts Can Only Be Comprehended Within Disciplines

The main theoretical objection to the development of a system such as we have recommended is the view, articulated by Hjørland (2002, 2008, 2009) that scholarly concepts can only be adequately appreciated within a particular scholarly community. That is, scholars belonging to different scholarly communities conceptualize (and talk about) phenomena or relationships in different ways and thus their disciplinary conceptual systems and languages are not commensurable. If so, then discipline-based classification is not simply a historical artifact of the emphasis on specialization at the time most major general classifications were introduced (see Chap. 4), but is the best that we can hope for. It would follow that interdisciplinary

© Springer International Publishing Switzerland 2016
R. Szostak et al., *Interdisciplinary Knowledge Organization*,
DOI 10.1007/978-3-319-30148-8_9

scholars and students can best be served by a cumbersome (and likely unfeasible) system of translation devices across each pair of disciplines.

The ubiquity of ambiguity and subjectivity in the world need not imply that a comprehensive classification is impossible (Kleineberg 2013). The key theoretical counter-argument is that complex concepts can usually be broken into more basic concepts that lend themselves to a sufficient degree of cross-disciplinary understanding for the purpose of information retrieval. These basic concepts generally refer to the entities (things) that we study or perceive, the relations that exist among these, and the properties of both things and relationships (Szostak 2011). Further clarification of meaning can then be achieved by placing phenomena in logical hierarchies, and employing a synthetic approach (see Table 7.1).

The vast bulk of scholarly research investigates how one or more phenomena influence one or more others. A system that allowed such research to be classified in terms of the phenomena studied and the relationships posited among these would provide the best possible information retrieval structure. The minority of research that examines the internal nature of a particular phenomenon would also be well served by synthetic classification in terms of phenomena and properties (see Chap. 8).

Philosophical Concept Theory

The idea that complex concepts can be broken into more basic concepts has been a cornerstone of philosophical concept theory for millennia (Margolis and Laurence 2011). Yet this cornerstone has long been challenged empirically: philosophers have signally failed to provide an accepted definition of such concepts as 'freedom' in terms of more basic concepts (Fodor 1981). But information science need not seek the same standard of shared understanding as philosophy: a comprehensive classification succeeds even if a few concepts prove hard to communicate and others allow some slight differences in understanding across groups or individuals. Moreover, philosophers may wish to identify 'primitive concepts,' the most basic building blocks, but the field of knowledge organization looks rather for common-sense shared understandings. Notably, the fact that 'freedom' lacks a precise definition *within any field* has not prevented information science from classifying works about freedom.

Nevertheless, it is important to engage philosophical concept theory. In present-day philosophical discourse there are five main types of concept theory (Margolis and Laurence 2011 provide a concise survey). Interdisciplinary scholarship would urge us to seek to integrate useful insights from each of these rather than claim that one is right and to reject all the others as fundamentally mistaken (Repko 2012). The Classical Theory was predicated on the idea that complex concepts were a combination of more basic concepts. As noted above, the main objection has been empirical: philosophers have not achieved the level of specificity in definition that they had sought. The Prototype Theory suggests that people classify to some extent in terms of typicality rather than logic; people may think an apple is somehow more of a fruit than is a watermelon. Information scientists can potentially classify the full set of subtypes of any concept, and thus provide a clear definition of that concept (albeit not in the form of shared characteristics as philosophers have long sought). The Theory Theory argues that concepts can only be understood within theories. It can be argued though that clarity in concepts precedes clarity in theories rather than the reverse, and thus the path to shared understanding lies in first clarifying the concepts (see below).[1] Conceptual Atomism argues that concepts are not related to each other but rather to the real world. This approach provides direct support for the idea that we should focus on the entities and relationships and properties that exist in the world (or that at least are thought to do so). Pluralism argues that there is some truth in all approaches. Information science is thus best advised to ground its classifications in multiple types of concept theory rather than, say, the most pessimistic incarnation of theory theory (Stock 2010 makes a similar argument with respect to epistemologies; Szostak 2015 urges a multi-dimensional pluralism). The approach of this book reflects elements of both classical theory and conceptual atomism, is consistent with prototype theory, and strives for consistency with at least some versions of theory theory. And the conclusion that can be drawn is that it may indeed be possible to break at least most complex concepts into basic concepts that represent things, relationships, or properties that we can readily observe in the world around us. We may not be able to achieve quite the level of precision dreamt of by philosophers but we may very well be able to achieve a level of shared understanding suitable for the needs of knowledge organization.

Hjørland and Szostak have disagreed on multiple occasions regarding the possibility of a comprehensive phenomenon-based classification (Hjørland 2008, 2009; Szostak 2008, 2011, 2013b; Fox 2012). The crux of their disagreement, it turns out, rests precisely on whether complex concepts can be broken into a set of basic concepts that can be understood similarly across groups. Hjørland draws heavily on the theory theory noted above to argue that concepts can only be understood within the web of beliefs and theories that characterize a particular group. Szostak responds that theory theory is by far the most pessimistic of the main philosophical approaches to concepts, and that a more balanced approach to concept theory indicates that shared understandings of basic concepts may be feasible for information science.

It is useful to provide some clarification. Basic concepts are not univocal: they do not need to be viewed in precisely the same way across groups or individuals. They need only to permit enough shared understanding for the purposes of classification: users from different groups must share similar enough understandings that they can be guided to relevant works. Information scientists need to appreciate when borrowing from philosophy that philosophers generally strive for precise distinctions: a concept is judged to be univocal or not. The sort of question of degree that lies at the heart of the classificationist's concern with concepts—is a term too ambiguous for the purposes of classification?—is rarely addressed directly

---

[1] Theory theory does support the goal of classifying documents also in terms of theory applied.

by philosophers. Information scientists can accept that ambiguity is ubiquitous and focus on whether the degree of ambiguity can be reduced to acceptable levels for the purposes of classification. It is also important to appreciate that we are not engaged in a reductive exercise: it is neither practicable nor desirable to reduce all of our understandings to the level of subatomic particles. Our desideratum is merely that broadly shared understandings are possible.

The Concept of Democracy

Different disciplines or cultures may treat a particular complex concept (say, democracy) quite differently. In such a case, these differences can then be identified in terms of more basic concepts. Members of one culture may for example think that severe limitations on who can vote or run for office are compatible with democracy, while members of another do not. At the level of these more basic concepts, the two groups may be able to understand what each other is talking about. When the former East Germany claimed to be democratic, others could have pointed out that it failed their definition of democracy due to the lack of free elections with multiple and self-selected candidates.

Hjørland (2009, 1079) would define democracy as 'A society in which the opposition(s) to the ruling power is (are) free to organize and has (have) opportunities to communicate their ideas in public media.' He argues that his definition is pragmatic because it speaks to 'what kind of society should we aim at' and how to organize our theories and concepts to achieve this. He thus unnecessarily conflates 'is' and 'ought.' It would be much better to define democracy in terms of what it is, and then engage in intelligent conversation about whether and how it can deliver certain (ideally well-defined) outcomes. Likewise, while I agree that 'freedom of speech' and 'open media' are necessary for 'democracy' to function well, this point is best made by carefully defining these distinct concepts and outlining the relationships among them rather than attempting to define one in a way that subsumes the others. That is, we should as scholars carefully specify and justify causal arguments (such as that freedom of the press is essential to a functioning democracy) rather than bury assumptions regarding several causal relationships in our definition of a single concept. Note that we can do a better job of classifying works about democracy if we distinguish works that discuss the role of freedom of the press [(freedom) (of) (press) (support) (democracy)] from those that address whether certain characteristics of democracy yield certain societal outcomes. That is, the basic concepts that arguably comprise the complex concept will prove more useful in classifying real documents (especially those that are clear in their arguments) than the complex concept itself. The term 'democracy' remains in the classification, but with a precise meaning grounded in elections, and works addressing the causes and/or effects of democracy can be found by users searching for works on democracy. Users with interest in a particular causal relation will be directed to works addressing that relationship.

The history of Egypt in recent years has highlighted for many the critical importance for successful democracies of constitutional protections of both individual and minority rights. Elections may establish governments that will not respect the rights of those they disagree with. A critical challenge in the early days of a democracy is to have those in positions of power place constitutional limitations on their own power (and establish institutions that can be counted on to enforce those limitations). Arguably, democratic societies have done a poor job of communicating the nature of successful democracy to others. These others may naively expect that free elections will result in governments that govern well. In fact free elections often result in corrupt and incompetent governments. Hence the importance of limitations on their power. Would the important purpose of educating the world about democracy be best served by a complex multi-faceted (and thus inevitably controversial) definition of democracy itself, or by carefully elucidated arguments—that are subject to scholarly analysis and clarification—regarding the relationship between certain constitutional guarantees and societal outcomes? The argument made in this section is that the latter strategy is superior. And thus we will want to classify works so that arguments about the impact of 'freedom of the press' or 'freedom of religion' or 'minority rights' are clearly distinguished but yet also clearly related to both the concept of democracy and the social outcomes that we hope democracy will deliver.

Disciplines and Concepts

It should be appreciated that theory theory implies serious communication problems even within disciplines, for no two individuals will share exactly the same set of beliefs. They cannot then share the same understandings of concepts if these are embedded in belief structures. We should thus be careful of assuming that the challenges of communication can be overcome within disciplines but not across disciplines. Rather we should investigate the degree of terminological ambiguity both within and across disciplines. Given that conversations do succeed across both disciplines and cultures (see O'Rourke et al. 2014), it must seem that some important degree of shared understanding is indeed possible.[2] This is perhaps not surprising given that psychologists (especially evolutionary psychologists) suspect that there are universals in how human beings think and perhaps in how they organize their conceptual maps (see Chap. 5).

The philosophers seeking precise definitions of 'freedom' clearly operate within the same discipline. Yet they are still troubled by their inability to agree on precise definitions of terms. That is, philosophers cannot communicate with each other as

---

[2] López-Huertas (2013) found that there were about 50 % of shared categories across three different cultures. The problem was that the citing order of categories was very different in those cultures. That is, hierarchies did not help in communication.

precisely as they would like. If the degree of ambiguity found troublesome by philosophers is also the degree of ambiguity that should trouble the practical field of knowledge organization, then even discipline-specific classification would be impossible. Knowledge organization of any type is possible only if we can abide a greater degree of terminological ambiguity than can philosophy. As noted above, it is then an empirical question as to whether the degree of ambiguity that can be achieved after all ambiguity-reducing strategies have been employed is less than the degree of ambiguity that a particular classificatory project can afford. Classificationists are certainly ill-advised to assume that there is too much ambiguity to allow a comprehensive classification but not enough to prevent a discipline-specific classification (Szostak and Gnoli 2014).

We can close with a brief reference to communications theory. Theories of communication argue that meaning is developed intersubjectively through communication (Keyton et al. 2010). It does not, that is, reside in independent minds but is created through interaction. Communications theory is to a degree supportive of the contention that meaning will be shared within disciplines. Yet it also indicates that meaning can come to be shared across disciplines through the act of communication. Scholars from different disciplines can work toward shared understandings conversationally. They can be trained in (imperfect) strategies for reducing the ambiguity that necessarily results. Success in reducing ambiguity will depend critically upon the development of compatible 'mental models' among participants. Notably this discourse within communications theory parallels the discussion in the literature on interdisciplinarity of the development of 'creoles' or 'pidgins' to facilitate conversation across fields. Thus, physicists and engineers working together on radar developed the concept of 'equivalent circuits' which was defined in a complementary but different fashion by the two groups: to accord with field theory by physicists and radio technology by engineers (Galison 1997). Researchers need not see the world in the same way, but must come to see it in compatible ways (Keyton et al. 2010). Breaking complex concepts into basic concepts and mapping the differences in meaning that different scholars may attach to complex concepts is a practice that can lead to compatible mental models.

Concepts Can Only Be Appreciated Within Theories

We have seen in the preceding section the importance of arguments linking concepts and theories. Hjørland and Nissen Pedersen (2005, 585) worry that 'if observations are theory-dependent, only very trivial observations may be shared among all observers, and consequently we have to base our classifications on trivial descriptions rather than on important or essential descriptions.' It thus deserves to be asked: Is it more likely that Newton arrived at the theory that force equals mass times acceleration, and then looked around for concepts to fit, or that he had a fairly clear idea of the meaning of force, mass, and acceleration before theorizing? It should seem fairly obvious that theories are often developed that utilize concepts that are already well appreciated. Even if, for the sake of argument, these concepts had been developed by some prior theorist, the important point is that Newton could apply them readily in his new theory. As theories are developed, they may of course suggest alterations in the meanings of concepts.

Concepts that are only utilized within a particular theory are not a huge problem. Only users familiar with that theory are likely to seek works that employ that concept. It is terms employed in different theories but with (allegedly and perhaps subtly) different meanings that would be problematic. Notably, Hjørland and Nissen Pedersen are confident that it should be possible to define concepts very precisely within a particular theoretical community. If so, then it should in principle also be feasible to compare the precise definitions given to a particular term within different theories. It could be that there is enough commonality that the concept can be defined in terms of common elements for use in a general classification. Or it could be that there are differences sufficiently important that they require scope notes or even the specification of different terms to reflect different meanings. But should we assume that there are incommensurable differences that we are simply unable to address? If we do so, then even Hjørland's hope that we can achieve translation devices across any pair of disciplinary classifications would fail. And thus it seems reasonable to explore in practice whether we can define (at least most) concepts in a theory-independent fashion sufficiently well for the purposes of classification.

We have indicated in Chap. 5 that phenomena should be defined in terms of their nature (for most natural phenomena) or function (for most social phenomena). A rock can be defined in terms of its nature in a manner that accords with a variety of geological theories. Likewise an institution can be defined in terms of its functions in a manner that accords with diverse theories of institutional change.

Theoretical disagreements need not imply conceptual disagreement. Theoretical differences reflect the causal links that are emphasized by a community of scholars much more than their definitions of phenomena or relationships. For example, it is often noted that natural scientists define gender physiologically while humanists define it culturally. Yet we can still define gender in terms of its physiological essence, recognizing some key physical differences (on average) at the core of gender. We can then study/classify the links between these and cultural attitudes. Such a classification has a place for both kinds of research (and indeed for works discussing how individuals that are physiologically of one gender may identify with the other). Classificationists need not and should not take a stand on the extent to which gender roles are culturally determined, but rather provide a classification system where there is an obvious place for all types of argument.

Indeed it might be argued that most (though not all) scholarly dispute—at least in the natural and social sciences—concerns how phenomena influence each other rather than the definition of particular phenomena. Moreover, scholars might agree about the possible ways in which one phenomenon might influence another but disagree about their relative importance. They might also agree about the set of properties that might adhere to a particular phenomenon (or relationship) but disagree about which actually do. That is, scholars will often agree on which concepts they are investigating but disagree about how they relate to each other and how important they are. The approach recommended in this book allows us to capture these disagreements in a manner that facilitates cross-disciplinary understanding.

There are some rare areas of scholarship in which an exception might be made to the foregoing analysis. On the frontiers of some fields of scientific research— notably the physics of sub-atomic particles—phenomena are defined provisionally with respect to certain theories. These phenomena are observed to change definitionally as the theory is clarified. In some cases, it could be best to treat such phenomena as aspects of the theories that imply their existence until scholarly consensus on theory is achieved. In general, though, the phenomena studied by scholars can and should be defined without any reference to theories.

Interdisciplinarians appreciate that each discipline chooses a mutually compatible set of theories, methods, and phenomena (see Chap. 1). That is, they choose methods that are effective means for investigating their theories, and then apply these theories and methods to suitable subjects. Interdisciplinary scholars recognize that there are advantages to this sort of specialization—scholars writing in a particular discipline need not defend or explain their choice of theory, method or subject matter—but that this is also accompanied by inherent biases within each discipline (and its subdisciplines). The success of interdisciplinary research indicates that it is possible to transcend disciplinarily defined blocs of theory and method and phenomena. Integration of disciplinary insights would be impossible if concepts could not be understood across theories. But interdisciplinary research will be hobbled if we reify such blocs in our classifications.

A Comprehensive Phenomenon-Based KOS Ignores the Skeptical Outlook of Our Time

We have in this book encountered arguments that there is too much ambiguity, or too little communication, or too limited human cognitive or perceptual capabilities (especially shared capabilities) for the project of a comprehensive phenomenon-based classification to be feasible. Our project could run afoul of yet other skeptical claims; in particular that there is in fact no external reality (see Szostak 2007) and thus that our hope that we can ground a comprehensive classification in perceptions of that reality is doomed. Though it is important to address these claims in turn, it is also important to say something about skepticism in general. Hjørland (2008, 2009) has suggested that his favored epistemological theories reflect the direction in which philosophical thought is moving. Should information science become skeptical because philosophy and literary theory are perceived to have become more skeptical?

Collins (1998), in a classic study, made several important observations regarding skepticism:

- Skeptical arguments tend to occur together. In a skeptical age, various types of skepticism regarding the possibilities of human understanding will be voiced.

- Skeptical thought has waxed and waned through the ages across all world philosophies. It is not, that is, the culmination of millennia of human thought, but something that has been around for a long time.
- Skepticism tends to emerge when there are 'too many' competing schools of thought. Religious zealots hardly need skepticism, for they know the answer. An individual faced by competing schools of thought, and unsure how to choose among these, can be easily tempted by arguments that understanding (especially mutual understanding) is a mirage.

There are of course good reasons for some degree of skepticism. We have seen in this book that ambiguity and subjectivity are ubiquitous in the world. There are also limits to human perceptual and cognitive capabilities. It is thus not our purpose to erase skepticism: this serves as a healthy antidote to over-confidence in the explanatory power of the theories one likes. But we should want the degree of skepticism in the world to be an accurate reflection of the difficulties humans face in comprehending the world we live in. In particular, we should not want the degree of skepticism to be artificially inflated by shortcomings in our KOSs that we are able to fix.

The implications of Collins' analysis for information science are profound. It is hardly surprising that there is deep skepticism in the contemporary world. There are a bewildering array of disciplines, theories, and methods in the contemporary academy. Scholars often start from widely different assumptions and reach widely different conclusions. How is even an educated person to choose between the arguments of economists and sociologists regarding free trade? Indeed, how can anybody be sure that they have even identified all relevant viewpoints within the vast scholarly enterprise on any issue that concerns them? (Szostak 2014c). Only knowledge organization can provide a solution to this last query, and thus set the stage for a positive answer to the preceding query.

The sort of classification urged in this book can make the scholarly enterprise appear both less intimidating and less epistemologically confusing. It will then become easy to find all relevant literature regarding any phenomenon or causal link. By placing all scholarly insights on a common 'map' of phenomena and relationships, and by clarifying the meaning of terminology, such a classification will serve to identify many cases where disagreement is apparent rather than real: that scholars were actually talking about different relationships or defining terms in quite different ways. When disagreements are real, it will be easy to identify the theories, methods, and perspectives that might generate conflicting insights. This on its own will reduce but hardly erase skeptical thought. The user can identify conflicting insights, and even the source of these, and still feel bewildered. Techniques for interdisciplinary analysis are helpful here, for they hold out hope that we can—both individually and collectively—integrate across differing insights in order to generate a more holistic understanding (Repko 2012).

Information science can address the sources of skepticism directly by providing both scholarly and general users with better access to the body of human understandings encoded in documents. And it can do so indirectly by fostering

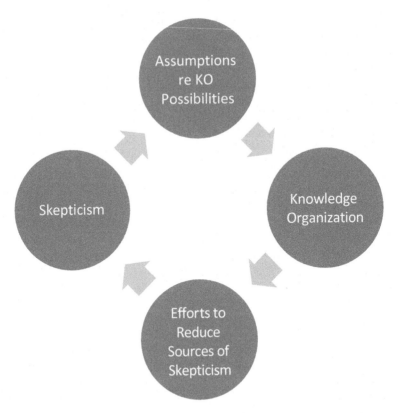

Fig. 9.1 Feedbacks between skepticism and knowledge organization

interdisciplinary analysis that can integrate across diverse conclusions. It would be both ironic and unfortunate if skeptical attitudes militated against the development of the very sort of classification that provides the best possible response to skeptical concerns (Szostak 2014c).

We can thus imagine two possible feedback processes between the degree of skepticism in the world and the strategies pursued in knowledge organization. These are captured in Fig. 9.1. If we start from the existing level of skepticism, we then doubt the very possibility of organizing knowledge coherently and thus reinforce a high degree of skepticism. Alternatively if we start by exploring the possibility of a more coherent organization, we can then reduce the degree of skepticism and invite further efforts toward providing a coherent organizing structure.

Interdisciplinary scholarship should benefit directly from efforts to establish what is effectively a multi-dimensional map of the scholarly enterprise. As noted above scholars will be much better able to identify scholarly disagreements and their sources. They will also be able to identify under-studied causal links, and perhaps draw on similar links to draw inferences about likely causal mechanisms. Beyond these practical benefits the recommended KOS serves also to firmly establish the necessity of interdisciplinary scholarship. If we understand that specialized groups of scholars apply a subset of scholarly theories and methods to a subset of the phenomena and relationships that we collectively care about—but that the scholarly enterprise as a whole potentially applies all relevant theories and methods to all phenomena and relationships—then interdisciplinary scholarship is essential to scholarly coherence. For every possible relationship between two phenomena, interdisciplinary scholarship can essay to integrate all relevant theories and methods. Only interdisciplinary research can synthesize specialized understandings into a complex but coherent whole. The value of interdisciplinarity within the academy is limited in both practice and appearance by a discipline-based approach to knowledge organization.

It Is Impractical to Shelve All Works on a Particular Phenomenon Together

Does it really make sense to group all works about 'fish' together? Surely a user interested in fish recipes has little interest in the zoological understanding of fish and perhaps even the catching of fish?[3] Yet researchers in the areas of environmental studies or sustainability science often do want to look at particular organisms from a variety of perspectives; these fields blend natural and social scientific understandings and sometimes humanistic viewpoints. Several points deserve mention here. These are summarized in Table 9.1

One point that is often made is that the field of knowledge organization is concerned for the most part with the classification of documents rather than the objects that these documents address (Gnoli 2008). It thus makes sense to classify documents in terms of the community that generated these rather than the objects they address. Two points seem particularly apposite in this regard. First, we facilitate search across databases (see Chap. 8) if we develop a classification that is well-suited to classifying both things and works about things. This is of particular importance in the study of art. Indeed, systems such as the *Art and Architecture Thesaurus* have been applied to both museum artifacts and the literature about these (see Gnoli 2010 and Szostak 2014b). A classification focused on documents will scatter studies of the same thing, but a classification focused on things is also well-suited to the classification of documents. Second, such a classification likewise allows us to classify both documents and insights, where insights involve some statement about the properties of one or more things or the relationships among certain things. We have seen above that the scholarly enterprise can be viewed as a

---

[3] The discussion in this section benefitted from an exchange between Aida Slavic and Claudio Gnoli on the website of the León Manifesto (2007). We thank Aida Slavic for bringing these important questions to our attention. We note that Brown's Subject Classification, the Bliss Classification, and some sections of UDC (such as the section on tourism) also allow for collocation of diverse works on a single phenomenon.

Table 9.1 Rationales for collocation

The user may indeed wish to follow their curiosity from one 'facet' of fish to another.
The use of synthetic notation leaves scope for the librarian to place a work on 'recipes for fish' with other works on recipes rather than other works on fish. This decision should be based on which phenomenon is the base theme of the work (Gnoli and Cheti 2013).
Even if the work is classified with works on fish, shelf ordering would separate works on fish recipes from works on fish catching.
The greatest advantages of the new classification come through searching online classifications, rather than browsing shelves (though the latter are also important), and there the advantages more clearly outweigh the disadvantages.
Perhaps most critically, and as we have seen throughout this book, the extant classifications in use in libraries place works that address very similar aspects of fish, or any other subject, in quite different places depending on the disciplinary affiliation of the author or the cataloguer's judgment of the discipline to which the book is best assigned.
The simple fact is that most works have multi-faceted subjects, and thus no classification can shelve them ideally for every possible user.
Users that need to know the disciplinary affiliation of the author can be provided with this information, along with other information regarding authorial perspective.
Arguably the most important thing for most users about a work on the "sociology of fish" is that it addresses fish rather than sociology.
Users interested in the sociology of fish are well served at present if their curiosity leads them only to other aspects of sociology but poorly served if their curiosity leads them to other aspects of fish.
The use of synthetic classification again allows us to serve both users interested in the *sociology* of fish and those interested in the sociology of *fish*.

coherent set of overlapping analyses of a large set of causal links. Once again, a discipline-based approach to classification scatters analyses of a particular (phenomenon or) link, but a classification grounded in phenomena and relationships allows us to classify both insights and documents in an accessible manner.

Ambiguity Has Its Uses

The argument above has been that we can quite possibly reduce ambiguity to the level necessary for a comprehensive phenomenon-based classification. Some degree of ambiguity is inevitable but this need not destroy the project. It deserves mention here that ambiguity is not entirely a bad thing (see Szostak 2014d). After all, poetry exerts much of its attraction precisely because words are employed in a way that simultaneously evokes different meanings. It is thus not surprising that the humanist Bal has been one of the staunchest advocates of the value of conceptual ambiguity (see especially Bal 2002). Yet Bal also appreciates that ambiguity imposes costs, and thus that concepts 'need to be clear, explicit, and defined' (2002, 22). Interdisciplinary analysis will be incoherent unless scholars can agree on what particular terms mean (2002, 28). There may then be some ideal degree and kind of ambiguity that somehow maximizes the benefit-to-cost ratio.

The fact that there are degrees and kinds of ambiguity was brought home forcefully decades ago in Empson (1970). Empson defines ambiguity as any phrasing that allows multiple interpretations. He then lists seven types of ambiguity. Empson's focus is on literature, and he suggests that in poetry especially the goal is to evoke multiple meanings that cohere. While such a strategy may at times be useful outside fiction, an author seeking to communicate a particular insight is encouraged to ensure that the meaning of words is clear in context, and avoid contradictions.

Nor are the advantages limited to the arts. Griffiths and Stotz (2014) argue that ambiguity in our understanding of concepts can sometimes stimulate scholarly research. Notably their examples are from natural science. In the early days of research on genes, researchers often defined the word 'gene' in quite different ways. Different researchers across several fields were thus excited in different ways by research on genes. Importantly, though, the different definitions were broadly consistent, and thus these different research agendas were broadly complementary. In other words these definitions differed largely in terms of which aspects of genes were emphasized but did not suggest incompatible characteristics. 'Gene' was thus an acceptable 'boundary object' about which researchers from various fields could constructively converse. It can also be seen as an element of a 'pidgin' language allowing fruitful conversation across fields (Galison 1997; Baird and Cohen 1999). On the other hand 'innateness' is a word with diverse and contradictory meanings, and thus research on 'innateness' has been incoherent. At present, researchers emphasize quite independent aspects of innateness and thus talk past each other (Griffiths and Stotz 2014; Szostak 2014d). Communication can survive a moderate degree of difference in emphasis, but is compromised when incompatible elements are associated with the same term. While clarifications of the meaning of 'gene' would have been helpful, the takeaway lesson for information science is that as long as users have broadly consistent understandings of what controlled vocabulary terms mean they will be able to navigate KOSs and find relevant research. This observation should not deter either information scientists or interdisciplinary researchers from the pursuit of greater clarity, but should encourage acceptance of the inevitability of some ambiguity. We can strive to achieve a degree of clarity sufficient for a comprehensive KOS.

We can usefully reflect on whether a comprehensive classification of the sort we have advocated is likely or not to generate the right amount and kind of ambiguity. Key arguments are summarized in Table 9.2.

We should stress that the 'right' or best level and kind of ambiguity differs by setting. As noted above, we may wish for greater ambiguity in literature than in scholarship. This accords with an argument made often in this book: that we need not and should not seek the same level of ambiguity in classification as has been sought by philosophers.

Noam Chomsky (2010) and other linguists speculated that the ubiquity of ambiguity must mean that language had not been evolutionarily selected for

Table 9.2 The proposed KOS and the kind and degree of ambiguity

The advantage of ambiguity comes through stimulating curiosity. The disadvantage comes when either researchers talk past each other because of incompatible definitions, or research is incoherent because of poorly-specified or incoherent definitions. Defining a phenomenon in terms of its core essence or function would seem to militate against each of the disadvantages. Such an approach, and especially an emphasis on causal (and other) linkages to other phenomena, is nevertheless supportive of curiosity, and is likely to direct this curiosity in productive directions.
One critical question is whether 'good' ambiguity is always temporary. In the earliest days of gene research, researchers could not know many key details of what a gene was and how it worked. If one hopes that scholarly conversation generates a narrowing of the range of plausible understandings, then it might be expected that ambiguity in definition should fade as the range of plausible understandings of what a thing is or how a certain process operates diminishes. Of course this process may be slow and uneven, and ambiguity may necessarily increase at times as new understandings are suggested.
Imagine that one group of scholars conceives of genes primarily in terms of their chemical makeup and pursues research designed to further clarify this, another group conceives of genes primarily in terms of the role they play in organisms and focuses on researching that aspect of genes, and a third group identifies genes in terms of how they evolve and studies that. In such a situation, we could well imagine that the three groups are able to achieve much. They will even be able to usefully borrow insights from each other *as long as their definitions are compatible*. But if one group's conception of the chemical composition of genes is inconsistent with another group's conception of how they evolve or how they work, then it may prove impossible to resolve (and perhaps even comprehend) this inconsistency without first achieving some shared understanding of 'gene' itself. A definition of 'gene' in terms of the biological function of genes would serve the purposes of scholarship well. The three types of research identified above could each then be reflected through compounds: 'chemical nature of genes,' 'evolution from one chemical composition to another,' 'particular effects of genes.' Such an approach allows the three groups of researchers a considerable degree of independence but also encourages cross-fertilization.
Advocates of theory theory might well imagine that the three definitions in the preceding section were inextricably tied to the theories of the three fields. But because they were consistent it was quite possible for a shared understanding to emerge across both fields and theories. More generally, interdisciplinarians and classificationists could strive to compare competing definitions in a way that would contribute to the all-important task of deciding which definition accords best with empirical analysis.
As noted elsewhere, we may find as we develop a comprehensive classification that different communities are utilizing a term in incompatible ways. It may then be necessary to identify separate terms in order to capture these different meanings. Economists define investment as increases in productive capital such as buildings and machines used for production. Accountants treat investment as any paper transaction where one buys an asset that will hopefully produce a return. The best strategy here may be to distinguish 'productive investment' from 'financial investment.' Such an approach serves to reduce the bad sort of ambiguity within the scholarly enterprise itself.
Resolving complex concepts into basic concepts can reduce the costs of ambiguity with limited or no effects on the benefits. In a case like gene research, outlining how each of the three groups conceives of genes in terms of more basic concepts—and especially mapping these overlapping understandings—would allow researchers in each group to better appreciate how they might learn from the others. But it would not at all prevent members of each group from continuing research as they had before.

(continued)

Table 9.2 (continued)

In cases where decreasing ambiguity does decrease curiosity, this will often be a good thing. Breaking a concept such as 'innateness' into its constituent basic concepts will expose the fact that the idea of 'innateness' abstracts away from the recognition that genetic inheritance and environmental circumstances interact in generating behaviors and personality. An appreciation of this might guide researchers away from analysis in terms of 'innateness' toward more carefully specified research into how particular aspects of genetic inheritance exert their effects within a (well-mapped) set of interactions. Griffiths and Stotz (2014) suggest that researchers would be better off if they organized research around what was 'in DNA.'

Those who value ambiguity should not fear the right kind of clarification. If one insisted on a definition of 'dog' such as 'annoying little animals that make loud noises and defecate in parks,' one would have an incomplete and biased definition that would naturally discourage many who might otherwise be interested in studying dogs. This sort of false clarity is to be avoided. An accurate but unbiased definition would not deter those who want to study human-dog bonds, dogs rescuing humans, dogs that do not bark, and so on. 'Dog' is in fact a concept that does lend itself to broadly shared understandings, and this fact has not at all interfered with treatments of dogs in either scholarship or poetry.

The key to the right kind of clarity is inclusiveness. Interdisciplinarians and classificationists should not casually ignore the interpretation of a term pursued by any group. They may need to make judgments regarding which of these are most important, but should strive not to exclude any. This is why we have stressed throughout this book the value of linking domain analysis to the pursuit of a comprehensive classification.

communication. But some scholars of linguistic evolution (see Larson et al. 2010) have argued that evolution must grapple with a tradeoff between precision and simplicity (in both memory and utterances). Humans must extend utterances significantly in order to achieve precision (and absolute precision is generally unattainable). In everyday conversation, context (plus the fact that there are often dominant meanings of particular terms) usually allows a fair degree of shared understandings of utterances couched in ambiguous wording and clausal structures. When precision is particularly important, as in legal documents, we sacrifice simplicity in its pursuit. Information scientists, then, should not be shocked or dissuaded by the ubiquity of ambiguity. Rather they should seek to ascertain whether they can achieve the appropriate level and kind of ambiguity for their purposes. This is what we humans do in every facet of our existence: strive to achieve the level of ambiguity needed. We only give up if we try and fail.

There are lessons here for practicing interdisciplinary scholars as well (Szostak 2014d). They also should strive for greater clarity, but neither demand nor expect perfection. In the early days of a new concept they should accept complementary definitions which stress different facets of that concept (and are thus inclusive, allowing researchers from different fields to participate). It is thus useful in the face of different definitions to ask whether these differ only in emphasis or are actually contradictory. Breaking complex concepts into basic concepts will expose contradictions, and logical or theoretical inconsistencies.

There Are Profound Difficulties in Classifying Phenomena

Hjørland and Nissen Pedersen (2005) provide several examples of practical difficulties with the approach to classification urged in this book. They thus set the stage
for a powerful test of the possibility of such a classification. If it can be shown that
each of these examples—provided by these authors in order to establish the
difficulty or even impossibility of cross-domain classification—can in fact be
dealt with, then we have good reason to expect that such a classification is indeed
feasible. First, Hjørland and Nissen Pedersen (585) note that pharmacology and
chemistry emphasize different properties of the same chemical compound. They
suggest that these two fields thus need quite different classifications of chemicals.
But this situation need be no barrier to a useful general classification. Compounds
can be classified in terms of their constitutive chemical elements, and chemical
elements can be classified in terms of their atomic composition.[4] That is, chemicals
and compounds are classified in terms of their constitution and structure. The
objective of chemists—to study how different elements or compounds combine—
can be served by identifying 'causal links' (or perhaps in this case we should think
of 'constitutive links') among different elements or compounds.[5] Likewise, physiological effects could be captured by links between particular chemical compounds
and some classification of physiological reactions. Both chemists and pharmacologists could easily find what they needed, as could those, like biochemists, who
wish to pursue both types of links.[6]

Hjørland and Nissen Pedersen then (588) discuss the possibility that a particular
substance is viewed as food in one society but not another. They suggest that it is
thus not possible to have a cross-cultural classification of food. Here again it is
possible to define (and thus identify) food fairly precisely in terms of whether a
substance has certain positive physiological effects when ingested. That is, we can
classify food in terms of its physiological function. Links between this category of
phenomena called 'food' and cultural attitudes could then indicate whether a
particular society disdains a substance with nutritive qualities, or celebrates a
substance with none. We thus carefully distinguish the physiological nature of
food from cultural attitudes surrounding this.

The role of causal links deserves emphasis: much of the ambiguity that
troubles Hjørland and Nissen Pedersen can be handled by defining phenomena
narrowly *but allowing scope for classification by causal links between phenomena.*

---

[4] Chemists, for good reason, prioritize the number of protons in distinguishing chemical elements,
and secondarily the number of neutrons and electrons. But a classification of chemicals can allow
for all three distinctions, by providing facets for these.

[5] In practice, this could be accomplished by using linked notation between phenomena, as
recommended in Szostak (2013a), or by using extra-defined foci as suggested in Gnoli (2006).
In the latter case, the notation for certain medical treatments using pharmaceuticals could follow
the notation for chemical compounds.

[6] If pharmacologists referred to a particular compound by a term that denoted its effects, a
thesaurus could lead them directly to the appropriate terminology.

Such a strategy reflects a key insight of facet analysis: the value of notationally linking subjects.

Hjørland and Nissen Pedersen follow their discussion of food by suggesting that the links between concepts depend on theories. Indeed, one theory may posit a link between phenomenon A and phenomenon B that alternative theories dispute. Scholars may disagree over whether a particular compound has a particular effect on a particular organ or biological function (591). But if these disagreements are buried in distinct domain-specific classifications, scholars may not be aware of this disagreement. The possibility that the disagreement can be addressed and even overcome will then be ignored through ignorance. If both sorts of study are instead classified as studying the same causal link within a general classification, the disagreement will be apparent to all who encounter both works. And the classification itself can signal the probable source of the disagreement by indicating the perspectives (including theories and methods) taken in the two studies. In other words, such scholarly disagreement need not, as Hjørland and Nissen Pedersen suggest, complicate the task of classifying documents, but rather provides a further rationale for a comprehensive approach to classification.

There Are Multiple Ways of Subdividing Phenomena

We noted above the (oft-heard) suggestion that pharmacologists might want a quite different classification of chemicals from what chemists want. Hope Olson has often suggested that this is a common problem: there are many ways to 'slice a pizza' or subdivide a class into subsidiary classes. It cannot be stressed too much that what pharmacologists want to classify is not chemicals themselves but the causal relationship between certain chemicals and certain physiological effects. We can proceed to classify chemicals according to their internal constitution and structure as chemists would want. We can capture the interests of pharmacologists quite well by linking chemicals and physiological effects (see Szostak 2014a).

Hjørland (2012) argues that this pizza-slicing problem means that there is no one best way to classify. That is, even domain analysis will suffer from this multiplicity of classificatory possibilities. But arguably a general classification would face greater challenges for different disciplines (as with chemists and pharmacologists) might prefer different classifications.

Mai (2010) argues, following Hjørland, that a stone in a field has information of different types for different users, and we cannot hope to classify all of these. Thus, no one mapping is the true mapping. But these different types of information largely reflect different uses to which the stone can be put: mining, building, skipping, and so on. We can capture these different uses through relationships. It is noteworthy that the word 'mapping' is used By Mai here in the sense of one-to-one mapping when the solution is a map that shows all relationships and thus allows one phenomenon to be mapped to many different relationships.

What about an area where there is intense scholarly controversy, such as in defining types of mental illness? Psychologists certainly disagree about how these are best classified (see Cooper 2011). Some psychologists would classify in terms of physiological symptoms and others in terms of psychological symptoms. Some would look for common causes, others for common effects. Note that even here compounding solves much of the problem, for we can link a particular illness defined with respect to symptoms to both its causes and effects. And if we are forced to privilege physical or psychological symptoms in classifying illness, we can link to the others. Note further that a domain analysis of psychology would struggle here as much as a comprehensive analysis. But domain analysis can suggest how best to employ compound notation to capture the psychological literature.

To reiterate: When a particular scholarly community disagrees about how to subdivide, this will be as great a problem for a field-specific classification as for a comprehensive classification. Classifying synthetically is the best way to address the challenge. When different scholarly communities disagree regarding subdivision, this generally reflects differences in the causal processes they address. A synthetic approach provides a direct solution to this challenge.

Mai (2010) also makes a reverse argument: that a particular subclass might be placed in many classes. He notes that likeness is not a quality of things but a relationship between them; we can find some similarity between any two things (e.g. plum and lawnmower). But what sorts of similarities exist between a plum and a lawnmower? Perhaps color, perhaps uses to which they can be put, perhaps places they are stored. All of these can be captured through relationships. The only singular class of which they are 'types of' is 'things.' Likewise, Mai notes that a cow can be treated as a type of food, an animal, and so on. As Mai's own use of the word 'relationship' suggests, compounding allows us to place any phenomenon in one class but link it to any others. A cow is an animal that can be used for food.

For Austin (1984, 80–1), the relationship between 'Cow' and 'Animal' would be a true generic relationship because it is a paradigmatic, a priori one (that is, all Cows are Animals), whereas the relationship between 'Cow' and 'Type of Food' is not (that is, 'Not All Cows are Types of Food' but only some cows in some contexts) and so is quasi-generic. The argument here is similar: concepts should be classed under their superordinate paradigmatic classes (i.e., 'Cows' should be classed under 'Animals') and then one should use relationship designators to link them to other concepts ('Cows' as 'Food').

In sum, we can proceed to classify subclasses that are either types of or parts of a particular class. We can then link these to other classes to which they may be related. The belief that multiple ways of cutting up the world render the construction of a truly comprehensive classification impossible is ultimately based on an undervaluation of the possibilities of synthetic classification to represent relationships. The kind of classification recommended in this book utilizes a synthetic approach to its fullest extent.

Possible Conflict Between a Comprehensive KOS and Respect for Diversity

In Chap. 1 we noted that our project for facilitating interdisciplinarity would intersect at many points and in diverse ways with another characteristic of the contemporary information environment: digitization. We can here address yet another characteristic of the contemporary information environment: a valuable and important concern with how KOSs can better reflect and respect social diversity of various sorts. Does our proposed approach to KOS facilitate social diversity?

Hjørland and Nissen Pedersen (2005, 593) worry that their preferred approach of exclusive reliance on domain analysis may disadvantage minority discourse: a classification system grounded in a particular literature could be expected to obscure the works of those with differing views. These will be thought by members of the dominant discourse to lie in a different domain. A congeries of classifications grounded in distinct discourses provides some solace: small communities of scholars can at least classify their own works, but will be invisible to others. Yet Hjørland and Nissen Pedersen themselves recognize (a key insight of the scholarship of interdisciplinarity) that 'it is important that users of a classification have access to different views.' But while views may differ within a domain, some of the most important differences occur across domains and thus will be obscured by an exclusive reliance on domain analysis. As we saw in Chap. 6, if gender studies is classified separately from other domains, its unique perspective is obscured.

On the other hand, an exhaustive general classification can provide an obvious place for all points of view. Yet this may carry a cost in that members of particular groups may have difficulty identifying the literature of their own group. And the information scientist should strive to facilitate both across-group and within-group communication (Szostak 2014a). Concerns with privacy may militate against authors indicating group membership. Happily, though, the approach recommended in this book of classifying works in terms of theory applied, method applied, discipline, and various other elements of authorial perspective, will greatly aid users in identifying works that reflect a particular point of view. A general classification that embraces a classification of authorial perspective is thus the best KOS for respecting social diversity.

The recommended approach will also alleviate one of the greatest challenges to respect for minorities inherent in existing classification systems. Systems that have evolved over decades or more, and that attempt to enumerate compound classes, tend to embody cultural values or expectations that are no longer acceptable. Male nurses or female engineers are treated as special cases rather than accorded classificatory equality with female nurses or male engineers. A synthetic approach, whereby conjunctions of occupation and gender (for example) are denoted through combination, ensures classificatory balance in such cases.[7]

---

[7] Olson (2007) had argued that a web-of-relations approach to classification would better serve the needs of women and various disadvantaged minorities than the extant reliance on hierarchy. Szostak (2014a) argued that the approach recommended in this book instantiates a web-of-relations approach. See chap. 2.

Key Points

The purpose of this chapter was to address in some detail a variety of theoretical objections that might be raised regarding the approach to classification urged in this book. It deserves to be stressed again that the feasibility of this approach is an empirical question and can only be answered definitively in practice. Yet theoretical analysis informs strategies for classification:

- It is possible to classify concepts comprehensively, but only if certain strategies—notably breaking complex concepts into basic concepts, classifying these logically within hierarchies, and utilizing a synthetic approach—are pursued.
- Concepts are not embedded in theories and should be classified in a manner that encourages cross-theoretical conversation.
- Information science (along with interdisciplinary practice) holds the key to reducing the sources of skeptical thought, and we should thus not take a skeptical outlook as given.
- The benefits of 'shelving' by phenomena rather than discipline likely outweigh the costs, especially in a digital environment.
- Ambiguity is not entirely bad, but we should avoid mutually incompatible interpretations of a concept. The strategies for clarification urged in this book should reduce the problematic kinds of ambiguity but not the good kinds.
- It is theoretically possible to classify phenomena comprehensively. Moreover, there is generally one best approach to subdivision into subclasses. The use of a synthetic approach is critical to both of these conclusions.
- We can best respect social diversity through use of a comprehensive classification that classifies works in terms of various kinds of 'perspective.' The synthetic approach mitigates the most common source of disrespect for diversity in existing classifications.

References

Austin DW (1984) PRECIS, A manual of concept analysis and subject indexing, 2nd edn. British Library, London

Baird D, Cohen MS (1999) Why trade? Perspect Sci 7(2):231–254

Bal M (2002) Travelling concepts in the humanities: a rough guide. University of Toronto Press, Toronto

Chomsky N (2010) Some simple evo-devo theses: how true might they be for language? In: Larson RK, Deprez VM, Yamakido H (eds) Approaches to the evolution of language. Cambridge University Press, Cambridge, UK

Collins R (1998) The sociology of philosophies: a global theory of intellectual change. Harvard University Press, Cambridge, MA

Cooper R (2011) Some classifications will be natural. Knowl Org 38(5):398–404

Empson W (1970) Seven types of ambiguity, 3rd edn. Chatto and Windus, London

Fodor J (1981) The present status of the innateness controversy. In: Representations: philosophical essays on the foundations of cognitive science. MIT Press, Cambridge, MA

Fox MJ (2012) Book. Review [of Szostak (2003) and Szostak (2004)] knowledge organization 39 (4):300–303

Galison P (1997) Image & logic: a material culture of microphysics. The University of Chicago Press, Chicago

Gnoli C (2006) The meaning of facets in non-disciplinary classification. In: Budin G, Swertz C, Mitgutsch K (eds) Knowledge Organization for a global learning society: Proceedings of the 9th ISKO conference. Ergon, Würzburg, pp 11–18

Gnoli C (2008) Categories and facets in integrative levels. Axiomathes 18(2):177–192

Gnoli C (2010) Classification transcends library business. Knowl Org 37(3):223–229

Gnoli C, Cheti A (2013) Sorting documents by base theme with synthetic classification: the double query method. In: Slavic A, Salah AA, Davies S (eds) Classification and visualization: interfaces to knowledge. Ergon Verlag, Würzburg, pp 225–232

Griffiths PE, Stotz K (2014) Conceptual barriers to interdisciplinary communication: when does ambiguity matter? In: O'Rourke M, Crowley S, Eigenbrode SD, Wulfhorst JD (eds) Enhancing communication and collaboration in interdisciplinary research. Sage, Thousand Oaks, pp 195–215

Hjørland B (2002) Domain analysis in information science. Eleven approaches—traditional as well as innovative. J Doc 58(4):422–462

Hjørland B (2008) Core classification theory: a reply to Szostak. J Doc 64(3):333–342

Hjørland B (2009) Concept theory. J Am Soc Inform Sci Technol 60(8):1519–1536

Hjørland B (2012) Is classification necessary after Google? J Doc 68(3):299–317

Hjørland B, Nissen Pedersen K (2005) A substantive theory of classification for information retrieval. J Doc 61(5):582–595

Keyton J, Beck SJ, Asbury MB (2010) Macrocognition: a communication perspective. Theor Issues Ergon Sci 11(4):272–286

Kleineberg M (2013) The blind men and the elephant: towards an organization of epistemic contexts. Knowl Org 40(5):340–362

Larson RK, Deprez VM, Yamakido H (eds) (2010) Approaches to the evolution of language. Cambridge University Press, Cambridge UK

León Manifesto (2007) Knowl Org 34(1):6–8. Available [with commentary] at: www.iskoi.org/ilc/leon.php

López-Huertas MJ (2013) Transcultural categorization in contextualized domains. Inform Res 18 (3), http://InformationR.net/ir/18-3/colis/paperC16.html

Mai J-E (2010) Classification in a social world: bias and trust. J Doc 66(5):627–642

Margolis E, Laurence S (2011) Concepts [revised]. Stanford encyclopedia of philosophy. http://plato.stanford.edu/entries/concepts/

Olson H (2007) How we construct subjects: a feminist analysis. Libr Trends 56(2):509–541

O'Rourke M, Crowley S, Eigenbrode SD, Wulfhorst JD (eds) (2014) Enhancing communication and collaboration in interdisciplinary research. Sage, Thousand Oaks

Repko AF (2012) Interdisciplinary research: process and theory, 2nd edn. Sage, Thousand Oaks

Stock WG (2010) Concepts and semantic relations in Information Science. J Am Soc Inform Sci Technol 61(10):1951–1969

Szostak R (2007) Modernism, postmodernism, and interdisciplinarity. Issues Integr Stud 26:32–83

Szostak R (2008) Classification, interdisciplinarity, and the study of science. J Doc 64(3):319–332

Szostak R (2011) Complex concepts into basic concepts. J Am Soc Inform Soc Technol 62 (11):2247–2265

Szostak R (2013a) Basic concepts classification. https://sites.google.com/a/ualberta.ca/rick-szostak/research/basic-concepts-classification-web-version-2013

Szostak R (2013a) Speaking truth to power in classification. Knowl Org 40(1):76–77

Szostak R (2014a) Classifying for social diversity. Knowl Org 41(2):160–170

Szostak R (2014b) Classifying the humanities. Knowl Org 41(4):263–275

Szostak R (2014c) Skepticism and knowledge organization. In: Babik W (ed) Knowledge Organization in the 21st century: between historical patterns and future prospects. Proceedings of the 13th ISKO conference Krakow. Ergon, Würzburg

Szostak R (2014d) Communicating complex concepts. In: O'Rourke M, Crowley S, Eigenbrode SD, Wulfhorst JD (eds) Enhancing communication and collaboration in interdisciplinary research. Sage, Thousand Oaks, pp 34–55

Szostak R (2015) A pluralistic approach to the philosophy of classification. Libr Trends 63 (3):591–614

Szostak R, Gnoli C (2014) Universality is inescapable. Paper presented at the ASIST Sig/CR Workshop, Seattle, November 2014. Advances in classification research 2014. Proceedings of the ASIST SIG/CR Workshop, 1 Nov 2014, Seattle. https://journals.lib.washington.edu/index. php/acro/article/view/14906

Chapter 10
Concluding Remarks and the Next Steps

We open this chapter by summarizing the conclusions reached in the preceding nine chapters. We then discuss avenues for further research, and also for public policy. We close with some reflections on the place of knowledge organization in the world.

Conclusions from Previous Chapters

We have reached a set of very strong conclusions in this book. We summarize these here, referencing the primary chapters in which these arguments are made:

1. Interdisciplinarity is of increasing importance in the academy (Chap. 1).

   • The success of interdisciplinarity indicates that it is feasible but challenging.
   • Critically for information science, the success of interdisciplinarity indicates that cross-disciplinary understanding can be achieved.

2. Existing classification systems serve interdisciplinary scholars very poorly (Chaps. 1 and 2).

   • They also serve the disciplinary scholar and the general user much less well than they might.
   • They are also poorly suited to the contemporary world of multiple online databases and the development of the Semantic Web.

3. We can identify a handful of key knowledge organization needs of the inter-disciplinary user (which will also benefit disciplinary and general users) (Chap. 2):

   • Classification in terms of phenomena studied rather than disciplines.
   • Classification of the relationships between any pair of phenomena.
   • Classification of the theories applied in a work.

© Springer International Publishing Switzerland 2016
R. Szostak et al., *Interdisciplinary Knowledge Organization*,
DOI 10.1007/978-3-319-30148-8_10

- Classification of the methods applied in a work.
- Classification of the authorial perspectives applied in a work.
- Clarification of the terminology employed in a classification and in scholarship more generally.

4. These needs are best achieved through a comprehensive phenomenon-based classification that takes a synthetic approach, allowing any two or more concepts to be linked (Chap. 3).

   - Such an approach allows us to represent with precision in our classification the key ideas/arguments of a work.
   - A synthetic approach facilitates the work of the classificationist, classifier, and the user, for each can combine basic concepts.
   - A synthetic approach also alleviates an important source of social unfairness in existing classifications: male nurses are treated identically to female nurses.
   - Less obviously, the synthetic approach allows us to simultaneously satisfy what appear to be divergent preferences regarding how to subdivide a class into subsidiary classes.

5. While some of these characteristics of the desired classification (particularly classification in terms of theory and method applied) might be achieved through amendments to existing classification schemes, others cannot (Chaps. 3 and 5).

   - An entirely new approach to classification is thus called for.
   - The proposed new classification can either complement or replace existing bibliographic classifications.

6. A classification with these characteristics will aid users both when they know what they are looking for and when they are engaged in exploratory search (Chaps. 1–3).

   - Users of all types wish to search by phenomena, relationships, and perspective, including theory and method.
   - Such a classification would aid what is variously termed 'undiscovered public knowledge,' 'literature-based discovery,' or 'serendipity.'

7. Such a classification is also well-suited to the contemporary digital environment (Chaps. 5 and 8):

   - It should facilitate searching across multiple online databases.
   - It could support the development of the Semantic Web. With the addition of some semantic rules, it might serve as an ontology for the Semantic Web.

8. There are strategies that can be employed to reduce terminological ambiguity within the sort of comprehensive classification proposed (Chaps. 6 and 7):

- The complex concepts that are understood differently by different people/ groups can be broken into basic concepts for which there is enough shared understanding for the purposes of classification.
- A synthetic approach not only allows us to link any phenomena and relationships, but allows us to establish strictly logical hierarchies that clarify what sort of thing a particular phenomenon is and what sort of thing it is not. [This also assists computer navigation of the classification.]
- Domain analysis is critically important in identifying the meanings attached to a particular concept by different groups, and ensuring that these are captured in the classification.

9. A handful of other strategies are of critical importance in achieving such a classification (Chaps. 3, 5, and 6):

- A deductive strategy based on principles of logical classification must be blended with an inductive strategy of domain analysis (which starts from the observed vocabulary of a domain).
- As noted above, a synthetic approach so that entities (things), relators, and properties can be freely linked, is critical.
- Numerous more detailed practices were recommended in turn for the classification of phenomena, relationships, and perspectives in Chap. 5.
- Techniques of domain analysis, and how these might be employed in the development of a comprehensive classification, were outlined in Chap. 6.

10. Theoretical objections to the sort of project outlined above can be transcended (Chap. 9):

- Through the strategies outlined above, terminological ambiguity can (at least potentially) be reduced to a satisfactory level.
- In particular, concepts are not so embedded in theories as to prevent cross-disciplinary understanding.
- Skepticism of our ability to understand each other is rooted in the complexity of the contemporary scholarly enterprise; our recommended classification serves to organize scholarly understandings and thus facilitate communication and hopefully synthesis.
- The recommended approach to classification will also encourage both within-group and cross-group understanding for various social groups.
- Though the recommended approach is best suited to digital libraries, the advantages of shelving by phenomena rather than disciplines likely outweigh the disadvantages.

11. It is entirely feasible to develop a classification with these characteristics (Chaps. 4 and 5).

- This is an empirical question. None of the potential theoretical objections indicates that the project is not feasible, though some usefully point to difficulties that must be surmounted.

- The Integrative Levels Classification (ILC) and Basic Concepts Classification (BCC) each illustrate the feasibility of the project.

12. This kind of classification encourages and would be supported by the development of a comprehensive thesaurus (Thesauri are addressed toward the end of Chaps. 3 and 5).

   - This project is also feasible, and for similar reasons.
   - Such a thesaurus would be most useful with an expanded and elaborated set of "Related Term" indicators.
   - Such a thesaurus should address not just phenomena but relators and properties.

13. A variety of benefits, beyond aiding interdisciplinary research and teaching, flow from the recommended approach to classification (Chap. 8):

   - As noted above, it captures the unique attributes of a work.
   - It can also potentially classify both things themselves and ideas.
   - It allows new topics to generally be represented through novel combinations of existing terms.
   - Users of all types are better able to judge the relevance of works if these are classified with respect to theory, method, and perspective applied.
   - Several other advantages were noted in Chap. 8.

14. Though our conclusions are novel, they reflect a long and significant stream of thought in the knowledge organization literature (Chap. 4).

   - The sort of classification urged in this book would have been more difficult to achieve in an era of card catalogues.
   - It would also have been less advantageous in an era of disciplinary hegemony.
   - The dominance of discipline-based classifications reflects historical circumstances which have evolved.
   - The simultaneous rise of interdisciplinarity and digitization thus create a historical moment in which change may be possible.

Though we have listed these conclusions separately it deserves emphasis that they are complementary. Together they represent a detailed case for both the desirability and feasibility of an approach to classification that is very different from most KOSs in use today, yet one that reflects and is grounded in the best traditions of research in knowledge organization.

Further Developing Phenomenon-Based Classifications

The main task ahead is to further develop the sort of classification urged in this book. The simple fact is that a classification must be developed in significant detail before it can be used. This is especially the case for a classification that stresses a synthetic approach, for the value of such an approach increases geometrically as more schedules are fleshed out and thus available for combination. This book has devoted so much space to establishing the feasibility of the project in large part to encourage the further work needed to make such a classification a reality.

This is a task that is best pursued collaboratively. We have stressed the need to balance inductive and deductive, domain and comprehensive approaches in this book. But there is also an advantage of engaging with scholars beyond the field of information science. Interdisciplinary scholars can give detailed input regarding their needs, and help to identify terminology that facilitates cross-disciplinary understanding. Disciplinary scholars can ensure that the meanings and needs of their fields are also respected. It is perhaps not surprising that a classification designed to serve interdisciplinarity is itself best developed in an interdisciplinary fashion.[1]

It should be stressed that the new classification will be much less complicated than older systems in important ways. It will no longer require distinct headings for the same subject within different disciplines. It will explicitly code for relationships between phenomena, and thus do away with the many complex but unanalyzed classes in existing enumerative classifications. While each work will ideally be coded in terms of the theories and methods applied, this coding will use the same headings as must be applied to works *about* a particular theory or method (see Chap. 5). Nevertheless, much work remains to be done.

We have in this book discussed in some detail how to classify phenomena and relationships. We have devoted far less space to the classification of properties. Both the BCC and the ILC encourage the synthetic combination of properties with phenomena and relationships (as does the UDC to some extent). Both have identified inductively (that is, in the process of classifying works) a set of properties that can be employed (see Chap. 7). But there has been no attempt to explore a deductive strategy. There may (or, then again, there may not) be scope for the development of a more logical classification of properties.

Another area in which there is a critical need for more research is the study of the techniques employed within (and sometimes across) diverse scholarly methods. We need to identify an exhaustive set of such techniques, and in a manner that can be appreciated by scholars from all disciplines. More generally, there is scope for fleshing out the classification of authorial perspectives.

---

[1] Holland (2008) argues that information science draws on many fields, but often in a multidisciplinary fashion, when in many cases an interdisciplinary approach would be preferable. See also Bawden (2008).

While we can thus identify a couple of areas that we might prioritize, there is scope for additional clarification throughout the ILC or BCC. Scholars with expertise in a particular area are encouraged—indeed urged—to suggest improvements. We would stress again the value of performing domain analysis of various domains with the goal of contributing terminology to a general classification. This would involve establishing which individual concepts are to be represented as well as the structural relationships among concepts within the domain (and the degree to which classification itself lessens ambiguity). It would also involve clarifying the ontological and epistemological assumptions of the domain, and comparing these to other domains.

Though we would stress the empirical work of actually building the classification going forward, it would be naïve to think that this book will set to rest all theoretical disputes. Nor would this be desirable, for theoretical discussion does inform in important ways the practical development of a classification. As we have seen, once a classification is developed and applied it becomes difficult to make substantial changes. It is thus critical that a new classification reflect relevant literatures in philosophy, information science, cognitive science, interdisciplinary studies, and other areas of scholarly endeavor. We have sketched out a strategy whereby we seek to satisfy as many relevant theories as possible, and seek to identify (in good interdisciplinary fashion) common ground among different theoretical perspectives. Indeed, we can claim that there is both a broad and deep base of theoretical discourse in place to guide the development of a comprehensive phenomenon-based classification. Further theoretical discussion is openly invited.

We have mentioned the general (non-scholarly) user several times in this book. Nevertheless our main focus has been upon interdisciplinary (and to a lesser extent disciplinary) scholars. The general user has little natural interest in disciplines and is likely to state queries in terms of combinations of phenomena, relationships, and properties. More extensive exploration of the benefits that the general user might achieve from the sort of classification recommended here would be highly desirable.

At some stage it will also be advantageous to translate the classification into other languages. It is hoped that the very characteristics of the classification that facilitate cross-disciplinary understanding—the emphasis on synthesis of terms with broadly shared understandings—will also reduce challenges in translation.

Some thought must also be put into how a mature classification is best administered. As noted, it could be viewed as either a substitute for or complement to existing systems. Some classifications in the world today—notably the Library of Congress and Dewey Decimal Classifications—benefit from a dedicated bureaucracy that can both achieve regular updates and take care of day-to-day concerns. Many others struggle with a heavy reliance on volunteer labor. A new classification project based on a novel approach faces particular challenges in financing the achievement of the necessary level of detail. These challenges are not insurmountable (see Chaps. 5 and 8), but are significant.

A Complementary Thesaurus

The recommended approach to classification could usefully be supplemented by a comprehensive thesaurus that consists of terms pertaining to phenomena, relationships, and properties, and possesses a well-articulated set of Related Term (RT) indicators. Many of the theoretical and empirical arguments that apply to a comprehensive classification apply also to a comprehensive thesaurus. But we appreciate that this case needs to be made more fully. Consensus is necessary on the best set of RT indicators. And then there is the need to actually do the detailed work of developing such a thesaurus. We would speculate that WordNet may provide a useful basis for proceeding here, and that it may prove possible to integrate across field-specific thesauri as the NCI Metathesaurus (National Cancer Institute 2015) has attempted to do in the biomedical field. As with a classification system, the benefits expand exponentially as more entries are added.

Revisiting the Empirical Question

We stressed in Chaps. 7 and 9 that the feasibility of the recommended KOS is an empirical question. We have concluded that the theoretical arguments in favor are strong. But we welcome empirical testing of the resulting hypothesis that a comprehensive phenomenon-based classification is possible.

We can, following our discussion in Chap. 9, identify three related empirical questions: How much ambiguity is there?; How much can we reduce it?; and How much ambiguity can a KOS abide? (We draw here on Szostak and Gnoli 2014). With regard to the first we could expose users from different domains to a variety of terms employed in different classifications (including ILC and BCC), ask for definitions, and employ content analysis to investigate the degree of shared understanding.

Even those who might still be skeptical of our project should see value in identifying the quantitative importance of the ambiguity-reducing strategies we have discussed. The value of decreasing ambiguity should be widely esteemed. We could examine first how diverse users break complex concepts into basic concepts. If they do so differently (as we would anticipate) we can then examine whether the resulting basic terms are understood across groups or individuals whereas the complex concepts were not. Say one person interprets 'globalization' as meaning (international trade) (affects) (unemployment rate) and another defines it as (American movies) (Affect) (French) (cultural values): We can then investigate whether these latter terms are much better understood than was globalization itself.

Placing terms within sentence-like compounds is another strategy we have advocated. We can explore empirically first the feasibility of combining three or four or five terms in a subject heading: at what point does the notation for complex combinations of basic concepts become too convoluted to be useful? This was very rarely a problem in the translation exercise reported in Szostak (2011, 2013), but might (or not) be more of a challenge in natural science. We can also explore the degree to which placing a term in such a compound increases the degree of shared understanding. Special attention should be paid to the value of linking noun-like, verb-like, and property terms. More general tests of the value of facet analysis in general might be pursued, and the question of whether users should be acquainted with the facet structure employed or whether this can safely operate behind the scenes.

Furner (2010) worries that information science has made little contribution to philosophy. One contribution that might be made is to provide some empirical idea of how much ambiguity there is and how much this can be reduced through classificatory practice (Szostak 2015). The bulk of the literature that we hope to classify is likely not written in terms of those concepts that have most troubled philosophers through the ages. Nor should this be surprising, for most scholarly and general literature addresses the world as it is—and thus at least potentially involves concepts with obvious external referents.

As for the third question, user studies seem called for in order to establish how well users can navigate a particular KOS. The literature on user studies has produced some robust findings over the years: it suggests that multiple methods be employed and that different types of user and query be investigated separately (Tenopir 2003; Wilson 2006). If a comprehensive phenomenon-based classification were applied to a diverse corpus of works, we could then analyze how users fared in navigating the classification.[2] We might indeed imagine a host of tests, each guided by our discussion in previous chapters:

- Do users achieve the juxtapositions of related insights from different fields identified in the literature-based discovery literatures?
- What success do users have with the sorts of complex queries that interdisciplinary and general users often have? [Even in the early stages of development of a classification, interdisciplinary scholars might be asked to suggest search terms, and then translate these into the terminology of the classification.]
- What about queries that members of one group or discipline might make about the practices or beliefs of other groups or disciplines?
- How well can users access relevant information from different fields on public policy questions?
- Is the classification easy to understand, and if so does it provide users with a sense of a coherent body of human understanding?
- Do users find classifications of theories, methods, and more general perspectives applied useful in finding and judging relevance of works?

---

[2] Beghtol (1994, 9–10) follows Foskett (1962) in urging the development of classifications that could serve as the 'experimental data' with which to test theoretical propositions in knowledge organization.

We should ideally perform these tests with different types of user: academic versus general; scholars from different disciplines and those who are interdisciplinary; and novice users versus experienced users. We should also test whether (ideally novice) classifiers find it easy to apply the classification.

User studies often presume that a user seeks a particular type of work. But users with complex queries may instead need to be guided to multiple works that each address part of their query (Green 1995). User testing should thus not just investigate whether users find relevant works but whether they find works that address each component of a complex query. Here the ability to move along a web-of-relations from one work to a related work (see Chap. 2) could prove crucial.

There is an alternative to traditional user studies. We can start from the subject headings associated with different classifications, and see whether different types of potential users are able to provide similar understandings of what these mean. This sort of test can be performed if synthetic phenomenon-based classifications are applied to a moderate set of works.

There is also value in explicit comparisons of classifications. Szostak (2013) found many ambiguities when trying to translate DDC terms into BCC, and further issues have been identified in comparative classification by DDC and by ILC in the test reported in Chap. 4. DDC has large generalia classes which conflate works about the discipline, its key objects of study, its methods, and its theories. These deserve to be distinguished. Elsewhere, philosophical and scientific concerns are needlessly conflated. Inevitably vague classes contain works of quite different types. Further comparisons or translations could highlight the strengths and weaknesses of different KOSs.

Classifying Things and Ideas

We have mentioned a couple of times that our approach to the classification of documents is also well suited to the classification both of things and of the insights contained in works. Both of these attributes are potentially of immense value.

There is considerable classificatory interest in better serving the needs of museums, galleries, and archives as well as libraries. These are often referred to as GLAM (galleries, libraries, archives, museums), and it is recognized that users often want to search across the different elements of GLAM (Gnoli 2010). We might make special note of the value of being able to seamlessly search for both documents about works of art, and those works of art. The significant overlap in holdings across GLAM provides a further motive: An engraved silver bowl might appear in a museum or gallery; A rare book might be held in library or archive; A poster might be archived or held in a museum or a library; An art catalogue might be held in a gallery or library or (more rarely) archive. Museums and galleries and archives often now have an online presence, but it is generally difficult to perform subject searches on any one website much less across many (Menard et al. 2010). Museums, galleries, and archives have not adopted library classifications. It is very possible, though, that the sort of classification urged in this book, with its synthetic approach and focus on the things and relationships that we actually observe in the world, might serve the needs not just of libraries but of museums, galleries, and archives as well. It might then serve as the elusive cross-GLAM search tool (Szostak 2014a; 2016). It might also, be useful, as we shall explore in the next section, for commercial databases.

We noted, following Börner (2006) and others (Chap. 2), that in future scholarship may be represented more by a network of ideas than a congeries of overlapping documents. We have nevertheless focused for the most part in this book on classifying documents. Much more could be known about the advantages of classifying both things and ideas (Gnoli 2010). The synthetic approach urged in this book allows and encourages subject headings that capture the key causal arguments of a work: A has influence X on B. We can thus easily classify simultaneously both documents and the key insights that they contain.

It will be very useful moving forward to further investigate the possibilities of applying a synthetic phenomenon-based comprehensive classification to the purposes of classifying both things and ideas.

Applying the New Approach Digitally

It could be that the approach recommended in this book to serve interdisciplinary scholarship has uses that we scarcely imagined as we began this project. We have speculated on a couple of these in this book, but more research is necessary to establish these possibilities. Nevertheless it should be stressed that there is a natural symbiosis between efforts to encourage cross-disciplinary communication and efforts to encourage cross-database communication. We should not at all be surprised if a classification admirably suited to one of these goals serves the other as well.

Is it possible to develop a classification system that can be used by a diverse set of online databases, including those developed by various institutions such as museums, archives, government agencies, non-profit organizations, and private companies? These various enterprises have often tended to develop their own classifications. One reason for this is the difficulty of mastering the very complex classifications employed in bibliographic classification. If a positive answer is to be given to our question then a classification that is easier to master is necessary. Since administrators of these databases wish primarily to provide access to a set of things, and indicate their properties (and perhaps the relationships among them), a classification that stresses synthetic combinations of these very elements has the best chance of adoption. But more research is called for.[3]

---

[3] Interestingly, architects of many large corporate websites are applying principles of facet analysis—an indication that a common classification for libraries and other websites is indeed feasible.

The Semantic Web is structured around RDF triples, which must be coded to represent the specific information within any one database. For inferences to be drawn across databases—which is the goal of the Semantic Web—RDF triples need to be coded with respect to a common or at least interoperable controlled vocabulary. Given the nature of RDF triples, which take the form (subject) (predicate or property) (object) this controlled vocabulary must independently capture phenomena, relationships, and properties. The sort of classification urged in this book must have advantages relative to existing classifications that mix these three elements in individual non-analytic subject headings. It remains to be seen just how useful this classification could be for the Semantic Web. We could identify a set of research questions (Szostak 2014c):

- To what extent can the recommended classification (aided perhaps by a complementary thesaurus) meet the controlled vocabulary needs of the Semantic Web?
- What sort of syntactic rules are necessary in addition to the classification to serve the purpose of ontology on the Semantic Web?
- Many of the databases noted above find it useful to employ RDF triples, as search engines increasingly search for these (Hart and Dolbear 2013). Will this encourage database managers toward a more comprehensive usage of controlled vocabulary, and thus a comprehensive classification?
- More generally, how can the field of information science best influence the development of the Semantic Web in order to ensure that it is based on the soundest principles of classification theory?
- What challenges are faced in applying existing classifications or thesauri to the Semantic Web?
- The Semantic Web has developed slowly (by the standard of other web technologies). Can a novel approach to classification accelerate its development, and in a superior direction?

Revisiting Information Retrieval

As noted above, the success of the Semantic Web depends on the use of the same or interoperable controlled vocabulary across databases. This simple fact signals a wider recognition of the limits of full-text searching as a method of information retrieval. Within the information retrieval community, there is increased hostility to the 'bag of words' assumption that search terms operate independently in a text (Metzler 2011; Mengle and Goharian 2010). That is, there is openness to some sort of syntactic structure in searches. It may thus be time to narrow the gaps between the fields of classification and information retrieval (as Glushko 2013, among others, urges). Is there some way that controlled vocabulary—in particular an easier to master and more logical controlled vocabulary—can be integrated into information retrieval strategies?

Advocacy

What is the single greatest thing that could be done to facilitate interdisciplinary research and teaching at this point in time? There are many possible answers. Lyall et al (2011) provide a host of invaluable pieces of advice to university administrators, granting agencies, and journal editors and referees: All of these could change their rules and behaviors in ways that would facilitate interdisciplinarity. But we would argue that the single greatest contribution to the productivity of interdisciplinary teaching and research would come from the development of KOSs that would better serve interdisciplinarity. Such KOSs would serve three extremely important functions:

- Facilitate interdisciplinary searches by interdisciplinary scholars and students, both when they know what they are looking for and when they are seeking novel connections.
- Clarify terminology across disciplines.
- Facilitate the communication of research results to all relevant audiences.

Search and communication absorb a great deal of the interdisciplinary researcher's time. And failure to identify relevant information limits scholarly discovery. Advances in KOSs, then, can have a dramatic effect on the productivity of interdisciplinary scholars. Indeed, Szostak (2014b) argued that knowledge organization was thus the most important single scholarly field. It can unleash advances across the scholarly enterprise. Moreover, as we saw in Chaps. 8 and 9, it will at the same time bring greater coherence to the scholarly enterprise (in both appearance and reality), and thus discourage unnecessary skepticism regarding the possibilities of enhanced human understanding. And general users will also benefit from the proposed KOS, and thus there are potential advantages for both public discourse and personal fulfillment.

Governments and granting agencies worry about how to facilitate interdisciplinarity. They seek better policy advice, and recognize that complex problems require interdisciplinary analysis. [Enlightened policy makers also wish to raise the quality of public discourse.] But they do not generally recognize this as a problem of knowledge organization. *They know that there is a problem in connecting the insights of diverse scholars, but do not look to knowledge organization for a solution.* They need to hear that advances in knowledge organization are both feasible and important. They need to be exposed to the possibilities. And they need to recognize that fleshing out a detailed classification is not easy, but that the costs of doing so are trivial relative to the benefits we have outlined in this book.

It would be best if they heard this message from both specialists in knowledge organization and scholars of interdisciplinarity. It would be advantageous if those interested in the development of the Semantic Web were also to encourage the development of the sort of KOSs recommended in this book.

Tasks for Scholars of Interdisciplinarity

The work that needs to be done in knowledge organization was described above. We stress here that there are important tasks for scholars of interdisciplinarity. Foremost, we see the detailed development of the recommended KOSs as a collaborative effort: interdisciplinarians can make suggestions on structure, employ the strategy of redefinition in order to clarify terminology, and give invaluable advice on the detailed decision-making inherent in the development of a KOS. Secondly, advocacy from those who will use a new KOS is an invaluable complement to advocacy from the field of KO itself.

This book is itself an interdisciplinary effort, for it has sought to connect the literatures on interdisciplinarity and on knowledge organization. Interdisciplinary scholars can employ their skills to further integrate these two literatures. They might, for example, draw connections between the literature urging exclusive pursuit of domain analysis and the more general literatures on the advantages of specialization. And interdisciplinary scholars can also hopefully strengthen the connections drawn in this book between developing a KOS for interdisciplinarity on the one hand and the pursuit of ontologies and the Semantic Web on the other.

This book also has lessons for interdisciplinary practice itself. We have described strategies for clarifying terminology. We have encouraged all scholars to take care in specifying the causal arguments they make and the theories and methods (and ideally other elements of authorial perspective) that they apply. And we encourage interdisciplinary scholars especially to see how their research fits within a coherent multi-dimensional map of the scholarly enterprise.

The Wider Implications

We close with some reflection on the place of knowledge organization in our world.[4] It is often said that the fuel of the modern world is not energy but information. In this book we have stressed the advantages for scholarship of an approach to classification that would enhance scholarly discovery and communication. If knowledge organization could enhance scholarly productivity by even a fraction of a percent, it would still be by far the most important field in the entire scholarly enterprise. But the potential benefits extend far beyond the academy. Innovators, artists, and entrepreneurs each depend on creating something new by combining old ideas. Citizens are limited in their impact on public policy by the difficulty that they encounter in finding relevant information to further their projects to effect change in their world. Well-meaning public officials are less successful than they might be through lack of information, especially with regard to the (often unintended) side effects that any policy on which they are deciding might have.

---

[4] Some of the ideas here are explored in Szostak (2014b).

Individuals and groups face a host of decisions for which they struggle to find guidance.

It is hard (though desirable) to estimate the effect that an advance in knowledge organization can have on the world. But we should not for a moment doubt that it is worth doing. A better future lies ahead if we will only grasp it.

References

Bawden D (2008) Smoother pebbles and the shoulders of giants; the developing foundations of information science. J Inform Sci 34(4):415–426

Beghtol C (1994) The classification of fiction, the development of a system based on theoretical principles. Scarecrow Press, Lanham, MD

Börner K (2006) Semantic association networks: Using semantic web technology to improve scholarly knowledge and expertise management. In: Geroimenko V, Chen C (eds) Visualizing the Semantic Web, 2nd edn. Springer, Berlin, pp 183–198

Foskett DJ (1962) The classification research group 1952–62. Libri 12(2):127–138

Furner J (2010) Philosophy and information studies. Annu Rev Inform Sci Technol 44:161–200

Glushko RJ (ed) (2013) The discipline of organizing. MIT Press, Cambridge, MA

Gnoli C (2010) Classification transcends library business. Knowl Org 37(3):223–229

Green R (1995) Topical relevance relationships. 1. Why topic matching fails. J Am Soc Inform Sci Technol 46(9):646–653

Hart G, Dolbear C (2013) Linked data: a geographic perspective. CRC, Boca Raton, FL

Holland GA (2008) Information science: an interdisciplinary effort? J Doc 64(1):7–23

Lyall C, Bruce A, Tait J, Meagher L (2011) Interdisciplinary research journeys. Bloomsbury Publishing PLC, Huntingdon, GBR

Menard E, Mas S, Alberts I (2010) Faceted classification for museum artefacts: a methodology to support web site development of large cultural organizations. Aslib Proc 62(4/5):523–532

Mengle SSR, Goharian N (2010) Detecting relationships among categories using text classification. J Am Soc Inform Sci Technol 61:1046–1061

Metzler D (2011) A feature-centric view of information retrieval. Springer, Dordrecht

National Cancer Institute (2015) NCI Metathesaurus [Updated Monthly] http://ncim.nci.nih.gov/ncimbrowser/

Szostak R (2011) Complex concepts into basic concepts. J Am Soc Inform Soc Technol 62 (11):2247–2265

Szostak R (2013) Translation table: DDC [Dewey Decimal Classification] to basic concepts classification. http://www.economics.ualberta.ca/en/FacultyandStaff/~/media/economics/FacultyAndStaff/Szostak/Szostak-Dewey-Conversion-Table.pdf

Szostak R (2014a) Classifying the humanities. Knowl Org 41(4):263–275

Szostak R (2014b) The importance of knowledge organization. ASIST Bull 40(4), April/May. http://www.asis.org/Bulletin/Apr-14/AprMay14_Szostak.html

Szostak R (2014c) The basic concepts classification as a bottom-up strategy for the Semantic Web. Int J Knowl Content Dev Technol, June 2014. www.ijkcdt.net

Szostak R (2015) A pluralistic approach to the philosophy of classification. Libr Trends 63 (3):591–614

Szostak R (2016) Synthetic classification of museum artifacts using basic concepts. Paper presented at the Museums and the Web conference, Los Angeles, Apr 2016

Szostak R, Gnoli C (2014) Universality is inescapable. Paper presented at the ASIST Sig/CR Workshop, Seattle, November 2014. Advances in classification research 2014. Proceedings of the ASIST SIG/CR workshop, 1 Nov 2014, Seattle. https://journals.lib.washington.edu/index.php/acro/article/view/14906

Tenopir C (2003) Information metrics and user studies. Aslib Proc 55(1/2):13–17

Wilson T (2006) On user studies and information needs. J Doc 62(6):658–670

Index

© Springer International Publishing Switzerland 2016
R. Szostak et al., *Interdisciplinary Knowledge Organization*,
DOI 10.1007/978-3-319-30148-8

Printed in the United States
By Bookmasters